W9-BYP-310

THE UNIFICATION
OF GERMANY,
1989–1990

**Other Titles in the Greenwood Press Guides
to Historic Events of the Twentieth Century**
Randall M. Miller, Series Editor

The Persian Gulf Crisis
Steve A. Yetiv

World War I
Neil M. Heyman

The Civil Rights Movement
Peter B. Levy

The Holocaust
Jack R. Fischel

The Breakup of Yugoslavia and the War in Bosnia
Carole Rogel

Islamic Fundamentalism
Lawrence Davidson

Frontiers of Space Exploration
Roger D. Launius

The Collapse of Communism in the Soviet Union
William E. Watson

Origins and Development of the Arab-Israeli Conflict
Ann M. Lesch and Dan Tschirgi

The Rise of Fascism in Europe
George P. Blum

The Cold War
Katherine A.S. Sibley

World War II
Loyd E. Lee

The War in Vietnam
Anthony O. Edmonds

THE UNIFICATION OF GERMANY, 1989–1990

Richard A. Leiby

Greenwood Press Guides to
Historic Events of the Twentieth Century
Randall M. Miller, Series Editor

Greenwood Press
Westport, Connecticut • London

Library of Congress Cataloging-in-Publication Data

Leiby, Richard A.
    The unification of Germany, 1989–1990 / Richard A. Leiby.
        p.   cm.—(Greenwood Press guides to historic events of the
    twentieth century, ISSN 1092–177X)
    Includes bibliographical references and index.
    ISBN 0–313–29969–2 (alk. paper)
    1. Germany—History—Unification, 1990.   2. Church and state—
Germany (East).   3. Germany (East)—Politics and
government—1989–1990.   I. Title.   II. Series: Greenwood Press
guides to historic events of the twentieth century.
DD290.29.L45   1999
943.087—dc21   98–22904

British Library Cataloguing in Publication Data is available.

Library of Congress Catalog Card Number: 98–22904
ISBN: 0–313–29969–2
ISSN: 1092–177X

First published in 1999

Greenwood Press, 88 Post Road West, Westport, CT 06881
An imprint of Greenwood Publishing Group, Inc.

Printed in the United States of America

∞™

The paper used in this book complies with the
Permanent Paper Standard issued by the National
Information Standards Organization (Z39.48–1984).

10 9 8 7 6 5 4 3 2 1

Front cover photo: A demonstrator pounds away at the Berlin Wall. REUTERS/CORBIS-
BETTMANN.

Back cover photo: The mass exodus from the GDR began in the summer of 1989. Courtesy of
German Information Center.

Contents

A photo essay follows page 100

Series Foreword

As the twenty-first century approaches, it is time to take stock of the political, social, economic, intellectual, and cultural forces and factors that have made the twentieth century the most dramatic period of change in history. To that end, the Greenwood Press Guides to Historic Events of the Twentieth Century presents interpretive histories of the most significant events of the century. Each book in the series combines narrative history and analysis with primary documents and biographical sketches, with an eye to providing both a reference guide to the principal persons, ideas, and experiences defining each historic event, and a reliable, readable overview of that event. Each book further provides analyses and discussions, grounded in both primary and secondary sources, of the causes and consequences, in thought and action, that give meaning to the historic event under review. By assuming a historical perspective, drawing on the latest and best writing on each subject, and offering fresh insights, each book promises to explain how and why a particular event defined the twentieth century. No consensus about the meaning of the twentieth century emerges from the series, but, collectively, the books identify the most salient concerns of the century. In so doing, the series reminds us of the many ways those historic events continue to affect our lives.

Each book follows a similar format designed to encourage readers to consult it both as a reference and a history in its own right. Each volume opens with a chronology of the historic event, followed by a narrative overview, which also serves to introduce and examine briefly the main themes and issues related to that event. The next set of chapters is composed of topical essays, each analyzing closely an issue or problem of interpretation introduced in the opening chapter. A concluding chapter suggesting the long-term implications and meanings of the historic event brings the strands of the preceding chapters together while placing the event in the larger historical context. Each book also includes a section of short biographies of the principal persons related to the event, followed by a section introducing and reprinting key historical documents illustrative of and pertinent to the event. A glossary of selected terms adds to the utility of each book. An annotated bibliography—of significant books, films, and CD-ROMs—and an index conclude each volume.

The editors made no attempt to impose any theoretical model or historical perspective on the individual authors. Rather, in developing the series, an advisory board of noted historians and informed high school history teachers and public and school librarians identified the topics needful of exploration and the scholars eminently qualified to examine those events with intelligence and sensitivity. The common commitment throughout the series is to provide accurate, informative, and readable books, free of jargon and up to date in evidence and analysis.

Each book stands as a complete historical analysis and reference guide to a particular historic event. Each book also has many uses, from understanding contemporary perspectives on critical historical issues, to providing biographical treatments of key figures related to each event, to offering excerpts and complete texts of essential documents about the event, to suggesting and describing books and media materials for further study and presentation of the event, and more. The combination of historical narrative and individual topical chapters addressing significant issues and problems encourages students and teachers to approach each historic event from multiple perspectives and with a critical eye. The arrangement and content of each book thus invite students and teachers, through classroom discussions and position papers, to debate the character and significance of great historic events and to discover for themselves how and why history matters.

The series emphasizes the main currents that have shaped the modern world. Much of that focus necessarily looks at the West, especially Europe and the United States. The political, commercial, and cultural expansion of the West wrought largely, though not wholly, the most fundamental changes of the century. Taken together, however, books in the series reveal the interactions between Western and non-Western peoples and society, and also the tensions between modern and traditional cultures. They also point to the ways in which non-Western peoples have adapted Western ideas and technology and, in turn, influenced Western life and thought. Several books examine such increasingly powerful global forces as the rise of Islamic fundamentalism, the emergence of modern Japan, the Communist revolution in China, and the collapse of communism in eastern Europe and the former Soviet Union. American interests and experiences receive special attention in the series, not only in deference to the primary readership of the books but also in recognition that the United States emerged as the dominant political, economic, social, and cultural force during the twentieth century. By looking at the century through the lens of American events and experiences, it is possible to see why the age has come to be known as "The American Century."

Assessing the history of the twentieth century is a formidable prospect. It has been a period of remarkable transformation. The world broadened and narrowed at the same time. Frontiers shifted from the interiors of Africa and Latin America to the moon and beyond; communication spread from mass circulation newspapers and magazines to radio, television, and now the Internet; skyscrapers reached upward and suburbs stretched outward; energy switched from steam, to electric, to atomic power. Many changes did not lead to a complete abandonment of established patterns and practices so much as a synthesis of old and new, as, for example, the increased use of (even reliance on) the telephone in the age of the computer. The automobile and the truck, the airplane, and telecommunications closed distances, and people in unprecedented numbers migrated from rural to urban, industrial, and ever more ethnically diverse areas. Tractors and chemical fertilizers made it possible for fewer people to grow more, but the environmental and demographic costs of an exploding global population threatened to outstrip natural resources and human innovation. Disparities in wealth increased, with developed nations prospering and underdeveloped nations starving. Amid the crumbling of former European colonial empires, Western technology, goods, and culture increasingly enveloped the globe, seeping into, and undermining, non-Western cultures—a process that contributed to a surge of religious fundamentalism and ethno-nationalism in the Middle East, Asia, and Africa. As people became more alike, they also became more aware of their differences. Ethnic and religious rivalries grew in intensity everywhere as the century closed.

The political changes during the twentieth century have been no less profound than the social, economic, and cultural ones. Many of the books in the series focus on political events, broadly defined, but no books are confined to politics alone. Political ideas and events have social effects, just as they spring from a complex interplay of non-political forces in culture, society, and economy. Thus, for example, the modern civil rights and woman's rights movements were at once social and political events in cause and consequence. Likewise, the Cold War created the geopolitical framework for dealing with competing ideologies and nations abroad and served as the touchstone for political and cultural identities at home. The books treating political events do so within their social, cultural, and economic contexts.

Several books in the series examine particular wars in depth. Wars are defining moments for people and eras. During the twentieth century war became more widespread and terrible than ever before, encouraging new efforts to end war through strategies and organizations of international cooperation and disarmament while also fueling new ideologies and instruments of mass persuasion that fostered distrust and festered old national rivalries. Two world wars during the century redrew the political map, slaughtered or uprooted two generations of people, and introduced and hastened the development of new technologies and weapons of mass destruction. The First World War spelled the end of the old European order and spurred communist revolution in Russia and fascism in Italy, Germany, and elsewhere. The Second World War killed fascism and inspired the final push for freedom from European colonial rule in Asia and Africa. It also led to the Cold War that suffocated much of the world for almost half a century. Large wars begat small ones, and brutal totalitarian regimes cropped up across the globe. After (and in some ways because of) the fall of communism in eastern Europe and the former Soviet Union, wars of competing cultures, national interests, and political systems persisted in the struggle to make a new world order. Continuing, too, has been the belief that military technology can achieve political ends, whether in the superior American firepower that failed to "win" in Vietnam or in the American "smart bombs" and other military wizardry that "won" in the Persian Gulf.

Another theme evident in the series is that throughout the century nationalism has continued to drive events. Whether in the Balkans in 1914 triggering World War I or in the Balkans in the 1990s threatening the post–Cold War peace—or in many other places—nationalist ambitions and forces would not die. The persistence of nationalism is yet another reminder of the many ways that the past becomes prologue.

We thus offer the series as a modern guide to and interpretation of the historic events of the twentieth century and as an invitation to consider how and why those events have defined not only the past and present but also charted the political, social, intellectual, cultural, and economic routes into the next century.

Randall M. Miller
Saint Joseph's University, Philadelphia

Preface

Tucked away in a remote corner of eastern Germany, the tiny agricultural town of Struppen stands in stark contrast to the city of Dresden, just a one-half hour drive away. There are no museums or large churches here. Were it not for its picturesque setting in the Elbe River Valley, there would be no reason why tourists would be drawn to this locale. However, in 1987, long before anyone dreamed that German unification was possible, I led a group of thirty American college students to Struppen as part of their cultural experience of Europe. Our itinerary mentioned nothing more than that we were to meet an East German youth group for dinner and conversation. Consequently, some of the student travelers balked at the trip, fearing that they would have to endure a meal with uniformed communists extolling the virtues of communism. I admit that I, too, was more than a little concerned that the evening would turn out to be more an ideological debate than a social occasion. To our surprise, we disembarked to find our hosts wearing not the blue shirts of the communist Young Pioneers but the same blue jeans and T-shirts any typical Westerner might wear. We were treated to an evening of mutual discovery, sharing experiences with young people who wanted nothing more than to get to know us and to hear about the West. After dinner, we talked about our homes, our lives, and our aspirations; and then we danced to the recorded music of some rock-and-roll band or another. We left them reluctantly. Leaving was not as painful as was the realization that within days we would be again in the West, but they would still be the captives of a repressive government. It was a revelation equal to any on the tour.

Struppen has changed little since that evening over ten years ago. Except for the Western automobiles parked at the curbs and the abundance of Western products on the store shelves, there is little evidence that the German unification of 1990 has had much effect on the town. Looking deeper, however, it becomes clear that the town has undergone a dramatic transformation. It is the people who have changed. The citizens I met on my return visit in 1997 seemed leery of my questions. Perhaps they feared that I was a "Wessie" coming to settle a debt or lay claims against their property. Few would talk openly about the communist years, and those who did spoke of the terrible toll the collapse of communism and the unification took on their community. "Almost half of our soccer team fled to the West," one gentleman related. A younger man, who claimed to represent the present Struppen Youth Association, could tell me little of the members I had met ten years before. Many of them were now gone, and the records of those years were unaccounted for. Even the former meeting hall is temporarily closed. Like so much in East Germany, it is being rebuilt.

The students who accompanied me on that memorable evening in 1987 can appreciate the impact that the East German revolution of 1989 and the German unification of 1990 have had on the lives of ordinary Germans. They heard the longing for information in the voices of the East German students. They saw the joy that that short interlude with Westerners brought to the young people living under a communist dictatorship. Unfortunately, those students who witnessed German communism firsthand have been replaced by a younger generation of scholars for whom East Germany, or communism for that matter, is just an abstraction in their history lessons. It is for them, as much as anyone, that I wrote this book.

This is an attempt to present the German upheaval and unification of 1989–1990 in a concise and readable fashion for students of recent European history. It makes no claim to be a comprehensive treatment of the subject, and therefore scholars well versed in German history will find little that cannot be readily unearthed in newspapers, journals, periodicals, or research monographs. Instead, this is a book for the nonspecialist who needs an introduction to the "turnaround" (*die Wende*) which is grounded within a general discussion of German history since 1945. Perhaps, too, it will serve as a guide to propel students, young and old, to further study of the period.

I owe a debt of gratitude to the many individuals who helped me with this project. My thanks go to the librarians and staff at Harvard University; the Hoover Institution on War, Revolution and Peace, Stanford University; the Goethe Institute, New York; and the German Information Center (especially

John Alba) for their assistance in tracking down information and illustrations. I am also grateful for the help of Professors Randall M. Miller, Timothy O'Hara, and Erlis Wickersham, who lent valuable suggestions to the manuscript. Thanks also go to Anne Trotter and the entire library staff at Rosemont College, and to the Connelly Foundation for providing financial resources that made a research trip to Germany possible. Special thanks go to my student secretary, Cara Camiolo, for deciphering my handwriting and seeing me through the vicissitudes of word processing. Finally, I dedicate this work to my wife Cathy Jo, without whom none of this would be worthwhile.

Chronology of Events

1944

September 12   European Adivisory Commission creates three occupation zones for conquered Germany territory.

1945

August   Three-power conference at Potsdam reconfirms the partition of Germany into zones of occupation.

1948

March 20   Soviet delegation walks out of Allied Control Council meeting, effectively terminating four-power control over Germany.

June 16   Soviets withdraw representatives from the Allied Kommandatura, ending four-power control over Berlin.

June 24   Soviet blockade of western zones of Berlin begins in earnest.

June 25   Western powers begin a massive airlift to supply West Berlin.

1949

May 23   Federal Republic of Germany is created, following acceptance of the Basic Law by state governments.

May 30   An East German Congress approves a constitution for the German Democratic Republic (GDR); it goes into effect October 7.

1950

February 8   East German Ministry for State Security (Stasi) is created.

1951

January 15   Chancellor Adenauer rejects an East German proposal to create an inter-German council. He insists that free elections are a prerequisite to any unification initiatives.

1953

June 17   Soviet troops suppress an uprising of East German workers who are protesting increased labor demands.

1955

May 5   Western powers grant full sovereignty to Federal Republic of Germany.

September 20   The Soviet Union grants full sovereignty to the GDR.

1961

June 4   Soviet memorandum calls for demilitarization of West Berlin.

July 25   President Kennedy rejects Soviet demands and calls for free access to West Berlin and the assurance of West Berlin's security.

August 13   East German government begins construction on the Berlin Wall in response to increasing flight of East Germans to the West.

1969

September 28   Willy Brandt becomes chancellor of West Germany following elections, and he signals a change in relations between East and West known as *Ostpolitik.*

1971

September 3   Quadripartite treaty regularizing the status of Berlin is signed.

1972

May 26   West and East Germany conclude a treaty removing many restrictions on travel, thereby easing the flow of visitors between East and West.

1984

June 27   West Germany's mission in East Berlin is forced to close as East Germans crowded the building demanding permission to emigrate to the Federal Republic.

1988

January 17   East German police arrest 120 Peace Movement demonstrators.

1989

May 2	Hungary begins to dismantle the barbed wire fences along its border with Austria.
May 7	East German election results claim 98 percent vote for Socialist Unity Party (SED) candidates despite large dissident turnout; citizens take to streets to protest the obvious election fraud.
End of July	East German refugees seeking asylum flood to West German embassies in Prague, Warsaw, Budapest, and East Berlin.
August 19	At a Pan-Europa-Union festival at the Austro-Hungarian border, 661 GDR citizens flee *en masse* into Austria.
September 11	Hungary officially opens border with Austria; New Forum opposition movement is founded in East Germany.
September 30	Over 6,000 East Germans in Prague and Warsaw embassies receive permission to emigrate to the Federal Republic.
October 7	Fortieth anniversary of founding of the GDR is celebrated; demonstrations break out in major cities, put down by force; Gorbachev refuses to support Honecker's government and suggests that it should work toward its own "*perestroika.*"
October 9	"Monday Demonstration" in Leipzig draws 70,000; GDR security forces take no action against the demonstrators.
October 18	Erich Honecker resigns and is replaced by Egon Krenz.
October 27	Krenz's government offers amnesty to those arrested in demonstrations up to that point.
November 4	Demonstration in East Berlin attracts up to 1 million citizens.
November 7	GDR Council of Ministers resigns.
November 9	Berlin Wall is breached; East German frontiers with the West are opened.
November 13	Hans Modrow becomes Chairman of GDR Council of Ministers.
November 28	Kohl presents his Ten-Point Program to the Bundestag.
December 6	Krenz resigns.
December 7	"Round Table" talks begin.
December 8–9	European Council in Strassburg decides that German unification must be embedded in a larger European Unity framework.
December 17	SED adds "Party of Democratic Socialism" (SED-PDS) to its name.

December 19   Kohl travels to Dresden to meet with Modrow, delivers a pro-unification speech at the Frauenkirche.

1990

January 15   Stasi headquarters is seized by demonstrators.

January 20   SED-PDS recasts itself as the Party of Democratic Socialism (PDS).

January 30   During Modrow's visit to Moscow, Gorbachev refuses to support ideas to strengthen the collapsing GDR; hints at possibility of unification instead.

February 5   Modrow creates a "government of national responsibility" and brings members of opposition groups into Council of Ministers.

February 7   West German government creates "unity committee"; Kohl proposes currency union.

February 10   Kohl and Genscher meet with Gorbachev, discuss Soviet interests and German unification.

February 14   Foreign ministers of the United States, France, Great Britain, the Soviet Union, and the two German states agree to begin formal talks to reach international agreement on unification.

February 24–25 Kohl and Bush meet at Camp David.

March 18   First free East German elections result in a victory for the conservative "Alliance for Germany" coalition.

April 12   "Grand Coalition" government takes power in GDR with elements of Alliance for Germany, SPD, and others represented; Lothar de Maizière named Prime Minister.

April 24   Kohl and de Maizière agree to a target date of July 1, 1990, for economic unification.

May 5   First official Two-plus-Four meeting in Bonn.

May 18   Treaty establishing monetary, economic, and social union is concluded between the Federal Republic and the GDR in Bonn, to go into effect July 1.

June 21   Bundestag and Volkskammer approve identical resolutions regarding the sanctity of present borders with Poland.

July 1   The Deutschmark replaces the Ostmark as the legal currency in East Germany.

July 16   Kohl receives Gorbachev's approval for a united Germany's continued membership in NATO.

July 22	East German Volkskammer reestablishes five states in territory of GDR.
August 23	East German Volkskammer accepts October 3, 1990, as date for unification.
September 12	Two-plus-Four Treaty signed.
September 24	GDR leaves Warsaw Pact.
October 1	New York declaration grants sovereignty to a united Germany.
October 3	GDR formally accedes to the Federal Republic of Germany.
December 2	First all-German elections result in Kohl's reelection.

1991

June 20	Bundestag votes to make Berlin the capital of united Germany.
September	Border guard trials begin.

1992

January 1	Gauck Commission officially opens Stasi files for public inspection.
August	Riots against foreigners in Rostock and other major cities.

1993

May 28	German Federal Constitutional Court strikes down compromise legislation on abortion as unconstitutional.

1994

July 12	Germany's Constitutional Court rules that German military participation outside of NATO operating area was not unconstitutional.
October 16	Chancellor Kohl is returned to office following a narrow victory.

1995

January 1	*Treuhandanstalt* ends its work.

THE UNIFICATION OF
GERMANY EXPLAINED

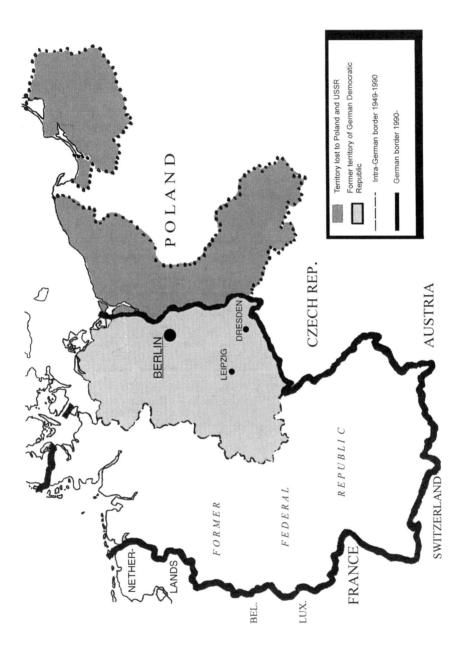

Germany's borders: Past and present.

I

From Division to Unification

Ever since its creation as a nation-state in 1871, Germany has had a most tumultuous history. In the short span of 125 years, it has experienced a monarchical government, a failed democracy, a brutal dictatorship, and defeat in two world wars. The last of these trials resulted in the division of Germany into two separate states, each with its own governmental, economic, and social structures. Many countries might never recover from such a litany or misfortune. Today, however, Germany is once again a single nation. Through skilled diplomacy and a little bit of luck, two very different states (one a failed communist dictatorship and the other a prosperous and stable Western democracy) somehow managed to merge into one political entity. That this unification occurred at all is amazing. What is even more astounding is the speed at which the transformation took place, for it took only twelve months to undo the previous fifty years of German history. Comprehending this acomplishment is a daunting task, and without an understanding of how Germany got to that point, such comprehension would be impossible. Chapter 1 attempts to provide that background through a brief explanation of German history since the close of World War II. This essay is the story of a bifurcated nation and the forces leading up to its unification.

Germany's history as a divided nation began in the waning months of World War II. By September 1944, with Hitler's war machine defeated and retreating on all fronts, Allied military planners divided the map of Germany into three zones, each to be administered by one of the victorious powers following the Nazi surrender or defeat. Great Britain was assigned the northwestern zone, which included the industrial heartland of Germany. The

United States was assigned the southeast, including much of the present states of Bavaria and Baden-Württemberg. The Soviet Union received the remaining (eastern) third, formerly the states of Prussia and Saxony. At the Yalta Conference in February 1945, President Franklin D. Roosevelt and Prime Minister Winston Churchill persuaded Soviet Premier Josef Stalin to accept France as a fourth "victorious power," with its own zone of occupation carved out of the American and British zones. Not only was Germany now partitioned, it also had to endure a constriction of its borders. German territory formerly known as East Prussia was severed from the occupation zones and ceded to the Soviet Union and Poland. In addition, the transfer of Prussian territory east of the Oder and Neisse Rivers effectively moved Poland's borders westward, compensating for the losses Poland suffered consequent to a similar westward readjustment of the Soviet Union's borders.

The reunification, or even the integration, of the four zones into a reconstituted nation was never an immediate concern. Although an Allied Control Council (composed of the four zonal commanders) did have decision-making power over the whole of Germany, it could not effectively coordinate the day-to-day activities of military government across four zones. Instead, each zonal commander had wide latitude to make administrative decisions in the area of his responsibility. The end result was that each zone began to assume the institutions and values of the nation governing it. A de facto division of Germany was already well underway.

Several more pressing issues kept the topic of German unity off the agenda. First, harsh weather and poor harvests forced zonal commanders to concentrate on the immediate food and energy needs of their zones, lest their populations starve and rebel against the occupation forces. Secondly, Allied policy had decided that the highly centralized Nazi governmental bureaucracy would have to be replaced by a more decentralized political system. Consequently, occupation authorities ordered that German political life should be rebuilt first at the local levels. Although the decision hindered the reestablishment of nationwide political institutions, prewar political parties did reemerge fairly quickly. The Social Democratic Party (SPD), traditionally Germany's largest political organization, was among the first to reappear. As the heirs to the socialist tradition, the SPD still sought the support of working-class populations for its platforms of social responsibility and economic planning. The prewar German Communist Party (KPD) also resurfaced, with the blessings of the Soviet occupiers, to resume the pursuit of a worldwide proletarian revolution. These left-wing parties were counterbalanced by other parties, most notably the Christian Democratic Union (CDU), a market-oriented, socially conservative party. With its ally the

Christian Social Union (CSU), the CDU represented primarily rural, agricultural, and Christian interests.

By 1947 the breakdown of the wartime alliance all but ended any chance for political revival of a single united Germany. Unable to achieve quadripartite agreement on how best to proceed with Germany's future, Great Britain and the United States merged their zones into a single administrative unit called "Bizonia." If this were not enough to drive a wedge between the Western powers and the Soviet Union, the American proposal to rebuild Europe under the Marshall Plan and the subsequent currency reform in the western zones fractured what was left of four-power control in Germany. In March 1948, the Soviet military governor Marshal Sokolovski stormed out of an Allied Control Council meeting, thereby effectively ending that body's activities. Three months later, Soviet troops blockaded the land and water routes into the western zones of Berlin in an attempt to force the West either to retire from the city or yield to Soviet demands on currency and political union. The Allies responded by supplying the beleaguered city with tons of food, fuel, and medicines by air. The effort became known as the Berlin Airlift and clearly demonstrated the West's determination both to protect the freedom of the western zones and to halt the advance of communism. The airlift worked. After a ten-month siege, the Soviets lifted the blockade. Unfortunately, this would not be the last such confrontation. As the Iron Curtain descended across Europe, the capitalist West and communist East each did its best to prove the superiority of its political system. Thus, caught in the crossfire of competing ideologies, Germany and Berlin became the focal points of a much larger conflict. The Cold War had begun.

THE GERMAN QUESTION TO 1989

The Soviet blockade of Berlin not only failed to bring West Berlin to its knees, it further hardened the West's resolve to create a German national government, with or without Soviet participation. While the blockade was underway, civilian authorities of the western zones received permission to hold elections for a constituent assembly to draft a constitution. Some Germans welcomed this assembly as a step toward self-determination, but others argued that the creation of a constitution without the participation of the citizens in the Soviet zone would automatically, and perhaps permanently, partition the country. In deference to the latter's wishes, the constituent assembly proceeded cautiously, carefully adopting language that addressed all Germans. The resulting document was called the Basic Law to avoid any sense of exclusion and finality, and was intended to be a temporary instru-

ment, effective until "the day on which a constitution adjusted by a free decision of the German people comes into force."[1]

As expected, the eastern zone retaliated with its own constituent assembly. While espousing civil rights and political freedom, the East German
constitution stifled political initiative by granting the newly formed Socialist
Unity Party (*Sozialistiche Einheitspartei Deutschland*, or SED) virtual monopoly status. Other political parties were permitted and expected to ally
themselves with the SED and follow its lead. Unlike West Germany, where
delegates were democratically elected from the major political parties, East
German deputies were elected from "unity lists" of SED party members or
their allies. In May 1949, only one week after the Western states accepted the
Basic Law, delegates to a People's Council in the Soviet Zone voted to accept its own separate constitution. On October 7, the German Democratic
Republic was born.

Germany was now officially two states, and to all the world a symbol of a
continent divided by rival ideologies. As each country set out on its own political and diplomatic path, the goal of unification became less and less realistic. West Germany adopted Western institutions, including a bicameral
legislature (the Bundesrat and Bundestag) and a "social market economy"
premised on capitalism and free enterprise. Thanks in part to the Marshall
Plan, which pumped much needed capital into the West German economy,
West Germany experienced an economic revival in the 1950s that many observers have called "miraculous." In 1950 West Germany joined with France
in creating the European Coal and Steel Community (ECSC), a supranational organization to oversee shared resources and steel production. Its success led West Germany and five other nations to form the Common Market
in 1957. As West Germany's economic stature grew, so too did its diplomatic
stature. Under the leadership of Konrad Adenauer (CDU), the Federal Republic aligned itself firmly with the United States and western Europe. The
postwar occupation ended officially in 1955, when the Western powers
granted sovereignty to West Germany and approved its membership in
NATO. By the mid-1960s, West Germany had not only become an industrial
power of some magnitude, it also had become one of the most stable, prosperous, and politically reliable nations in the Western alliance.

In contrast, the German Democratic Republic (East Germany) set out to
create a model socialist society. Its government appeared democratic, complete with a legislature (the People's Chamber or Volkskammer) and popular
elections, but such institutions were a façade to mask the dictatorial
decision-making power of the SED and its chairman, Walther Ulbricht. Further, East Germany instituted a centrally planned economy in which the state

owned the factories, set production quotas, and delegated resources. At least at first, the GDR enjoyed a reputation as a "showcase" of socialist achievement. Statistically, the GDR was the most productive country in COMECON, the Soviet Union's answer to the Common Market. Its citizens boasted the highest living standards of any nation behind the Iron Curtain. And considering its position along the border with the West, East Germany became the keystone in the Warsaw Pact, the Soviet defensive military alliance of eastern European satellites.

As impressive as these accomplishments seem, they were achieved at the expense of the country's natural resources, both mineral and human. In a race to stay on par with the West, the GDR's economic planners looked away while their factories plundered and polluted the environment. Over time, the stultifying socialist economy could no longer compete with its capitalist competitors. Durable goods such as telephones, washing machines, and automobiles were scarce, and those which were produced were of substandard quality. More important, the regime maintained its hold on society by enforcing rigid political uniformity. Citizens lived in the shadow of the state security police (Stasi), whose operatives might be a neighbor, a co-worker, or even a family member. Its network of secret informants enabled the Stasi to reach into every town and village to frighten and coerce obedience. Dissent was not tolerated. Those who did protest, such as the Berlin workers who struck against higher work quotas in June 1953, quickly discovered that the police and the military stood ready to quell any disturbances with force. Clearly, deviation from the "correct" (i.e., socialist) path was unacceptable.

Many East Germans chose to flee to the West rather than live under such repression. From 1945 to 1961, nearly 3.5 million refugees took advantage of West Germany's offer of immediate citizenship. In 1961, as Soviet Premier Nikita Khrushchev's bellicose language heightened fears of superpower confrontation, the pace of emigration quickened, and the GDR cordoned itself off from the West. In East Berlin, where the alienated could defect simply by crossing the street, construction troops erected concrete walls separated by barbed wire, land mines, and tank traps. The Berlin Wall, which soon became the most hated symbol of divided Germany, did discourage many from fleeing. Most who tried were caught in the attempt or felled by gunfire from the guard towers overlooking the expanse. A nation, a city, and even families were now physically separated, first by barbed wire and then by an ugly concrete barrier. East Germans became the captives of a brutal, repressive government bent on restricting their liberties in the name of communist solidarity.

Clearly, the two Germanys were developing into completely different societies. Nevertheless, neither side had given up totally the idea of unification. The East German government, taking its cue from the Soviet Union, often held out the carrot of unification in exchange for the neutralization of central Europe. Given Adenauer's policy of grounding the Federal Republic in the West, the Federal Republic was not about to abandon NATO. Adenauer and his successors refused to recognize the existence of East Germany, claiming that the Basic Law was the sole legitimate expression of the will of the German people. The CDU leadership insisted that there would be no unification until the Germans in the East could elect representatives freely. By the mid-1960s, West Germans showed little sorrow at the division of their country. The status quo afforded them both security (under NATO's nuclear umbrella) and considerable prosperity. Unification seemed highly unlikely.

Then, in 1969, the election of Willy Brandt (SPD) as chancellor marked a departure from Adenauer's policies. Instead of estrangement, SPD foreign policy stressed "change through rapprochement"; that is, the two Germanys would be more likely to come together through cooperation and mutual acceptance than through confrontation. Brandt's new policy, called *Ostpolitik*, set out to mend fences with the communist bloc. Within four years, the Federal Republic concluded nonaggression pacts with East Germany and the Soviet Union, signed treaties recognizing the inviolability of East German and Polish borders, and reached agreements on the status of West Berlin. With *Ostpolitik*, the two German states finally came to terms with each other's existence while, paradoxically, simultaneously reaffirming Germany's right to unify. Both Germanys could now set aside World War II animosities and work together as much as their ideological differences could tolerate. The GDR eased restrictions on travel to the West, and the Federal Republic abandoned its position as the only legitimate representative of the German people.

For the next fifteen years, the two states coexisted in relative peace, secure in the knowledge that unification would not occur without concomitant change in Europe's Cold War security arrangements. Indeed, by the early 1980s, unification suddenly seemed less important than survival. The threat of superpower confrontation reappeared in 1982 as the United States began deploying Pershing missiles in Europe to counter Soviet SS20 missiles. Soviet leadership, determined to keep pace with the West militarily despite the drain on their overburdened economic system, soon responded by placing more short-range missiles near the border with West Germany. Many Germans on both sides of the Iron Curtain felt caught in the middle of a disagreement that could easily lead to a war—with Germany as the battleground. Then, in 1985, the inconceivable happened. Mikhail Gorbachev, a young and energetic champion of reform, became premier of the Soviet Union and embarked on a new course for the ailing Soviet empire. His policies of *glasnost* (openness) and *perestroika* (restructuring) promised to relieve the Soviet Union of its defensive burdens by allowing its satellites in east-central Europe to find their own path to socialism. Gorbachev's actions were a monumental *volte face*. Not only did this imply an easing of military tensions internationally, it also meant hope for the dissident populations of eastern Europe. The Polish government embarked on its own *glasnost*, allowing referenda that eventually led to round table discussions between government and the governed. In Hungary, a group of liberal communists ousted the party hard-liners and began a reform movement. The shackles of four decades of communism were slowly loosening.

While dejected populations all over eastern Europe welcomed these changes, Gorbachev's ideas were less than well received by the hard-line governments that Moscow had propped up for decades. The reaction was particularly vehement in East Germany, where an aged Erich Honecker led a government that had lost all touch with reality. When asked what Gorbachev's new approach would mean for East Germany, one *apparatchik* (party functionary) glibly responded, "If your neighbor put up new wallpaper, would you feel obligated to have your wallpaper changed too?"[2] While their government might have been hesitant, the population of East Germany had become increasingly receptive to redecoration. Dissident groups that had emerged during the 1970s and flourished during the nuclear debate had become increasingly vocal about their hopes for peaceful change. Emboldened by the movements within other eastern bloc nations, more and more East Germans became politically active. Overt protests and demonstrations, which in previous decades were rare, had become more frequent. East Germany responded with prison sentences, fines, and exile for anyone so involved. Honecker's proclamation—"The Berlin Wall will stand for another century"[3]—seemed ominous. He had no way of knowing the wall would be torn down within a year.

THE GENTLE REVOLUTION

The year 1989 was one of discontent. Revolutionary movements caught fire in Romania, Bulgaria, and China as citizens tried desperately to persuade their governments to adopt reforms similar to those already underway in Hungary and Poland. In the midst of all the activity, East Germany's leadership seemed as unwilling to change as ever. Honecker's government held its regular elections on May 7, and despite a large turnout of dissenting voters, the official tally showed that 98 percent of the votes cast approved the government's slate of candidates. Egon Krenz, Erich Honecker's heir apparent, publicly supported the Chinese government's brutal reppression of the Tienanmen Square demonstrations in June. Other East German officials criticized the wisdom of *perestroika* and had the temerity to question Mikhail Gorbachev's ability to lead.

That July, as the French celebrated the bicentennial of their revolution against oppression, thousands of East Germans considered how best to achieve their own liberation. Whether they chose emigration, flight, or political demonstrations, their cumulative efforts ultimately undermined the East German state.

Exodus

The GDR was accustomed to a certain amount of migration. Every year, tens of thousands of East Germans left their country to seek freedom and a better life in the West.[4] To put a good face on what was clearly a referendum against communism, the SED regime permitted individuals to apply for emigration to the Federal Republic. This largesse came with a price, however, as those who applied lost their jobs and were forced to work at menial labor, sometimes for months or years, until the bureaucracy rendered a final decision. Nevertheless, by the end of summer 1989 nearly 120,000 East Germans had submitted exit applications.[5] Hundreds of others took advantage of their vacations to flock to the West German embassies in Warsaw, Budapest, and Prague demanding West German citizenship and passage to the Federal Republic.

While these emigrants waited, the less patient decided to flee. For the determined, illegal border crossings remained the quickest, if not safest, avenue of escape. In early May, the Hungarian government announced that henceforth part of its border with Austria would be open to unrestricted travel. Honecker's government received the news with a mixture of anger and horror. They realized that any East German who held a valid visa to visit Hungary might escape by crossing into Austria and freedom. Initially, Hungarian guards detained East Germans at border checkpoints, but they could not stop crossings of the "green border" (the unmanned sectors where barbed wire had been dismantled). Over the next three months, approximately 1,600 East Germans left Hungary for freedom in the West.

By August, the traditional month for vacations, the SED regime faced a severe emigration crisis. On August 19, 661 East Germans attending an outdoor gathering near Sopron, Hungary, slipped en masse into Austria. To everyone's amazement, Hungarian border guards did not try to stop them. To make matters worse, on September 10 the Hungarian government halted any pretense of border delays. By the end of the month, East Germany had lost 25,000 citizens to Austria.[6]

The emigration of East Germans had quite an impact on West Germany as well. The Bonn government had a humanitarian duty to aid the fleeing masses of Germans since the Basic Law recognized their German citizenship. Consequently, the government threw together makeshift camps to provide shelter, food, and "welcome money" for each emigrant. Despite its early exuberance, West Germany could not afford to invite further defections. The East German press already had blamed West Germany for the current difficulties, and Chancellor Kohl did not wish to risk destroying intra-German relationships. Furthermore, as the stream of fleeing citizens became a flood, West German social services strained under the weight of all the work. Certainly, West Germany could not take in an indefinite number of emigrants. Thus, Chancellor Helmut Kohl, while privately jubilant at Honecker's misfortunes, had to appeal publicly to the East Germans to stay at home. The appeal had little effect. Despite the government's efforts to stabilize the situation, the West German media inadvertently encouraged further migrations. Every night, East Germans who remained behind tuned in West German television stations to witness the spectacle firsthand on news broadcasts. The images of jubilant men, women, and children crossing the border to freedom emboldened others, who had not believed it possible, to flee themselves.

The SED regime soon closed its border with Hungary and temporarily patched the "Hungarian hole," but it could do nothing to halt the rush of East Germans who were seeking asylum in West German consulates in Poland and Czechoslovakia. As increasing numbers of refugees crammed into makeshift shelters on embassy property, the world's attention focused on their plight. What began as a minor diplomatic matter had quickly become an international embarrassment that threatened to spoil the GDR's fortieth anniversary celebration. To save face, the GDR decided to expel these citizens by shipping them to West Germany in sealed railroad cars. As the trains passed through Dresden, crowds of people gathered at the train station in the hope that they too might jump on board. In a final, desperate attempt to stem the tide of refugees, the GDR suspended permission to travel to Poland and Czechoslovakia. East Germany was now isolated—even from its own allies.

Protest

As thousands of East Germans took flight, thousands more took to the streets to protest the regime's rigidity. Mass demonstrations were nothing new, but they had never been very successful, given the government's willingness to subdue them with force. By the mid-1970s, however, the undercurrents of dissent had coalesced into organizations founded to advance environmental, peace, and human rights agendas, among other concerns. While at first these organizations stayed in the background of East German society, many were now coming forth to voice their dissent more openly. Nevertheless, their ability to effect change remained marginal until the coming of Mikhail Gorbachev. It was his drive for reorganization that, for the first time in history, put the weight of the Soviet Union behind the reform movements. Governments now had to think twice before cracking down on such groups, as they could no longer be certain Moscow would back up their decisions with tanks. As reformers sensed this change, the scope and scale of protests increased dramatically. Suppressing them would become even more difficult.

The first widespread demonstrations of 1989 followed the rigged election in May. Marchers took to the streets by the thousands, many brandishing whistles, to poke fun at the election results. The police broke up the demonstrations and made arrests as usual. In spite of the danger, the agitators vowed to commemorate the "election lie" by holding similar demonstrations on the seventh of every month. Their actions were only the tip of an iceberg of protest submerged in East German political life. By July and August, political and social groups once considered illegal were now coming out publicly. Generically referred to as "civic action groups," these organizations advanced a variety of political platforms. The first of these, called the New Forum, was created by artist Bärbel Bohley, pastor Jochen Tschiche, molecular biologist Jens Reich, and others. Its political agenda called for, among other things, an open dialogue between civic groups and government officials on the problems of the nation. Two other groups, Democracy Now! and Democratic Awakening, launched similar appeals for a democratic transformation of East German society. Some civic action groups advanced environmental or feminist causes. The Green Party brought its anticapitalist environmental agenda to the fray, calling for East Germans to reject the "cut-throat society" of the West.[7] By the end of summer, such groups had evolved into de facto political parties. In direct defiance to established authority, they held open meetings to discuss the political future of their nation and how they might best renew their society.

October 7, 1989, proved a pivotal date for the dissident movement. It had been five months to the day since the falsified May elections and it was also, coincidentally, the fortieth anniversary of the East German Constitution. In other years, typical anniversary celebrations featured military parades, political speeches, and visits by foreign dignitaries. This year was special, since the accomplishments of forty years of "real existing socialism" would be on display to the world. Although Chairman Honecker wanted nothing to spoil the festivities, crowds of young people took the streets for their monthly "whistle concert" in protest against the election fraud. To make matters worse, his featured guest, none other than Mikhail Gorbachev, stoked the fires by openly revealing his sympathies with the dissident movement in his keynote speech. Clearly, Gorbachev had suffered Honecker's leadership too long. In private conversations, the Soviet premier urged the SED leadership to seek a rapprochement with the people since "life punishes those who are late."[8] His message was a clear signal that Moscow would support a move to dismiss Honecker. Would anyone act?

As the official ceremonies continued, trouble brewed in the streets. Despite the government's notices that disruptions would not be tolerated, the dissidents refused to cower. As groups of protesters formed, police units swept them quickly and brutally from the streets. At the Gethsemane Church where a week-long vigil for imprisoned citizens was underway, crowds gathered for a peace march. As the marchers began, the police blocked their path and beat them with rubber truncheons. Participants and innocent bystanders alike were loaded up on trucks and taken to police stations. Two young girls from the Prenzlauerberg section of Berlin recounted:

When the police tried to break up the demonstration at Schönhauser street, we ran for our lives down the Danenstrasse. There, we came upon a group of police officers who struck us with their clubs. A friend of ours lived at Danenstrasse 4. She wasn't at the demonstration but she saw us and called us to come upstairs. When we got there, we locked ourselves in and watched everything from the window—we were photographed. After half an hour there was a terrible banging and knocking. We didn't open. Then my friend and I went to a neighboring apartment to use the phone. In the two minutes we were gone, the police had entered the apartment building and arrested everyone.[9]

The police showed little discretion in breaking up the demonstrations. Another witness remembered: "The worst experience for me was that someone whacked my 14-year-old daughter's hand with a rubber truncheon, just because she was holding a candle. He knocked this candle brutally from her hand. I naturally got pretty angry, then the man said,

'Clear the streets or you'll be loaded up.' "[10] Over 1,000 Berliners were arrested that Saturday and Sunday. Police detention centers filled so quickly that many of the arrested were taken to police garages where they were forced to stand at attention for hours while pressed up face-first against a wall. This ordeal lasted through the night until the next morning when the officers released the detainees.[11] Those with ties to civic action groups were less fortunate. Many faced indefinite terms of imprisonment.

Berlin was not the only city to have citizens voice their dissatisfaction publicly that night. In Dresden, 30,000 men and women demonstrated in open sympathy; in Plauen, another 10,000 marched. Smaller but equally volatile demonstrations took place in Magdeburg, Potsdam, Arnstadt, and Karl-Marx-Stadt (Chemnitz).[12] While unarmed civilians had to muster a great deal of courage to take to the streets, the possibility of confrontation was not attractive to many policemen either. In Leipzig, as a crowd of 10,000 protesters gathered, many officers balked at the use of force. In one account, five auxiliaries questioned their superiors when ordered to use their pistols if clubs proved insufficient. When one asked what to do about the children in the crowd, he was told, "They are out of luck." The five men then did what they could to avoid service. Some volunteered for kitchen duty; others just lay in their beds and cried, unsure what to do.[13]

Leipzig got no respite from the political tension. Two days later, on October 9, a general feeling of dread swept over the city as crowds gathered for that evening's traditional Monday peace rally. As in Berlin, local party newspapers had warned earlier in the week that police were "ready and willing to suppress these counterrevolutionary activities effectively and finally . . . if necessary with weapons in hand."[14] Shops closed their doors by five o'clock to keep the city center empty. Parents were advised to pick up their school children before the late afternoon and leave the city. Rumors circulated that hospitals had stocked up on blood (had police commanders issued shoot to kill orders?). Tanks took up their stations outside the city, and security troops gathered at key points in the city limits. Everything pointed to a confrontation.

By the time the peace rally began, approximately 70,000 people already had crowded the city center. The original Prayer for Peace service at the Nikolai Church filled to capacity, so four other churches opened their doors to the marchers. As the crowds made their way on the ring street around the city, individuals shouted "Gorbi, Gorbi" and taunted police to put down their weapons and join the march. In the midst of the mayhem, six brave gentlemen mounted a platform to address the crowd. Among them were

Kurt Masur, then the director of the Leipzig orchestra, Pastor Peter Zimmerman, the cabaretist Bernd Lutz Lange, and three SED functionaries. They called for moderation not confrontation, and pleaded for a peaceful dialogue between citizens and state. No one knows how many people heard them that evening, or if their words had any direct effect on the marchers or the police. Nevertheless, their message captured the moment. The crowd did not riot, and the security forces did not act.

Reform or Revolution?

To this day, no one is quite sure who issued the orders for the troops to stand fast. Perhaps the disagreement within the SED was sufficient enough to allow those reformists who wanted to avoid a bloodbath to maneuver Honecker out of the decision. This interpretation is supported by Egon Krenz, Honecker's heir apparent and self-styled champion of *perestroika*, who later claimed that he had countermanded shoot-to-kill orders. It is also probable that local police and security troops were unwilling to obey any shoot order. At least one commander is on record as telling his troops not to fire since the demonstrators were fellow citizens.

Although we may never know the complete truth surrounding the decision, it is safe to say that the evening marked a turning point in the struggle between people and government. By allowing the crowd its say, the regime lost what little authority it had left to command the people's obedience. In an attempt to stave off a complete collapse, the SED removed Honecker and his hard-line supporters. Krenz, now elevated to party secretary, quickly positioned himself as the East German Gorbachev. Within days, Krenz had reopened the Czech border, promised a reform of the travel laws, and sought to begin a dialogue with the civic action groups. For many dissidents, those concessions were insufficient. Every week more and more citizens joined the marches—not the rowdies or malcontents whom the government had claimed were involved—but average citizens with families and jobs. By the end of the month, some demonstrations drew 200,000 people, and the flight from the country continued unabated.

The collapse continued, largely because East Germans had little faith in the new leadership. Krenz was never a popular choice for leader. While most people welcomed Honecker's dismissal, they also remembered Krenz's involvement in the election fraud of May and his support for the Chinese government. Consequently, Krenz took a desperate chance in an attempt to win favor with the people. On November 6, the Politburo drafted new travel regulations that would permit all GDR citizens the right to hold a passport and travel abroad for thirty days. However, in a televised press conference

announcing the pending change in law, Berlin party boss Günther Schabowski seemed to say that anyone wishing to visit West Berlin could immediately obtain a visa at the border. Many citizens interpreted this to mean that
unrestricted travel would begin forthwith. To test their assumptions, thousands of East Berliners walked or drove to the border checkpoints. The border guards, confused by the announcement and lacking precise instructions,
let them pass. East Germans were now free to travel for the first time in
twenty-eight years. Overnight, the Berlin Wall had become a curious anach-
ronism. Students, dissidents, and fun seekers climbed the wall with pick-
axes, hacking off pieces as personal mementos or for future resale. With the
damage already done, Krenz's government dared not try to correct its error.
Soon, transit points all along the border opened to unrestricted travel.

Krenz's blunder set in motion a chain of events that would end East Germany's forty-year history as a communist dictatorship. On November 13,
the People's Chamber chose Hans Modrow, a noted moderate and party up-
start, to lead the Council of Ministers. His election symbolized the continuing success of the reform movement, which by now had infiltrated even the
ranks of the SED. Following revelations of the good life lived by former
party brass, the reform wing of the SED purged the remaining hard-liners.
On December 1, the People's Chamber voted to strike the SED's monopoly
of power from the constitution. With the passage of power to the
Volkskammer, East Germany became a parliamentary democracy. Egon
Krenz resigned shortly thereafter, and Hans Modrow became East Germany's provisional head of state, pending elections.

TRANSITION AND UNIFICATION

Krenz's departure and the resulting political infighting left the SED badly
shaken and nearing disintegration. Faced with its almost complete rejection
by the citizenry, the SED membership tried to salvage the party by transforming it into the Party of Democratic Socialism, or PDS, and expelling
former SED leaders from its ranks. In the confusion, the SPD and CDU (the
so-called "bloc parties"), which at one time had cooperated with the SED,
also resurfaced and asserted their independence. The tasks confronting Modrow's government were formidable. Citizens were still fleeing in ever
larger numbers, precipitating a monumental economic crisis. Further, with
the wall gone and travel liberalized, unification suddenly seemed attainable.
The shouts "We are the people" were now becoming "We are one people."
Could reforms salvage a working socialist society, or would Modrow's

government ultimately collapse under the weight of economic distress, political unrest, and the clamor for unification?

These questions would not be solved by government action alone. Instead, the People's Chamber opened up negotiations to include representatives of the dissident movements. The so-called Round Table discussions, based on a format that Polish reformers had used with some success, brought together leaders of the civic action groups with delegates of the established political parties to discuss problems and possible solutions. The first discussions revealed a wide gulf between the participants. Modrow's government had hoped that the Round Table format would mollify the civic action groups, co-opting them into the government's plans. The groups, however, never intended to cooperate with or replace the existing government. Instead, they distanced themselves from decision making, preferring instead to act as a sounding board for ideas and a watchdog over implementation. Once he discovered he could not control the Round Table, Modrow wanted to have little to do with it and did what he could to limit its effectiveness.

It did not take long, however, to determine which side held the initiative. In January 1990, Modrow insisted that any new East German state would require a secret police force similar to the Stasi. The Round Table opposition was vocal and called for a complete repudiation of all state-sponsored secret police activity. Modrow remained unconvinced of his error until January 15, when crowds of angry citizens occupied Stasi headquarters in East Berlin, destroyed records, and vandalized the property. Soon after this display of civil disobedience, the Round Table persuaded the government to dissolve the dreaded Stasi apparatus. Modrow got the message, and thereafter paid more serious attention to the civic action groups. Further concessions to the popular will followed, including advancing the date for scheduled elections to March 18.

Despite its revolutionary demeanor, the Round Table proved a remarkably moderate assembly. Although it demanded a new constitution, its members openly advocated the GDR's continued survival as a democratic socialist state. While many delegates accepted the idea of unification in theory, they felt that unity ought to take place pursuant to Article 146 of the Basic Law. This would allow for the gradual merger of the two sovereign states and ensure the preservation of many of the "achievements" of socialism.

Most East Germans did not share the Round Table's opinions of the "achievements" of socialism. When comparing the Federal Republic to the GDR, many East Germans simply shook their heads and said, "We have wasted forty years." Consequently, while the Round Table debated, the flight of East German citizens continued unchecked. Younger professionals were generally the first to leave, lured by the prospects of a better (and more profitable) life in the West. Unskilled workers, who now felt the enticement of the capitalist system following their visits to the Federal Republic, followed closely behind. Suddenly, there were labor shortages in practically every sector of the economy. As more and more workers left, an already terrible economic situation became much worse. According to one estimate, East German industry was losing about 80 million Deutschmarks each day.[15] One official quipped that all Germany would someday be reunited—in the West. Given the steady stream of workers leaving the GDR for West Germany, the joke was not far from the truth.

Getting Unification Started

In the Federal Republic, reactions to the imminent collapse of East Germany were mixed. While most people welcomed the opening of the borders and the liberalization of the GDR government, the unification question was more contentious. Conservatives, especially Chancellor Helmut Kohl and the CDU, saw unification as the opportunity of a lifetime and resolved not to let the chance slip away. The opposition party was more cautious. While agreeing to the idea of unification in principle, the SPD did not want the effort to translate into higher taxes for West Germans. Party ideology aside, everyone agreed that unification—if accomplished at all—would take years of negotiation and compromise. Both Kohl and Modrow devised unification plans that reflected that assumption. Modrow's plan called for a federation of separate states with a gradual integration of the two societies. Chancellor Kohl's Ten-Point Program anticipated four years of negotiations aimed at eventual unity. In February, Kohl created a Bundestag committee to investigate the possibilities of unification.

The upcoming March elections in the GDR became a referendum on unification as the traditional political parties (now linked and receiving support from their counterparts in West Germany) and the various civic action groups mobilized voters in an effort to increase their electoral strengths. As the polling date approached, most pundits expected an SPD victory. Assuming that the electorate would be eager to preserve the social net that had once existed under communism, the "experts" figured that the SPD's traditional sensitivity to social issues should make it the most favorable choice of voters. Furthermore, the SPD was also publicly pro-unification, even though its leadership privately preferred a slow pace of negotiation and compromise. The CDU, on the other hand, enjoyed a more developed organization in East Germany and benefited from its relationship to the ruling West German CDU, the backing of its astute leadership, and the efforts of Chancellor

Kohl. These advantages were apparent during Chancellor Kohl's campaign stop in Dresden on December 19–20 in support of East German CDU candidates. During his speech, Chancellor Kohl peered out over the large gathering at the multitude of banners calling for immediate unification, not the lengthy drawn-out process most politicians envisaged. Evidently, he was duly impressed. Gambling on his ability to sense the popular will, Kohl abandoned the ill-received Ten-Point Program and committed his party to rapid unification under Article 23 (accession to the Federal Republic's Basic Law). In February 1990, he forged a new political entente called "Alliance for Germany," consisting of the western and eastern CDU parties, their Bavarian and Saxon allies (the CSU and DSU), and the civic action group Democratic Awakening. In the March elections, the Alliance scored a stunning triumph, drawing almost half of the East German vote (see Table 1).

Table 1
Results of All-German Elections: May 18, 1990

	Percent of Vote
Christian Democratic Union (CDU)	40.9
Social Democratic Party (SPD)	21.8
Party for Democratic Socialism (PDS)	16.3
German Social Union (DSU)	6.3
Alliance of Free Democrats	5.3
Alliance 90 (New Forum, Democracy Now! et al.)	2.9
Greens	2.0
Democratic Awakening	0.9
Other	3.6

Source: D. Philipsen, *We Were the People* (Durham, NC: Duke University Press, 1993), 401.

The victory elevated Lothar de Maizière, the East German CDU chairman, to the position of East Germany's first (and, as history would have it, last) freely elected chancellor. Surprising as the conservative victory was, the poor showing of the civic action groups is even more revealing. Their inability to draw votes may have been the result of poor organization or insufficient funding. Regardless, their defeat killed any last hopes to revive the socialist state. The two states were now on the fast track to unity.

The Unification Process

Now that the issue of method had been decided, the task at hand was to remove the obstacles hindering East German accession to the Basic Law. By necessity, economic matters received immediate attention since East Germany's economy was eroding more and more each day under the weight of absenteeism, unemployment, and inflation. The need for an economic solution was just as great across the border, as the Federal Republic's ability to see to the needs of East German refugees was rapidly becoming overtaxed. To stabilize the East German economy, Kohl suggested that the two countries form an economic union with the Deutschmark (DM) as its official currency. Despite the fears of economists, the currency exchange went well. East Germans could trade in their worthless East German Ostmarks (OMs) for DMs at the rate of one-to-one for savings up to 400 DMs. Wages and salaries were also converted at one-to-one, but debts were exchanged at the rate of two-to-one. For its part, the de Maizière government enacted legislation to introduce capitalism to the former communist state. The long and arduous negotiations ended with the signing of a treaty establishing monetary, economic, and social union on May 18. On July 1, the Deutschmark became the legal currency of both halves of Germany.

The final obstacle to political unification was beyond the direct control of the two Germanys; the international community had yet to agree. Unification was a diplomatic problem on any number of levels. Germany's neighbors, many of which had fallen victim to Nazi aggression, feared that a restored Germany might again become expansionist. Poland was particularly sensitive to this issue, since a unified Germany might lay claim to the Oder-Neisse territories ceded to Poland after World War II. The security of the Soviet Union also had to be addressed. Gorbachev's insistence that a new Germany be neutral—that is, a member of neither NATO nor the Warsaw Pact—seemed the best the Soviets could offer. After all, the Soviet Union could ill afford further NATO encroachment on its borders. Would the West accept his reasoning? Would Germany rearm? Might it possess nuclear weapons?

Official negotiations on these vexing questions began on May 5, 1990, in Bonn. The so-called Two-plus-Four talks brought together a cadre of highly skilled foreign ministers. Representing the two German states were Hans-Dietrich Genscher and Lothar de Maizière. The four wartime powers were represented by James A. Baker (US), Roland Dumas (FR), Douglas Hurd (GB), and Eduard Shevardnadze (USSR). The Polish border issue demanded immediate attention, if only to allay the Polish government's rapidly growing fear of German intentions. Resolution came fairly quickly. Kohl and de Maizière introduced identical resolutions to their respective parliaments promising that the German states and Poland would "respect each other's sovereignty and territorial integrity without restriction."[16] Kohl assured that an all-German parliament would ratify the resolutions by treaty following unification. Although the compromise was not the complete abrogation of Germany's claim on the Oder-Neisse territories that it wanted, the Polish government acquiesced.

The issue of NATO membership was much more disruptive. A united Germany, still in NATO, would have been perceived by many Soviets as a blow to the security of the Soviet Union. On the other hand, the West did not intend to allow Germany to be neutral and therefore free to pursue its own foreign policy path without the mitigation of other nations. Fearing that this issue might scuttle unification just as the object came into sight, Kohl flew to Moscow to meet with Gorbachev in person. It turned out to be Germany's most significant state visit in recent history. At his summer retreat in the Caucasus, Gorbachev told Kohl that the USSR would no longer insist on neutrality. Undoubtedly, Gorbachev's change of heart was in part a ploy to woo German economic support. However, it was also a positive gesture toward NATO's pledge to revise its mission in Europe to emphasize political, not military, goals.

The Two-plus-Four negotiations produced a carefully worded treaty designed to remove all the diplomatic obstacles to German unity. By the terms of the document, the Soviet Union, the United States, France, and Great Britain divested themselves of their postwar authority over the German nation. Although the final product was more a Soviet concession than a compromise, the treaty did embody both Soviet and Western interests. Germany would be free to join whichever alliance(s) it wanted, even though everyone understood that it would join NATO. In deference to the Soviet Union, the treaty restricted NATO from stationing troops on former GDR territory until all Soviet troops left. In addition, the agreement limited the size of the future German military and prohibited the possession of atomic, biological, and chemical weapons.

With the international aspects settled, only the inter-German treaty of union remained. On August 31, 1990, the Unification Treaty established agreements and compromises on a wide range of issues from constitutional law and internal justice to sports, culture, and education. Having thus chosen a common infrastructure, the two Germanys had little left to do but unite. The GDR People's Chamber chose October 3, 1990, as the day it would officially accede to the Basic Law and vote itself out of existence. As that day approached, Germans looked back on the previous twelve months with a mixture of amazement and trepidation. Forty years of division had ended in only nine remarkable months. In the early evening on October 2, Unity Day celebrations took place all over East and West Germany. Many communities opted for low-key observances, while others favored fireworks and political speeches. In Berlin, the Philharmonic played Beethoven's *Ode to Joy* under the direction of Kurt Masur, the hero of the Leipzig demonstrations the year before. Chancellor Kohl's address that evening proclaimed that the new Germany would work toward "a common peaceful future in trustful cooperation with all countries and peoples."[17] Those were comforting words, designed to soften the transition as Germany and Europe entered a new era. Germany's position within the European Union and its role in world diplomacy would need to be redefined. As of 1990, those and other problems still lay ahead.

NOTES

1. Article 146, 1961 translation.

2. Quoted, inter alia, in H. A. Turner, *Germany from Partition to Reunification* (New Haven: Yale University Press, 1992), 223.

3. A discussion of *Torschlusspanik* (gate-closing panic) and the fear that East Germans would forever be captive to an unchanging society can be found in the article "Das droht die DDR zu vernichten," *Der Spiegel* 33 (August 14, 1989): 19. See also Turner, *Germany*, 225.

4. As of 1989, over 4 million East Germans had changed their citizenship. See Bundesministerium des Innern, Übersiedler report, August 6, 1990, German Subject Collection, Box 96, Hoover Institution on War, Revolution and Peace, Stanford, CA.

5. Manfred Görtemaker, *Unifying Germany, 1989–1990* (New York: St. Martin's Press, 1994), 62.

6. Ibid., 64.

7. Konrad Jarausch, *The Rush to German Unity* (New York: Oxford University Press, 1994), 42.

8. The German text, as published in the East German print media, reads: "Wer zu spät kommt, den bestraft das Leben."

9. "Ich hörte nur noch Schreie," *Der Spiegel* 42 (October 16, 1989): 22 (translated by the author).

10. Ibid.

11. Guards physically abused prisoners with truncheons, often striking individuals in the legs or head. See Hannes Bahrmann and Christoph Links, *Wir Sind das Volk* (Berlin: Aufbau Verlag, 1990), 7–15.

12. Neues Forum Leipzig, *Jetzt oder nie—Demokratie* (Munich: C. Bertlesmann, 1990), 306.

13. In the end, only two of them saw action in the city that night (ibid., 92–93).

14. The actual German text of the announcement, which was printed in the *Leipziger Volkszeitung* on October 6, 1989, is quoted in the following: Hans-Jürgen Sievers, *Stundenbuch einer deutschen Revolution* (Göttingen: Vandenhoeck und Ruprecht, 1990), 65–66; Jörg Swoboda, *Die Revolution der Kerzen:*

Christen in den Umwälzungen der DDR (Wuppertal: Onckenverlag, 1990), 22–23; and Bahrmann and Links, *Wir Sind das Volk*, 16 (translated by the author).

15. Mike Dennis, "Perfecting the Imperfect," in Gert-Joachim Glaessner and Ian Wallace, *The German Revolution of 1989: Causes and Consequences* (Oxford: Berg, 1992), 72.

16. Resolution on the German-Polish Frontier, *The Unification of Germany in 1990* (Bonn: Press and Information Office of the Federal Government, 1991), 61.

17. Message from Chancellor Kohl to the Governments of the World, ibid., 163–65.

2

Emigration and Flight

For most working-class Europeans, July and August are usually the beloved months of the year. During these eight weeks, families put aside their troubles and depart for vacations. So, too, is this time special in Germany, as many families take their *Urlaub* in August. For the citizens of East Germany, however, the summer of 1989 would be like no other. For the first time in their lives, they had a realistic opportunity to flee the oppression of their country. As hundreds fled, hundreds of others agonized whether to risk everything and flee or play it safe and continue their existence in "real existing socialism." By the end of the year, tens of thousands had opted to "vote with their feet" and escape to the Federal Republic to claim their right of citizenship. In doing so, these refugees destabilized the once-mighty East German Communist Party enough to bring down both the Berlin Wall and the East German government.

How is it that a nation that had survived for forty years by imprisoning its citizens behind concrete walls and barbed wire fences was now powerless to stop this latest exodus? What threat did the flight of citizens pose to the existence of the East German socialist movement? This chapter shall tell the story of the largest migration of Germans since the Allied occupation after World War II. It will explain how the East Germans' flight to freedom contributed to the chain of events that culminated in the unification of the German people.

BACKGROUND

Ever since its founding in 1949, East Germany lost a fairly steady stream of citizens who emigrated to the Federal Republic in order to claim citizenship as guaranteed by the Basic Law. Before 1961, such emigration proved fairly easy in that one needed only to cross from the eastern to the western zones of Berlin. The building of the Berlin Wall put a halt to such direct emigration, but not before the Federal Republic received the staggering total of 3,419,042 emigrants from the East.[1] Thereafter, the numbers of resettlers and refugees declined as more and more East Germans resigned themselves to their captivity. Gradually, emigration reached predictable yearly levels, ranging from approximately 42,000 in 1963 and 1964 to 12,000 in the late 1970s. The pace again quickened in the 1980s as the Polish and Hungarian reform movements encouraged East Germans to turn their backs on their government. Illegal border crossings were now more risky than ever. Practically every meter of the GDR border was protected by sentries in watchtowers and by attack dogs, and the unmanned sections were equipped with machine guns that fired automatically when "tripped." Those who did not want to risk their lives found that a safer avenue of escape was available. One might always seek refuge in the diplomatic consulates of foreign nations.

The GDR handled asylum cases with extreme diplomatic care. Given that they had to deal with the missions of foreign countries, East German leaders always had held that it was better to permit the refugees to emigrate than risk a diplomatic incident. Typically, the East German government promised asylum seekers that they would not be punished if they returned home and that they would be allowed to emigrate following successful completion of a police check. This formula was put to the test when fifty-five refugees occupied the West German mission[2] to East Germany in 1984. In this instance, the crisis was resolved peacefully, setting a precedent for the resolution of any future incidents. The East German government would have plenty of opportunity to apply this formula in 1989.

Why Leave?

Although each refugee had his or her own grounds for fleeing, several common motivations stand out. The most frequently cited reason for leaving was economic. Despite its well-acclaimed high standard of living within the communist bloc of nations, the East German economy could not compare to the capitalist West. Goods and services were scarce, if available at all. As one disgruntled consumer noted, "You cannot get screws or nails. There are no bananas, and when there are, they're the ones the monkeys wouldn't eat."[3] Many times, scarce household items were removed from regular stores and put into specialty *delikat* shops at much higher prices. When items were available, one faced the ever-present queues East Germans often derisively called "socialist waiting collectives."[4] For appliances and durable goods, the delay could be endless. In 1989 a number of citizens finally received the Trabants they ordered in 1974.[5] They were the lucky ones. The average wait for a new automobile was sixteen years. A few disgruntled families planned twenty-fifth anniversary celebrations—of their application to receive a telephone.[6] The lack of services only made such deficiencies worse. Many apartment complexes built in the immediate postwar reconstruction period had never been updated, and even the simplest of repairs was difficult to come by unless one had the means to strike a "private arrangement" off the books of government services.

Although the economic hardships of East German life might be reason enough to leave, the stultifying effects of communist ideology on everyday life took its toll as well. East German society was full of social ironies. Government officials who approved and relayed exit visas to workers for visits to West Germany were themselves not allowed to leave the country. Similarly, border patrol police had to watch enviously while their neighbors came home with packages of Western goods purchased with Deutschmarks at Intershops, since special rules prohibited the border police from holding Western currency.[7] Engineers or company supervisors who shouldered the responsibility of meeting production quotas were rewarded for their efforts with even more travel restrictions than the laborers whom they supervised. Considering the added stress, lower pay, and longer hours that such positions demanded, it is not surprising that the most capable individuals did not go into management.

The two most damning reasons for the flight of East Germans concerned the absence of freedom.[8] Freedom of travel was also a luxury afforded the very few. While travel to other socialist satellites was easy and acceptable, travel to West Germany was most difficult until 1975, when the regime relaxed its travel restrictions. As signatory of the Helsinki Final Act (the international agreement guaranteeing human rights), East Germany liberalized its policy to allow citizens to visit West Germany for personally important events such as weddings or other family matters. Nevertheless, such travel was still restricted to thirty days. One had to think twice about using this as an avenue of escape, given that family members forced to remain behind might be subject to retribution.

It might have been easier to deal with these travel limitations had they been uniformly applied. However, these laws did not apply to party functionaries and the intelligentsia. These fortunates enjoyed privileges unavailable to the rest of society, including such luxuries as lavish automobiles and well-furnished apartments. They could travel as they wished, and they vacationed in the best locales where Western goods and fine restaurants were readily available. Workers, on the other hand, spent their vacations in company resorts alongside the same people with whom they worked every day. Typically, such resorts lay along the Baltic Sea coast, a pleasant enough locality were it not for its unstocked shops, the paucity of restaurants, and the typically dreadful weather.

The absence of freedom also manifested itself in the suppression of thought. Although every citizen had the right to submit grievances, those who did received form letters in return, assuming they got an answer at all. Those who pursued their grievances further faced mountains of red tape and officious bureaucrats who cared more about protecting their careers than effecting change. Some dissenters, including those who protested the falsified May 1989 elections, kept quiet once they were threatened with prosecution for slander. This insensible treatment of dissent produced a societal malaise whereby citizens derided their country as a place where nothing ever changed. Despite the ever-present dissatisfaction deep within society, party leadership remained oblivious to the need for change. While communist regimes all over eastern Europe were disintegrating, the SED steadfastly held that it knew the correct path to socialism. Government newspapers continued to publish stories about how much better life was for East Germans than for West Germans. Those who had seen the alternatives knew better.[9]

ESCAPE TO FREEDOM

The Iron Curtain began to show small holes in the spring of 1989. In an attempt to expand their connections with the West, the Hungarian government of Prime Minister Nikolas Nemeth and Foreign Minister Gyula Horn announced that it would open portions of its Austrian border to unrestricted travel on May 2. With this one announcement, all of the GDR's border defenses could be rendered useless. Although Hungarian border guards would continue to patrol the major crossing points and stop illegal exiting, anyone who could find an unguarded section could escape. Thousands of East Germans had already been given visas to travel to Hungary on holiday. Thousands more might try to use their visas to Czechoslovakia to slip into Hungary illegally and then to freedom. For the millions of East Germans who had been penned up in a restrictive totalitarian state, there was suddenly a way out.

From May to August, word spread of the "green border." As many as 100,000 East Germans escaped during the first nine months of 1989.[10] In no time, the Federal Republic's immigration offices were overburdened. Each day, more and more trains arrived in Frankfurt full of former East Germans carrying their few possessions in backpacks or plastic bags. Although this was not their final stop, many disembarked to marvel at the Bahnhof and the well-stocked terminal shops. Their final destination was a reception camp near Giessen, where they would spend three to seven days being processed. On the first day of the process, the refugees took an oath to uphold the Basic Law and received linens, clothes, eating utensils, and temporary lodging. Refugees spent the next few days completing bureaucratic requirements and following a list of camp regulations that made their experience here much like a boot camp. Finally, each received two hundred Deutschmarks as welcome money and set out into society.

In order to disperse the newcomers across West Germany more evenly, the Federal Government established quotas for each of the states. The system worked reasonably well for refugees with no specific final destination. However, certain states were much more likely to receive immigrants than others since many refugees preferred to settle with relatives or friends in order to make their transition easier. One such example was West Berlin, the chosen target for as many as one-fifth of the acceptances. Given its already high unemployment rate, West Berlin could barely absorb any more population. It needed 70,000 new living spaces just to keep pace with the growth of population. Rents skyrocketed, even for the simplest of domiciles such as construction trailers or efficiency apartments. Those who could not pay for such lodging settled in tents within the city. Conditions could only worsen; the city expected a total of 100,000 refugees. Undoubtedly, homelessness awaited many.[11]

Seeking Asylum

As thousands of East Germans vacationing in Hungary awaited their chance to escape, other East Germans, fearing capture,[12] decided instead to seek asylum at the nearest West German embassy. In August, 131 East Germans jammed onto the compound of the West German mission in East Berlin, forcing the mission to close pending a solution to the diplomatic impasse. Almost simultaneously, East Germans who had failed in their attempts to cross the Austro-Hungarian frontier flocked to the West German embassy in Budapest. By August 14, the entry of 180 refugees (among them thirty children) forced officials to close the Budapest embassy.[13] Within ten days, the West German embassy in Prague was occupied by one hundred would-be refugees. The embassy in Warsaw would also receive such "visitors."

To the dismay of these squatters, the Federal Republic could do nothing to aid them. The embassies could process citizenship applications and issue

West German passports but, as exit documents, such passports were invalid. Therein lay the snag. The Basic Law guarantees citizenship to ethnic Germans everywhere, but it grants citizenship only to those who arrive at West German borders. Since the West German legations could not legally provide refugees with travel documents, the best they could do was advise their guests to return home and apply for permission to emigrate through usual channels. Pursuant to the same policy that had worked well in 1984, East Germany's interior minister Wolfgang Vogel assured asylum seekers that no one who returned home would be punished. This time, however, government policy did not work. In a letter sent to the German publication *Der Spiegel*, weary squatters in the embassy in Budapest exclaimed that "each of us knows that despite the GDR's promises regarding freedom from punishment 'back home,' harassment and psychological pressure nevertheless await anyone who returns."[14] The squatters occupying other embassies echoed their sentiments. The overwhelming majority would not budge.

Solving these crises proved a daunting task. The occupation of the West German mission in East Berlin might have been the easiest, given that such inter-German matters were usually resolved routinely. The occupation of the Budapest embassy was a much more difficult diplomatic problem. Hungary was bound by treaty to return East German citizens who were caught fleeing to the West. However, these refugees were on West German property, and the Hungarian government, eager to improve relations with the Federal Republic, did not want to risk antagonizing Bonn by forcing the issue. The Czechoslovakian government was not as sympathetic to the West, but it too faced the international diplomatic as well as humanitarian pressures brought to bear by the refugees and their plight. It seemed that the usual solutions would not apply this time.

As the refugees occupying the consulates in Prague, Warsaw, and East Berlin languished, those in Budapest got lucky. On August 19, 661 East Germans who had gathered at Sopron for an international festival escaped en masse across the border into Austria. As it became clear that thousands more were poised to flee, the necessity of detaining a mere 131 refugees in the embassy came into question. Consequently, the Hungarian government agreed to fly 108 of the refugees by charter plane to Vienna and to bus the remainder to a transit camp in Nuremberg. While the solution relieved the pressure on the Budapest compound, the respite proved only temporary. September approached, and with the end of the vacation period came the return to work or school. Faced with a certain immediacy, more and more East Germans applied for visas for Hungary in the hopes of attaining freedom while they still could. Eventually, the East German government curtailed issuing vacation visas, citing the exhaustion of their Hungarian currency supply as an excuse. Many of those who could not obtain a Hungarian visa tried to obtain a visa for Czechoslovakia and then cross the Czech frontier into Hungary. Given what was at stake, no route seemed too circuitous.

Refugee Profile

Who were these refugees? Demographically, they constituted the best and the brightest of East German society. Over half were under the age of thirty, and only 17 percent were over forty. The vast majority were skilled or semiskilled workers (some were professionals such as physicians), and roughly 87 percent had left some job behind them.[15] Few had been in trouble with the police. Ludwig Kerscher, a waiter from Karl-Marx-Stadt, was a typical refugee with an atypical history. For fifteen years, Kerscher had tried every avenue of escape he could imagine. His determination took him to Bulgaria, Poland, and even Tajikistan, but he never succeeded. He once built an airplane (despite never having seen the inside of an actual airplane), but abandoned the effort when he could not find an engine to propel it. Kerscher made seven failed attempts to cross from Hungary into Austria, but on the eighth he succeeded.[16]

Like thousands of others, Kerscher had traveled to a tiny corner of the Austro-Hungarian border near the Neusiedl Sea, where the Iron Curtain bulged out into Austria. By the end of August, the Neusiedl Sea area was awash with 20,000 Germans. The towns of Sopron and Zugliget soon became refugee centers reminiscent of the centers for displaced persons after World War II. Three makeshift tent cities sprang up to house refugees, many of whom had brought with them next to nothing. At Zugliget's church, a Roman Catholic relief organization ministered to roughly 600 Germans camped out in the courtyard while in a nearby garage, West German officials issued passports. The luckiest refugees found shelter in private homes. For the estimated 2,000 others, the nearby tent camps supplied the only lodging available.[17] Campers dined on little more than bread, and water was about the only potable available. The lack of food was tolerable only because these refugees found sustenance in the hope that they might soon succeed in finding their own path to freedom.

The best routes were the ones that worked. Finding a route was not hard; but since border guards and police patrolled the highways and major access points, it often took a little imagination. One group of twenty individuals had driven to the border and, after finding the highway blocked, abandoned their vehicles and worked their way through a dense forest to the Austrian town of

Moerbisch. In another instance, one enterprising man joined a wake at a cemetery that lay directly on the border. Abruptly, in the middle of the proceedings, he scaled the wall protecting the border and ran through a cornfield into Austria. Some venturesome individuals waded or swam the shallow Neusieldl Sea to freedom. Perhaps the most imaginative solution was that of an East German who sailed a rubber dinghy out on the Neusiedl Sea with a partially emptied case of beer. When stopped by Hungarian patrols, he flashed the passport he had received from the West German embassy (in Budapest) and exclaimed that he was a West German who had lost his way. Taking him at his word, the guards figured him as an intoxicated tourist and allowed him to continue to the Austrian shoreline.[18]

As diplomatic negotiations dragged on into September, the Hungarian government decided to take the initiative. An estimated 20,000 East Germans remained in Hungary, each one a potential refugee. To forestall a crisis, the Hungarian government announced plans to allow any East German presently in Hungary to cross the Austrian border without detention. However, in deference to their ally, the Hungarian government delayed implementation of the plan until East German officials had a chance to persuade their citizens to return home.[19] At midnight of September 10–11, the Hungarian border opened completely. East Germans could now cross by showing only an identification card. Thousands of refugees streamed across the border that night in cars or in buses. Once across, those without transportation boarded special trains the Austrian government had provided to take them to Bavaria for processing. One estimate put the number of refugees arriving that night at the Bavarian border at 8,100.[20]

When the first trains and buses of emigrants arrived at Passau in Bavaria, crowds greeted them with what one observer called a "carnival atmosphere." West Germans showered the newcomers with balloons, beer, and soft pretzels. Some drank sparkling wine or champagne brought along to toast freedom. Bananas—the almost nonexistent fruit in East Germany—became a standard welcoming gift. Many people were overcome by emotion and simply paused to cry. However, once the reception died down, there followed the difficult task of assimilating so many new citizens. Five long-established tent cities near towns surrounding Passau accepted newcomers. Each was equipped with only enough tents, transportable kitchens, and food for 1,000 refugees. Consequently, the tent cities soon filled to capacity, making life even more difficult for the immigrants. To win much needed space, government officials commandeered schools, gymnasiums, army barracks, civil defense bunkers, and town halls for use as shelters.[21] In Passau, the Niebelungenhalle became a makeshift branch of the Giessen immigration office where hundreds of bunk beds, sleeping bags, and pillows afforded the weary some rest. Local charities established a station inside the hall where refugees (many of whom had brought no luggage) could get a change of clothing. One could also get advice and local information as well as register for jobs. Most important, government workers handed out 250 Deutschmarks of "welcome money" to each arrival.[22] Until they got jobs, the newcomers would have to make do with that sum.

While Hungary's humanitarian gesture paved the way for thousands to reach the West, the Czechoslovakian government had no such intentions. East Germans trying to pass through Czech territory to get to Hungary were summarily detained (in some cases dragged from railroad cars) by police and had their passports seized. With no place to go, the would-be emigrants flocked to the West German embassy in Prague to join the 250 asylum seekers who had been there since August. Until now, August temperatures made life in the tents outside the embassy building tolerable. Throughout September, as the weather turned colder and rainier and the numbers of occupiers swelled to over 3,000, conditions within the compound deteriorated rapidly. Women and children slept on foam rubber pads while the men took turns sleeping in shifts. There was little to eat, save for bread and jam and stew prepared by field kitchens. Despite the conditions, only a small percentage left the compound to return home and pursue emigration properly, as over 100 of the refugees in East Berlin had done earlier in the month.[23]

Erich Honecker's regime faced a diplomatic nightmare. With the fortieth anniversary of the GDR approaching, the SED leadership thought it best to deal with the problems rather than allow them to cast a pall over the festivities. They decided to allow passage to the Federal Republic, provided that the asylum seekers first return to East German soil so that their citizenship could be revoked as a prelude to an official expulsion. The plan was to transport the refugees from Prague and Warsaw to East Germany aboard special railroad cars, which would be locked from the outside. Then, once the trains arrived in East Germany, officials were to disseminate emigration documentation in return for the passengers' East German identity cards. It was an elaborate procedure designed solely to save face.

The East Germans occupying the embassy in Prague were informed about this plan directly by Hans-Dietrich Genscher, foreign minister of the Federal Republic. When other East Germans outside the compound heard the news, an avalanche of people descended on the embassy in the hope of securing a place on the trains. The Czech police spent most of the day trying to decide what to do. For a while, the police barricaded the streets leading up to the embassy, then for some reason later allowed many families (especially those with infant children) to pass. Desperate individuals climbed the embassy walls and jumped fences to enter. By October 3, 11,000 East Germans were safely within the embassy's protection, awaiting transportation to freedom. Now, faced with a situation similar to the one in Hungary, the GDR had no choice but to close the border to Czechoslovakia as well.[24]

Honecker had gambled that the release of the refugees would end the problem. It did not. As the first trains approached the station at Dresden, hundreds of East Germans crowded the platforms to get at the locked cars. Riot policemen wielding rubber truncheons and water cannons dispersed some 10,000 demonstrators who fought back by hurling stones. In Karl-Marx-Stadt, police cordoned off the train station and denied everyone access to the tracks. These measures did not stop the determined. Some East Germans hid in forests along the rail routes and tried to hop on when the train slowed down. Clearly, East German society was hemorrhaging, and it seemed that nothing could stop its ultimate collapse.

EPILOGUE

The first trains arrived at Hof in Bavaria on Thursday, October 5. On Monday, the Leipzig demonstration sealed the fate of Erich Honecker and his hard-line supporters. Within a week, Egon Krenz would lead a reform government and promise more liberal travel laws. On November 1, Krenz's cabinet lifted the ban on travel to Czechoslovakia in the hopes that their citizens would stay at home and accept the new reform movement. The bleeding did not stop, however, as another 1,300 East Germans made their way into the Prague compound. This time, leaving was easy. The new refugees were bused to the East German embassy in Prague where they were stripped of their citizenship and given new identity papers listing them as "stateless." Once through the procedure, the emigrants could leave for wherever they chose. Within days, events back home made this procedure unnecessary. On November 10, the GDR government announced complete freedom of travel. With the Berlin Wall breached, there seemed no need for restrictions whatsoever. East Germans could now traverse the border at will.

As thrill seekers danced on the wall to celebrate the end of an era, the majority of people who came to see the West spent their time with more mundane activities such as sightseeing or shopping. Many had brought shopping lists and had planned to buy groceries, cosmetics, or luxury items not available in the East. Banks, besieged by East Germans wanting their welcome money, stayed open into the weekend. One family was surprised by the products available, especially fresh strawberries and asparagus. On Sunday, the family loaded up their Trabant with soap, shampoo, canned vegetables, and six bottles of beer. Then, like most of the others, they returned home to East Berlin.

With so many of their countrymen fleeing, it seems odd that so many returned home. "Our lives are here," said one couple. "Our friends are here, we don't have any relatives in the West. Now that we can come and go, why should we leave?"[25] They had a point, and it was a feeling shared by many of their compatriots. For example, out of the estimated 60,000 who visited the town of Helmstedt over the weekend, less than 1 percent defected.[26] Perhaps this is an indication that the majority of East Germans preferred remaining in the homes and towns they knew. Norbert Jacobs understood this feeling as well as anyone. The twenty-one-year-old husband and father from Schwerin left his family behind to flee through Hungary to the Federal Republic. After two weeks of living in a campground near Hamburg, Norbert found a job. Unfortunately, like many other refugees, the transition to life in West Germany proved difficult. After four weeks, he had to admit that "he had expected something different" and felt that he just did not fit in. That November, he embarked on yet another journey—this time back home to his family and the GDR. Norbert's case is not an exception. Approximately 100 former East Germans who had fled to the Federal Republic chose to return to East Germany by December. Many others considered returning too, but did not do so, for fear of being laughed at or singled out for shame. Often, refugees said that they would not have risked life and limb to flee East Germany had they known that their government would eventually liberalize travel laws. Others, especially older refugees, were disillusioned with the differences between East and West Germany. Many lamented that in West Germany, "older people don't count for much."[27]

These cases lead to two very important conclusions. First, the fact that the vast majority of East Germans had no plans to flee suggests that most East Germans preferred to reform their government, not run away from it. This raises an interesting question. Should those citizens who fled be chastised for their unwillingness to fight their government directly? Many who had stayed behind thought so. Even though the most effective pressure on the SED regime came from the crowds of citizens who marched in the streets, it is difficult to condemn those who opted to leave. It seems natural that when imprisoned, one's first thoughts are to escape, not to reform the prison. After all, citizens who decided to take flight did not do so capriciously. Family members left behind faced untold hardships and retribution from state authorities. Those who fled may not have been heroes, but neither were they cowards.

Second, these examples prove that many East German refugees had over-estimated how much their quality of life would improve in the West. Home-lessness, high rent, and unemployment awaited those who were forced to start anew. Everyone faced years of social integration and a relearning of the rights and responsibilities of citizenship. For the tens of thousands who crossed the border in those months of 1989, life would never be the same. For some it would improve, for others it would not. Nevertheless, despite the adjustment difficulties, four out of every five refugees refused to consider re-turning to the GDR under any circumstances.[28] The East Germans had "voted with their feet," and they had no urge to change their ballots.

NOTES

1. Report on Übersiedler, Bundesministerium des Innern, August 6, 1990, German Subject Collection, Box 96, Hoover Institution on War, Revolution and Peace, Stanford, CA.

2. Since the Federal Republic refused to accept officially the existence of a separate German state, the West German government refused to call its legation to the GDR an embassy.

3. John Tagliabue, "Leaving Behind a Land of Shortages but Also Friends and Relatives," *New York Times* (hereafter *NYT*), October 4, 1989.

4. Ferdinand Protzman, "Thousands Swell Trek to the West by East Ger-mans," *NYT*, September 12, 1989.

5. Serge Schemann, "Refugees in Prague to Leave for West," *NYT*, October 4, 1989.

6. "Das droht die DDR zu vernichten," *Der Spiegel* 33 (August 14, 1989): 21.

7. Ibid., 20.

8. Nearly three-fourths of all who responded to questionnaires in 1989 listed restrictions on travel and the absence of free expression as the two most important motives for leaving East Germany. See Richard Hilmer and Anne Köhler, "Der DDR läuft die Zukunft davon," *Deutschland Archiv* 22 (December 1989): 1385.

9. According to *Der Spiegel*, roughly 2.73 milion East Germans had visited the West in 1988. See "Das droht die DDR zu vernichten," 21.

10. Übersiedler Report, Bundesministerium des Innern.

11. The onslaught of the expected 15,000 emigrants to West Berlin that August is comparable to the flight of 20,000 East Germans in June 1961, just before the completion of the Berlin Wall. See "Zusammenrücken—ja, wo denn?" *Der Spiegel* 22 (August 14, 1989): 29.

12. Leaving East Germany without permission was an offense punishable by up to ten years' imprisonment.

13. "West Germans to Shut Embassy in Budapest Today," *NYT*, August 14, 1989.

14. "Wir bitten nicht, wir fordern," *Der Spiegel* 33 (August 14, 1989): 24 (translation by author).

15. Pressemitteilung, Bundesministerium für innerdeutsche Beziehungen, Bonn, September 12, 1989, German Subject Collection, Box 96, Hoover Institution. See also Ferdinand Protzman, " 'Help Wanted' Signs Sprout in West as East Germans Continue to Arrive," *NYT*, September 13, 1989.

16. Kerscher's story can be found in "Wir wollen nichts mehr," *Der Spiegel* 33 (August 14, 1989): 30.

17. Henry Kamm, "East Germans Put Hungary in a Bind," *NYT,* September 2, 1989.

18. "Wir wollen nichts mehr," 31.

19. The GDR had set up a special trailer in Zugliget for that purpose, but few accepted the offer. See Serge Schemann, "Hungary Allows 7,000 East Germans to Emigrate West," *NYT*, September 11, 1989.

20. Serge Schemann, "Smiles From the Guards in Hungary, Then Sips of Champagne in Austria," *NYT*, September 12, 1989.

21. "Alles knüppeldicke voll," *Der Spiegel* 36 (September 4, 1989): 18.

22. Bonn provided 200 Deutschmarks, local charities the extra fifty. See Protzman, "Thousands Swell Trek to the West by East Germans," *NYT,* September 12, 1989.

23. Serge Schemann, "East Germans Swell Embassy in Prague," *NYT,* September 29, 1989.

24. Serge Schemann, "Refugees in Prague to Leave for West," *NYT*, October 4, 1989.

25. Craig R. Whitney, "2 East Germans Back Home Because 'Our Life Is Here,' " *NYT*, November 13, 1989.

26. Alan Riding, "The 'True Unification': Clunkers on the Autobahn and Sunday Shopping," *NYT*, November 13, 1989.

27. "Rübe plätzt," *Der Spiegel* 47 (November 20, 1989): 61–63 and passim.

28. Anne Köhler, "Ist die Übersiedlerwelle noch zu stoppen?" *Deutschland Archiv* 23 (March 1990): 429.

3

Pastors as Protestors:
The Role of the Clergy

The exodus of East Germany's citizens put substantial pressure on the SED government to change, but it was the actions of those who stayed behind that actually toppled the regime. The massive demonstrations in Berlin, Dresden, and Leipzig revealed that dissent was not limited to a handful of disgruntled emigrants but was prevalent in almost all of society. That September and October, Honecker and his lieutenants had only two options: suppress the crowds by force, as the Chinese had done at Tienanmen Square, or yield to the reformists. That no blood was spilled on the path to peaceful change is a testament to the brave men and women who risked all in defiance of a corrupt system.

Who were these dissident leaders, and what philosophies guided their actions? Surprisingly, there is no good answer to that question. In other eastern European countries, the intelligentsia (the artists, writers, and intellectuals) played visible leadership roles in bringing about change. In East Germany, however, the intelligentsia was curiously withdrawn and marginalized, prompting Joachim Fest, the well-known West German journalist and biographer of Adolf Hitler, to write that this was the first revolution "that has not been preceded by its theorists."[1] While it is true that the East German revolution did not produce the equivalent of Vaclav Havel in Czechoslovakia or Lech Walesa in Poland, this was not a rebellion bereft of leaders or ideology. Although they might reject the description, the GDR's Protestant clergy were the "revolutionaries" who—sometimes willingly, sometimes reluctantly—nurtured the dissident groups, worked to promote change, and provided the movement's philosophical underpinnings of peace, justice, and righteousness. This chapter will examine the motivations and goals of the East German clergy in order to determine why ministers felt it necessary to mix politics into their religious activities. The discussion should help explain how religious institutions, especially the dominant Evangelical Lutheran Church, could wield such political power in a Marxist state officially pledged to atheism.

BACKGROUND

The unique position that religious institutions enjoyed in East German society is partially a product of their roles during the Nazi era. Many clergymen resisted coordination in the Nazi state and some, most notably Martin Niemöller and Dietrich Bonhoeffer, suffered and died for their convictions. Following the defeat of Germany, the Soviet occupiers elected not to subordinate the churches to communist orthodoxy. Ostensibly, this was a gesture of gratitude, but it was more of a ploy to gain the churches' cooperation; after all, the religioius community might prove to be a useful tool to help stabilize and legitimize the new communist regime. Further, the Soviets could ill afford to alienate the Protestant population of their zone, which in 1946 totalled nearly fifteen million, or 80 percent of the population.[2] Consequently, the constitution of 1949 incorporated the freedoms of religion and conscience in its articles and acknowledged that churches had a right to exist. In return for these constitutional safeguards, the churches "acquiesced" to the imposition of the Soviet-style government in the eastern zone. The phrase "Church within socialism" later became a popular slogan to describe the role of Protestantism in the Marxist state. The formulation implied neither support nor condemnation of the regime, simply acceptance of its existence. The churches thus became semi-autonomous within the GDR's communist superstructure, and as such had to temper the religious needs of the population with the political needs of the state. This balancing act often proved quite difficult.

The cordiality in church-state relations evaporated once the GDR was well established. In the early 1950s, as Stalinist repression across eastern Europe brought a return of Marxist atheism, the SED did its part by establishing secular rituals and organizations to compete with religious ones. Despite repeated attacks on religious freedom, the churches refused to battle with the government openly. Instead, pastors publicly disagreed with and even criticized governmental decisions, but they also urged parishioners not to resort to violence in search of political change. Consequently, church leaders escaped harassment or imprisonment as counterrevolutionaries, even though the state was suspicious of their motives. As a result, while many other eastern European states suppressed or restricted their churches, the GDR government allowed the Evangelical Lutheran Church (and other demoninations) to function quite independently.[3]

Over the next two decades, East Germany's Protestant churches became society's moral voice. Like a "natural conscience," they occasionally forced a totalitarian government to look at itself critically. As the GDR's only non-integrated institution, the Church enjoyed a freedom to communicate not shared by the rest of society. Here, young people could gather to discuss ordinarily taboo subjects such as homosexuality, rock music, and conscientious objection to military service. Ordinary citizens soon looked to their churches as havens from the stark socialist reality they faced in everyday life. Social activist groups also found refuge in the Protestant Church. Many sympathetic ministers granted protection to the environmental, equal rights, or social justice groups with which they agreed. Many even gave a limited amount of institutional support by placing their facilities and their "independence" from government scrutiny at the group's disposal. Nevertheless, there were limits. Many clergy tried desperately to keep religious and political agendas separate. To argue for justice was proper; to attack the unjust was not Christian.

The most visible manifestion of this church-sponsored activism was the Peace Movement, an antiwar, prodisarmament political activism that grew out of heightened military tensions in Europe and the world of the 1980s (i.e., the Soviet invasion of Afghanistan and the debate over stationing nuclear missiles in central Europe). The movement soon found a home in the churches, which helped advance the cause by holding peace vigils and prayer sessions. Between November 9 and 19, 1980, East German Christians observed the first national "Ten Days of Peace" (*Friedensdekade*) by holding a series of church services across the country that called for peace and international security. The movement galvanized the political discontent hiding beneath the surface of GDR society. Borrowing a phrase from the Old Testament Book of Micah, youth groups seized the issue and called their movement "Swords into Ploughshares." Members could be identified by decorative patches on their clothing that bore the image of the Soviet monument to peace at the United Nations Building in New York, which happens to be a statuary depiction of that very biblical verse. Their political agenda was rather simple: East Germany should disarm and adhere to the Helsinki Final Act principles of international human rights. By 1982 the common interests shared by the churches and peace groups led the two groups into a mutually advantageous relationship. More and more young people were attracted to the Protestant Church and its activities, and the Church provided the sanctuary wherein such issues could be discussed freely.

Ironically, the Church's stance on peace complemented the GDR government's stance on détente and international disarmament quite well. Like other communist nations, the GDR envisioned itself as the protector of the Marxist utopia—that is, as the defender of communism against the (capitalist) enemies who sought to destroy it. Consequently, Honecker's government welcomed the Peace Movement and supported the youth groups' efforts. In a 1980 letter to a Protestant bishop, GDR Prime Minister Willi Stoph openly praised the Church and expressed his satisfaction that the "peace policy of the GDR [was] borne by both Christians and churches."[4] Such gratuitous accolades evaporated once the government realized that the Church's definition of "peace" included tolerance of different opinions, respect for human rights, and open exchanges of information—ideals, the dissidents asserted, that applied not just to the external dealings of nations but to internal political realities as well.[5] Suddenly, the Peace Movement became "subversive." Students were now forbidden to wear the "Swords into Ploughshares" emblem in public, so many students cut off the patches but wore their tattered garments in silent protest. Those who defied the ban risked losing their student status in universities and faced imprisonment. Such reprisals merely drove the Peace Movement further into the arms of the Church where it continued to hold other, more clandestine, activities. The Honecker regime then found itself in a quandary. As signatory to the Helsinki Final Act that guaranteed human and civil rights, the government had to think twice before attacking the Church openly. Consequently, as the movement grew, the state found itself ever more unable to act decisively against it. By equating internal accord with international peace, the Protestant Church had seized the moral high ground and provided a sanctuary for citizens critical of government policy.

PRELUDE TO REVOLUTION

Mikhail Gorbachev's accession to power in the Soviet Union gave an external validation of the Peace Movement's program. As the GDR stubbornly refused to reform, churches became the assembly points for those who wanted to bring about an East German *perestroika*. National peace seminars held under Church auspices became weekly events attended by believers and nonbelievers alike. Many dissident groups, emboldened by growing numbers and the tacit support of the Soviet Union, broke away from their Church protectors to go public with demands for change. Eventually, the

Church would abandon its restrictions on criticizing the regime in public. On February 13, 1986, Church leaders called for an ecumenical meeting for Justice, Peace and the Preservation of Creation to analyze social ills and prepare suggestions for consideration. The appeal received widespread response, drawing 150 delegates from nineteen churches and church societies across the GDR. The convocation proved so successful that it continued to meet yearly to discuss suggestions sent from churches or parishioners. In 1987 Honecker's patience for clerical "interference" waned. That summer, East German Secret Police (Stasi) and peoples' police units raided East Berlin's Church of Zion (Zionskirche) in search of illegal printing presses. Seven people were arrested; and despite protests all over the GDR, arrests continued unabated in the weeks following. By March 1988, the SED increased the censorship of church newspapers, and Stasi or police agents physically prevented citizens from attending church services. [6]

As state repression worsened, Church rhetoric got more heated. In June, the Church community of Wittenberg prepared a list of twenty theses for a renewal of society. Pastor Friedrich Schorlemmer, a lecturer at the Wittenberg Divinity Seminar, presented the text to the regional church day meeting in Halle. Part of the document listed environmental, ecological, and energy conservation concerns. The bulk of the document, however, was an explosive, revolutionary manifesto. It not only attacked the dogmatic and conformist nature of the East German state, it poked fun at the "rose-colored glasses" shading the SED's eyes from their own mistakes and malfeasance. Among its many demands were the elimination of the party's monopoly of the "truth," free and open elections with a choice of candidates, and an open dialogue among all groups in society.

Disagreements turned into open rebellion following the May 1989 elections. In a cynical attempt to appear open to reform, Honecker's government had asked firefighters, sports groups, and other *apparatchiks* to suggest candidates for inclusion on election lists. Many Church-sponsored environmental and peace groups submitted lists, but their suggestions were summarily dismissed. The state's disregard for the people's wishes angered enough clerics to urge parishioners to hold the government accountable for the accuracy of the vote count. The state synod of Saxony took the unprecedented step of suggesting that citizens might even abstain from voting. When the official results revealed that the state had rigged the elections as usual, protests broke out all over East Germany. Particularly vehement protests occurred at the Sophia and Gethsemane churches in Berlin. The Evangelical Lutheran Church's central organization protested the election, only to draw even more fire from an increasingly hostile state leadership. When

Bishop Gottfried Forck, head of the church in Berlin Brandenberg, attempted to present his case to party leadership, the SED brass refused to meet with him.

In April, the Church released the conclusions of the meeting of the ecumenical "Conference of Christians and Churches for Justice, Freedom, and the Preservation of Creation" held in February 1988. The final document, which represented the work of thirteen committees working for over a year, railed at the evils of a repressive society. In one section, entitled "More Justice in the GDR—Our Task, Our Expectations," the delegates made a number of particularly vehement attacks on the government, blaming it for much of society's problems.

Why are so few people prepared to take responsibility for the common good? Many don't get involved out of laziness or fear of rocking the boat. Others believe it isn't worth it; it will only bring reprisals. This attitude is born from daily experience:

When citizens gather outside of social organizations to pursue common interests, they quickly come under suspicion for subversive activities.

Whoever proposes uncomfortable suggestions often meets a bureaucrat who must go through all the red tape, and seldom is prepared to make decisions in his area of responsibility.[7]

Although the document contained very sharp words, the conference called not for a revolution but for a national dialogue on how to solve East Germany's difficulties. There was no time for such a dialogue. Within weeks, the GDR's very existence was in doubt.

In August, as the stream of citizens fleeing to the West turned into a raging flood, churches became meeting places for people who were considering flight. Most clergy tried to find a middle ground between their disgruntled parishioners' wishes and an ever more defensive government. Nevertheless, as church attendance fell, individual pastors did what they could to keep their parishioners at home. Their leaders, meeting at the Evangelical synod in Eisenach, took bolder action and drafted a letter to Erich Honecker that listed what they believed were the reasons that citizens were chosing to flee East Germany and called for a national dialogue in search of solutions. The church leaders suggested discussions on democratic party politics and economic reforms, and urged the government to create a new electoral system that permitted choices between competing personalities and ideologies. The latter suggestion called into question SED leadership and the communist nature of the government—a stance that was bound to get the party's attention. The official party response to the letter callously brushed aside the demands as "quixotic and completely unrealistic."[8]

Not all the Protestant clergy welcomed the synod's initiatives. Many clergy believed that the church's true mission (namely, to save souls) was being compromised by an unwise foray into politics. Other ministers, particularly those who had already been active in their own political movements, welcomed the opportunity to further their agendas. Among the most notable of these were Pastor Schorlemmer, Bishop Forck, and Rainer Eppelmann of Berlin's Samaritan Church, who along with others founded the civic action group Democratic Awakening. Using Schorlemmer's Twenty Theses as its manifesto, the Democratic Awakening called for a "socialist society on a democratic basis." This was not the only group with roots in the Church. Clergy also participated in the creation of Democracy Now! (Pastor Wolfgang Ullmann) and the New Forum (Pastor Jochen Tschiche).[9] The historical understanding to keep religion separate from politics—which kept church and government at arm's length for fifty years—had now completely broken down.

As the political authority of the state withered away that September, more and more people transferred their allegiances to the moral authority of the church. Nowhere was that moral authority more evident—or more important—than in Leipzig. Here, where Martin Luther stood fast on his conscience four centuries earlier, a new brand of civil disobedience had achieved notoriety. Ever since the early years of the Peace Movement, the Nikolai Church held weekly "Prayers for Peace" gatherings that were part religious services, part social gatherings. Typically, a service began with an exchange of information, often regarding the whereabouts of individuals arrested in demonstrations. Thereafter came prayers or meditations followed by a sermon that was often more political than spiritual in substance.[10] Throughout the services, worshippers sang traditional hymns; among them, most appropriately was *Dona Nobis Pacem* (*Give Us Peace*). The services then ended with the usual blessings and paternosters.[11]

The Nikolai Church and its "Prayers for Peace" soon became a rallying point of Leipzig's reform movement. It may have been the most notable protest service, but it was not the only one. By now, churches all across East Germany had followed its lead to provide both believers and nonbelievers alike with reliable information. By September, churches drew crowds of citizens who were seeking news about loved ones or information on routes of escape. As the crowds grew, civic action groups that had previously used the churches as a shield took to the streets in open defiance, risking imprisonment or physical abuse. Police and security units habitually encircled the Nikolai Church, often armed with rubber truncheons and accompanied by attack dogs, to discourage attendance. Occasionally, the Stasi mounted cameras on church doors to make a record of those who entered.[12] On certain days, police vans whisked worshippers away to headquarters for registration and harassment. Sometimes, punishment included having your citizenship revoked, ironically making church attendance one way to escape East Germany.

On October 9, many people feared an approaching Armageddon. The previous week, riots broke out in Dresden as the trains bearing refugees from the Warsaw and Budapest embassies passed through the city on their way to the West. The memory of the fortieth anniversary celebrations in Berlin, which had ended in counterdemonstrations and violence only two days before, was also fresh in the public's mind. Monday evening, as citizens gathered for their usual "Prayers for Peace" services, Leipzig's Lutheran clergy feared a replay of the Tienanmen Square massacre. Pastor Christian Führer found Nikolai Church packed that evening, not just with the usual parishioners but with a number of Communist Party loyalists sent to disrupt proceedings. Outside, a tense crowd grew nervous as the church closed for lack of space. Eventually, three other churches opened their doors to accommodate the masses in the streets. What had once been a church service had become a dangerously large political gathering made even more volatile by the presence of armed riot police.

The messages from the pulpits that evening were uniform and direct. Johannes Hempel, the Bishop of Saxony, related to all four churches the simple message that "force does not solve any problems."[13] In St. Thomas's Church, Pastor Johannes Richter asked his parishioners to be courageous but patient. Reading from the Book of Proverbs, he preached a sermon on temperance and nonviolence,[14] and in the end he implored the congregation to go directly home so that there would be no bloodshed. His words of restraint reached only a minority of the 70,000 individuals who took to the streets that night, but the message of nonviolence held the moment. Within days, Erich Honecker would resign, and a new government under Egon Krenz promised dialogue with the populace. The worst had not materialized. Weeks later in the town square where protest banners had once flown stood a solitary placard with the message, "We Thank You, Church."[15] It was a simple gesture, but one that recognized the moral and political leadership that the clergy had exercised during the years of travail.

AFTERMATH

The Leipzig demonstrations that brought down Honecker's government turned out to be the climax of the Church's role as a major player in the rebellion. Until now, most clergy had seen themselves primarily as intermediaries between a totalitarian government and a voiceless populace. Now that a new government promised dialogue, what role should the Church play? Some clergy suggested that the time was right to withdraw from the debate, but many others asserted that the Church had an obligation to see the process through the upcoming negotiations. Consequently, when the central "Round Table" discussions between the national civic action groups and the bloc parties of the central government began, it was Church officials who set up and moderated the initial sessions. Local round tables frequently turned to their ministers for leadership as well.[16] Given the Church's widespread involvement in the ensuing discussions, it is easy to agree with the comment of one observer, who remarked that it seemed as if East Germany "was being taken over by Protestant pastors."[17]

These discussions put the clerics in an unusual and uncomfortable position. As moderators, clergy often had to mediate disputes in which other clergy (as members of civic action groups or bloc political parties) were taking part. This dilemma forced many Church leaders to announce their intention to withdraw from the discussions once they were well established, leaving the leadership in the hands of the participants themselves. Lay people were reluctant to let them leave, however. Consequently, many pastors stayed on and continued to work toward their vision of a reformed, albeit socialist, East German state.

The March 1990 election dealt a crippling blow to that vision. The CDU Alliance for Germany victory was a clear repudiation of socialism in favor of quick unification with the capitalist West. German clergy were suddenly at odds with the very parishioners whom they had once worked to protect. Although many activist ministers continued to work for reform (four clergy found their way into de Maizière's cabinet), many other clerics retreated with dejection and resignation. The Evangelical Lutheran Church finally withdrew officially from the central Round Table, much to the relief of many pastors who were happy to remove their political cloaks and don their clerical vestments again. Some clergy rationalized the public's rejection of their hopes for reform by questioning whether the Church should have ever gotten involved at all. In a moment of self-deprecation, a few Church officials debated whether they had been too supportive of the communist dictatorship.[18] After all, the Church had given its tacit support to the SED regime for many years. Was it equally culpable for the government's excesses and failures?

With the inevitable unification approaching, many Church leaders stepped back and took a close look at what they had wrought. Some clergy, seeing potential difficulties in the merger of two such different societies, urged that reforms be made deliberately and cautiously. In what may seem as a last act of desperation to slow down the pace of unification, Church leader Manfred Stolpe remarked in June 1990,

The question of the hour for Germany is how and when national unity will occur. There are significant reasons for speed, although a transition period of a good two years would have made sense. Though we do not have that much time, the problems remain. Two years of solid work after the fact should be a compulsory requirement, during which urgent economic and social matters can be dealt with humanely.[19]

Stolpe's plea for a slow unification fell on deaf ears, even within his own synod. Although the Eastern and Western Evangelical churches had agreed to "grow together," and then over the next few years work on a new unified constitution, the East German synod voted in late September to invite East German churches to merge with the West German Evangelical churches, thereby ending any separate East German church administration.[20] Days later, Germany was reunited.

On Unification Day, many church bells in the former GDR were silent.[21] In Leipzig, where freedom was won only a year before, the doors of the Nikolai Church were closed. Some ministers suggested that the government request that churches ring their bells to proclaim unity amounted to undue political interference. That rationalization masks the deeper resentment that their parishioners opted for unification with West Germany. "I'll always think of myself as a part of the GDR," said one pastor. Another agreed, adding, "You can't ignore forty-five years of history. We are not starting in 1945."[22] Their comments reflect a feeling common to many of the pastors: East Germany had sold out to capitalism.

The Reverend Christian Führer explained why his church did not celebrate Unity Day. "We could hold a service of thanksgiving to celebrate the fact that the borders are open and that the security police are gone. There are others for whom we could better hold a service of intercession—the people who have lost their jobs . . . and don't have any idea what's to come. . . . So instead we will simply keep quiet, and let the silence move people to think."[23]

It would be easy to dismiss these sentiments as the grumbling of communist dupes; yet for those clergy who had fought a corrupt system to create a better society for their flock, the economic hardship immediately following unification must have been a bitter pill to swallow. Their parishioners' delight at the union with prosperous West Germany had soon dissipated in the wake of unemployment and the rising taxes that were needed to pay for social services that were no longer free. As some clergy concluded, East Germans were no better off than before: The political tyranny of Marxism had been replaced by the economic tyranny of capitalism. This bitter interpretation would persist for years to come.

NOTES

1. Harold James and Marla Stone, eds., *When the Wall Came Down: Reactions to German Unification* (New York: Routledge, Chapman, Hall, 1992), 53.

2. Robert F. Goeckel, *The Lutheran Church and the East German State: Political Conflict and Change under Ulbricht and Honecker* (Ithaca, NY: Cornell University Press, 1990), 14.

3. The situation is in some ways analogous to the relative independence that the Catholic Church enjoyed in communist Poland.

4. Goeckel, *Lutheran Church*, 258.

5. Pedro Ramet, "Church and Peace in the GDR," *Problems of Communism*, 33 (July–August 1984): 46.

6. John Sandford, "The Peace Movement and the Church in the Honecker Years," in Gert-Joachim Glaessner and Ian Wallace, eds., *The German Revolution of 1989: Causes and Consequences* (Oxford: Berg, 1992), 138.

7. Jürgen Israel, *Zur Freiheit Berufen: Dir Kirche in der DDR als Schützraum der Opposition, 1981–1989* (Berlin: Aufbau Taschenbuch Verlag, GmbH, 1991), 227–28 (translation by author).

8. As printed in the party newspaper, *Neues Deutschland*, "Was haben solche abenteuerlichen, völlig unrealistischen Parolen noch mit Kirche im Sozialismus zu tun?" *Deutschland Archiv* 22 (Oktober 1990): 1178. See Bernd Alsmeier, *Wegbereiter der Wende: Die Rolle der evangelischen Kirche in der Ausgangsphase der DDR* (Pfaffenweiler: Centarus, GmbH, 1994), 49 (translation by author).

9. For a more complete discussion of the civic action groups and their origins, see Konrad Jarausch, *The Rush to German Unity* (New York: Oxford University Press, 1994), 39–44.

10. That September, sermon topics included a remembrance of the German invasion of Poland fifty years earlier, news from the reform movements in other countries, and techniques for peaceful resistance.

11. Sebastian Feydt, Christiane Heinze, and Martin Schanz, "Die Leipziger Friedensgebete," in Wolf-Jürgen Grabner et al., eds., *Leipzig in Oktober* (Berlin: Wichern-Verlag GmbH, 1990), 133–34.

12. Ibid., 125.

13. Jarausch, *Rush to German Unity*, 34; and Jörg Swoboda, *Die Revolution der Kerzen* (Wuppertal: Onkenverlag, 1990), 28.

14. Feydt et al., *Leipzig in Oktober*, 130. The message contained in Proverbs 25:28 is: "A man who cannot control his anger is like a city without walls."

15. Philip Yancey, "What Erich Honecker Didn't Know," *Christianity Today* 34 (March 19, 1990): 72.

16. Reinhard Henkys, "Die Kirchen im Umbruch der DDR," *Deutschland Archiv* 23 (February 1990): 177–78.

17. Sandford, "Peace Movement and Church," 140.

18. Quoting from a document issued by the Conference of Church Leaders: "For many years we spoke out publicly while many kept quiet. But we have also

kept quiet when we should have spoken" (translation by author). See Henkys, "Die Kirchen im Umbruch der DDR," 180.

19. Konrad H. Jarausch and Volker Gransow, *Uniting Germany: Documents and Debates, 1944–1993* (Providence, RI: Berghahn Books, 1994), 169.

20. Sandford, "Peace Movement and Church," 141.

21. "Churches Uneasy Over Reunification," *Christianity Today* 34 (November 5, 1990): 65–66.

22. William E. Downey, "For German Pastors a Bitter Taste," *Christian Century* 107 (October 31, 1990): 988–89.

23. "Germany Unites After 45 Years of Division," *Facts on File* 50 (October 5, 1990): 733.

4

Four-Power Diplomacy and German Unification

Germany's rush to unity raised some troubling diplomatic issues and created potentially dangerous international problems. While most of Germany's neighbors welcomed the opening of the wall and the eventual liberalization of the GDR, the drive toward unification was another matter. Suddenly, wartime fears of German expansionism resurfaced. Would a unification of Germany lead to claims on Pomerania, East Prussia, and the other territories lost to Poland after World War II? Even if a new German government renounced its irredentist claims, there would still be a need to readjust existing European security arrangements. Should a new Germany belong to NATO or the Warsaw Pact? Both? Neither?

These questions would be difficult enough to answer even in the easiest of diplomatic circumstances. However, these negotiations would be further complicated by the fact that the wartime alliance between the United States, Great Britain, the Soviet Union, and France still had controlling rights over any united German state. Forty-five years had passed since the end of World War II, but there was no more agreement on how to solve the "German Question" in 1990 than there had been in 1945. Each nation had developed its own set of assumptions regarding German unification and was willing to defend those interests in the international arena. Considering that four very different approaches to the problem had to be reconciled, it is amazing that any diplomatic solution could be reached at all. Nevertheless, in only two months, the four powers had forged an agreement on the unification of the two German states. How was it possible? It was due to equal parts of diplomatic skill, bribery, and luck.

This chapter is a study of multinational decision making at its best. First, French, British, American, and Soviet reactions to the fall of German communism and to the unification drive are discussed. Then, the chapter continues with an account of the Two-plus-Four diplomacy that led to the treaty that settled the disposition of Germany. The startling conclusion is that the four powers did *not* define the emerging Germany in light of their national interests. Instead, they were forced to redefine their national interests in light of the reemergence of Germany.

REACTIONS TO THE GERMAN COLLAPSE

The French Stance

The French government reacted to the events in the two Germanys with a mixture of support and suspicion. Since the end of World War II, France and West Germany had been partners in creating a new Europe. Their cooperation in such historic ventures as the European Coal and Steel Community and the Common Market bore evidence of the friendship begun by Konrad Adenauer and Charles de Gaulle. The two nations, in many ways, neatly complemented each other. Germany was the more powerful country economically, but as a defeated and divided nation it had never been a postwar political powerhouse. France, while economically weaker, did well to maintain what was left of its prewar political prestige with its United Nations Security Council seat and its status as an atomic power. An enlarged Germany might upset this delicate balance and shift the diplomatic and economic center of the European Community (EC) away from the Atlantic toward central Europe. Thus, France was caught between two conflicting desires. How might France support German self-determination without jeopardizing France's extremely fragile position as a major player in European and world politics?

The first diplomatic exchanges proved fairly cordial. At the 54th Franco-German summit on November 3, 1989, Chancellor Helmut Kohl and President François Mitterrand seemed to reach an agreement on the "German Question." As Egon Krenz's socialist government was collapsing, Mitterrand confided in Kohl his worst fear—namely, that the future course of German events would lead Kohl to forsake the drive toward European unity for Germany unity. Kohl did what he could to reassure his friend that Germany's problems could be solved in a European framework and implied that Germany's days of playing off the West against the East were over. Despite such reassurances, Mitterrand's policy remained cautious. In the concluding press conference, Mitterrand asserted that he was "not afraid of German unification."[1] Privately, he tried to make sure that the rapid pace of German events did not overtake French interests.

The camaraderie ended abruptly on the 28th of that month, when Chancellor Kohl announced his Ten-Point Program. Mitterand, angry and publicly critical of the plan, had neither been informed nor consulted. His negative reaction was understandable since the announcement invoked images of past German governments that acted first and sought consensus later. In the hopes of restraining this "loose cannon," Mitterand responded to journalists that he considered German unification "a legal and political impossibility."[2] In private conversation, he lectured German Foreign Minister Hans-Dietrich Genscher that Europe would not tolerate another unbridled Germany. There was even talk in unofficial circles of rapprochement with the Soviet Union (much like the old Franco-Russian entente before World War I) to keep the Germans from isolating France.[3]

Mitterand then embarked upon a number of scheduled personal visits over the next few weeks that would enable him to see if others shared his opinions. His first stop was to the GDR on December 20, 1989; but in a carefully considered quid pro quo, he did not inform Chancellor Kohl of his departure date. In East Berlin, Mitterand told an audience that the German people should decide their own future, provided the decision maintained European peace and recognized existing borders. His presence there sent a clear message to Bonn not to ignore French interests. Nevertheless, Mitterand, always the consummate politician, was careful not to embarrass Kohl. He understood that their working relationship would have to continue long after the unification issue ended. His next stop took him to Moscow to meet with Gorbachev, where the two men agreed that the existence of two separate Germanys was a "stabilizing influence" and that unification was not on the agenda.[4]

As the new year approached, Kohl and Mitterand worked to reform their friendship. In early January, Kohl met with Mitterand at Gascogne in southern France for what would be the first of many such meetings throughout the year. During the conference, the two men set forth their fears and aspirations regarding a possible German unification. Kohl purposely "stroked" the French, by telling the press that he believed that only France could legitimize German unity. In more private conversations, Kohl reaffirmed his commitment to work toward unity within the framework of the EC, and said that the process would not alter Germany's long-standing partnership with France. The ever-cautious Mitterand answered cooly, "I shall adhere to that."[5]

At best, Mitterand's tactics might slow the pace of unification, but he realized that he could not stop it completely. By February, Mitterand had refashioned his foreign policy toward Germany in order to salvage as much as he could of the French agenda. Since an enlarged Germany would most certainly further reduce France's role as an international leader, Mitterand devoted most of his attentions to forging a consensus on German unity within the EC. Thereafter and entering the Two-plus-Four negotiations, French diplomats downplayed their concerns about keeping Germany linked to the EC and committed to European unity. Roland Dumas, the French foreign minister, summed up his government's position in an article published in the *New York Times* on March 13, 1990. He wrote:

I always believed that the arbitrary division of Germany was senseless. Since no one can permanently divide a nation, a people, a country, German unity will put an end to one of history's anomalies. And it is up to the Germans themselves to determine the pace and internal coalitions of this unification. But the situation inherited from the war cannot be improved without the participation of countries other than the two Germanys.

Everything revolves around a simple idea: German unification must be accompanied by a strengthening of European stability. . . . A unified Germany will have to be part of this strengthening of the community.[6]

On the eve of the Two-plus-Four negotiations, Germany and France had largely mended their differences. However, even as late as September, President Mitterand still could not bring himself to be positive about German unification, which was now only days away. In his speech following the Franco-German summit conference in Munich, Mitterand implied that there were still many unresolved "conflicts, rivalries, and misunderstandings." Harmony was still a long way off.

Great Britain

British reactions to the fall of the Berlin Wall and the drive toward unification were predictably similar to the French reactions. Although popular opinion in both countries favored unification, older generations remembered the wartime hardships brought on by German aggression and could not help being more than a little suspicious. For Prime Minister Margaret Thatcher and her cabinet, themselves members of the latter generation, the reemergence of the "German problem" in 1989 would pose a number of difficult foreign policy paradoxes. Her government feared that the rapidly changing political scene in central Europe might upset stability and alter the status quo—to Great Britain's detriment.

Even though Britain had always supported the idea of German self-determination, the rapidity of the East German collapse caught many policy makers off guard. Thatcher, who grew up during the wartime hatreds of Nazism and anything German, seemed ill-disposed to deal with the issue. It was no great secret that she did not hold Germans in high regard and that she particularly had no love for Chancellor Kohl.[7] Much of England's conservative press picked up on her dislikes. Anti-unification articles, such as those arguing that there might be a "Fourth Reich"[8] and that the "only thing worse than a bad German is a good German,"[9] frequently appeared on English newsstands. Nevertheless, as news of the breaching of the Berlin Wall reached London, the official reaction expressed optimism and hope for the future. The prime minister welcomed the events of November 9, proclaiming that day to be "a great day for freedom, a great day for liberty."[10]

Such exuberance quickly faded once German unification had become a distinct possibility. Several potentially severe consequences for England were evident. A union of the Germanys would most certainly produce an economic colossus and possibly upset or disrupt established market relationships within the EC. Still worse, such a powerhouse might command increased diplomatic respect abroad and threaten Great Britain's status as intermediary between the United States and Europe, a position it had enjoyed ever since 1945. Finally, and perhaps most important, was the question of Germany's role in Europe's existing security arrangements. Great Britain did not want to see Germany neutralized. The best way to hold a reunited Germany in check would be to adopt the French suggestion and submerge German institutions into those of the EC. Such a solution, however, would require an ever-wider integration among the EC member states. Given that Thatcher vehemently opposed surrendering any more British sovereignty to the EC, this proposal did not seem tantalizing either.

Consequently, Great Britain's policy makers were caught between two conflicting goals: the desire to see Gorbachev's reform movement succeed and the need to watch over and contain Germany. The dilemma proved so difficult that during the initial discussions on the possibility of unification in January 1990, the best policy the prime minister could devise was to delay. In an interview with the *Wall Street Journal*, Thatcher accepted the eventuality of a single Germany but said that unification "must come at a rate which takes account of other obligations and which gives us time to work things out."[11] This was a polite way of saying that she preferred German unification to take place in conjunction with a more general democratization of Eastern Europe, a process that she privately hoped might take ten to fifteen years.[12]

Thatcher never got the chance to try out her ideas, for the March elections in the GDR rendered her dilatory strategy obsolete and forced yet another change in policy. Faced with the new reality of a rapidly unifying Germany, Thatcher convened a meeting of experts at the prime minister's country estate, Chequers, to discuss Germany and their expectations for its future. The four prominent history professors and two political commentators in attendance characterized the Germans by reeling off a litany of negative personality traits that stereotyped Germans as insensitive and self-absorbed people. Although most of the group thought that Europe need not fear the Germans, there remained a minority who thought that the lessons of past aggression should not be lost upon the present. The Chequers Memorandum,[13] as the notes of the meeting came to be known, might never have seen the light of day had it not been for the debate over the comments of Nicholas Ridley, the Cabinet Secretary of Industry. In an interview with *The Spectator*, Ridley blasted the proposed German monetary union as "a racket designed to take over the whole of Europe."[14] The British public did not share Ridley's contentions. Nevertheless, the parliamentary debate on the affair and the subsequent leak of the Chequers Memorandum led many citizens to question Thatcher's policy toward Europe. Britain's relations with Germany suffered accordingly.

It was under this dark cloud of controversy that the Thatcher government had to prepare for the Two-plus-Four negotiations. As far as Great Britain was concerned, unification should be accomplished gradually, within an all-European context, and only upon the successful conclusion of the four powers' rights and responsibilities vis-à-vis Germany. Further, Great Britain could accept East German participation in the EC provided that such participation did not destabilize the EC. Finally, the new Germany would have to be a member of NATO.[15] This final insistence put British policy on a collision course with the interests of the Soviet Union.

United States

The United States had a long history of supporting the idea of unification. As early as the middle of 1989, State Department bureaucrats saw that unification was finally within the realm of possibility and worked to formulate policy. As the East German government began to destabilize, many in the Bush administration thought that the United States should come out quickly in support of unification and thereby win favor from Germany. However, the West German government in Bonn still had not clarified its own position on unification, and thus the State Department did not rush to formulate a policy for fear of appearing "more German than the Germans." Consequently, as the East German revolution gained momentum in October, the policy of the United States was still in flux. The general strategy was to support Chancellor Kohl and pay lip-service to the idea of unification, but to do nothing to speed it along.[16]

While the rest of the world responded joyously to the opening of the Berlin Wall, President George Bush was busy deflecting criticism that he did not seem very happy about the events in East Germany. Bush's response was more measured than it was unemotional. He, like his Secretary of State James A. Baker, had to temper his personal euphoria over communism's troubles with his role as diplomat. Neither of them wanted to give the impression that they were taking political advantage of the misfortunes of others.[17] Further, the situation was still far from stable. It would have been unwise to send the impression that the United States would come to the demonstrators' aid should a military crackdown (á la Tienanmen Square) ensue. The rapidity of the East German collapse soon forced a more deliberate plan of action. Kohl's Ten-Point Program received a mixture of cautious optimism and disapproval at not being consulted. State Department spokesperson Margaret Tutweiler announced that the United States was sympathetic to Germany's drive to unify, but her announcement stopped short of endorsing the plan. In private conversations, President Bush told Foreign Minister Genscher that although unification was a matter for the Germans to decide, the United States would insist on certain conditions including, among others, that Germany retain membership in both NATO and the EC. In addition, Germany's borders and other security arrangements would have to be settled by international agreement before the United States would agree to relinquish its postwar responsibilities toward Germany.

By December, it was clear that the United States had taken a more positive approach to German unification than had France and Britain. In February, Chancellor Kohl and his wife came to Camp David for a weekend visit, during which the issues of unification received attention. Kohl and Bush agreed on almost every issue, including German membership in NATO. One bit of friction occurred when Kohl refused to renounce publicly German claims to the Oder-Neisse territories and guarantee Poland's borders. President Bush was not pleased, but he refused to press the issue either. Apparently, the Bush administration took seriously Henry Kissinger's comment that "if the Germans see us as obstructing their aspirations, we'll pay a price later on."[18] Clearly, the United States did not want to risk alienating Kohl and thereby jeopardizing the American-German partnership.

Soviet Union

Of the four postwar powers interested in the fate of Germany, the Soviet Union had the most at stake. Soviet leaders had invested much effort into turning their World War II "prize" into the cornerstone of Soviet ideology in central Europe. East Germany was a symbol of communist achievement—a bastion of Marxist ideology bravely confronting a capitalist enemy to the west. In the previous decades, such a confrontational paradigm had meaning. But by 1989, Gorbachev's reform movement held out the promise for change. *Glasnost* and *perestroika* might have liberalized East Germany and kept it allied to the Soviet Union. Unfortunately, Erich Honecker's intransigence and Egon Krenz's failures pushed East Germany beyond reform into revolution. The Soviet Union now had to face its worst nightmare. East Germany was now on track for unification with West Germany. Was unification compatible with Soviet interests?

Gorbachev did not think so. In 1987, two years before unification became a possibility, the general secretary remarked that there would be "serious consequences"[19] for any movement seeking to alter the status quo in Germany. During a state visit by Chancellor Kohl in October 1988, Gorbachev bluntly remarked that "the current situation is a result of history. Attempts at overturning what has been created by it or to force things by an unrealistic policy are an incalculable and even dangerous endeavor."[20] However, by the next spring, Soviet officials were singing a different tune, hinting that their government might support a unification of Germany. In October, Soviet spokesperson Yevgeny Primakov told the *New York Times* that there was "no formidable obstacle to reunification."[21] In a speech before the United Nations in December and again to the Communist Party Central Committee in February, Gorbachev conceded that all peoples have the right to choose their social and political systems freely. In each speech, he implied that governments must be responsive to the wishes of citizens. The Brezhnev Doctrine, which retained for the Soviet Union the right to interfere in the internal affairs of communist nations, had died a sudden death. What caused such a dramatic *volte-face*?

The relatively sudden turn in the Soviet Union's German policy was based on the old formula that a united *and neutral* Germany might not necessarily be detrimental to Soviet interests. Gorbachev had to find a common ground between two opposite approaches to the German problem. On the one hand, the German issue would test his image as a champion of liberty. Any attempt to limit the East Germany's right to self-determination would bring into question his own commitment to *glasnost* and *perestroika*. On the other hand, Gorbachev still had to answer his enemies back home who were highly critical of any plan to surrender territory to the West. When Chancellor Kohl's Ten-Point Program forced a reckoning with the issue, Gorbachev reacted duplicitously. Publicly, he accepted the possibility of unification and asserted that the Germans themselves must decide their own fate but stressed, however, that unification was not of "urgent international importance."[22] At the same time, his message to the communist faithful back home was that East Germany's future as a member of the Soviet bloc was secure.

Evidently, it would be left to his foreign minister, Eduard Shevardnadze, to reconcile these apparent contradictions publicly and define the Soviet Union's stance on unification. In a speech to the political committee of the European Parliament in February 1990, Shevardnadze reiterated that the Soviet Union accepted the principle of German self-determination, provided it was accompanied with assurances against the buildup of hostile military power and future aggression. In other venues, Shevardnadze also demanded a recognition of existing borders, and a satisfactory resolution to the question of Germany's place in the defensive structure of Europe. However, he reserved his strongest language for the official communist publications. In articles published in *Pravda* and *Izvestia*, he reiterated that the USSR had "very important and legitimate rights" in respect to Germany that were won by "twenty-six million dead (and) many thousand destroyed cities and towns."[23]

Shevardnadze's words gave the impression that the Soviets could never accept a reunited Germany in NATO. Indeed, Gorbachev had no desire to move on this issue, since he still had hopes that the socialist reform movement inside the GDR would be successful. But as Egon Krenz's resignation signaled socialism's irrevocable failure, Gorbachev slowly came to accept the reality of the situation. During Hans Modrow's state visit to Moscow, Gorbachev let it be known that the Soviet Union would not oppose German unification provided Soviet interests were not jeopardized. The two men then discussed how this might take place. The resultant "Plan for Germany Unity," although officially credited to Modrow, clearly bore both men's hopes to preserve at least some of the GDR. The plan called for a confederation between the GDR and West Germany, one that would be a member of neither NATO nor the Warsaw Pact. Although this was an acceptable solution for the Soviet Union, this latter provision made it patently unacceptable to the other three powers.[24]

The March GDR elections and its call for unification could not have come at a worse time for Mikhail Gorbachev. Four years into the process, *perestroika* had not fared well. The promised economic prosperity still had not materialized and the long lines and food shortages that were customary under the communist economic structure still governed the marketplace. As the economic situation continued to deteriorate, Gorbachev's leadership came under attack from the right wing of the Communist Party, which also viewed the changes in eastern Europe as a retreat and defeat. In the midst of these personal and political difficulties, Gorbachev came to realize that a unification of Germany might actually be a blessing in disguise. A withdrawal of troops from East German soil would ease a terrible financial burden. In addition, Gorbachev might be able to exchange Soviet consent to unification for hard currency or credits, both of which Gorbachev desperately needed to prop up his ailing economy. Suddenly, Gorbachev saw in unification a means to silence his critics and simultaneously secure his political base at home.

Such a grand coup would never be possible unless Gorbachev could persuade his military and political opponents that the Soviet Union's security and economic interests were best served by surrendering control of East Germany. Given the British and American insistence that a new Germany remain in NATO, that prospect seemed remote. That spring, the Soviet Union suggested various plans for German involvement in European security. Shevardnadze proposed neutrality, joint membership in both NATO and the Warsaw Pact, and a complete revamping of both alliances to form a single pro-European security arrangement. All suggestions fell upon deaf ears. NATO membership remained the stumbling block that prevented an agreement. As the Two-plus-Four negotiations approached, Mikhail Gorbachev faced a difficult choice. He either had to agree to concede to Germany's membership in NATO and withdraw from East Germany at the risk of his own political future or submit to the pressure of his political opponents and hold fast in opposition to unification, thereby alienating potential sources of economic and foreign diplomatic support.

FINDING SOLUTIONS:
THE TWO-PLUS-FOUR TALKS

The idea for multiparty diplomatic discussions emerged in the middle of January 1990, shortly after the GDR's collapse. James Baker and his State Department aides are generally credited with the idea, which was subsequently dubbed the Two-plus-Four talks. The other three powers agreed to the talks after the Ottawa "Open Skies" Conference in February 1990.[25] The Two-plus-Four meetings would prove little more than a formality. The critical issues of Polish border guarantees, NATO membership, and Soviet security concerns would be settled in private, face-to-face negotiations.

Everyone agreed that a unified Germany was impossible without a renunciation of all claims to Polish territory. Kohl understood this well himself but had to worry about his own domestic political position. Many of Chancellor Kohl's closest supporters were refugees from Polish territory and, given the upcoming selections, Kohl did not wish to alienate a major part of his electoral base by renouncing the territory outright. Instead, Kohl insisted that only an all-German parliament could give up such claims, a position that engendered open disagreement with President Bush at the Camp David meeting. Although there was precedent for such an argument, Kohl realized that unification would go nowhere without some sort of guarantee of Poland's borders. As a possible compromise, Kohl decided to seek joint resolutions from the Bundestag and the Volkskammer that renounced all territorial claims. Further, he promised that once unification was accomplished, he would present those resolutions to the first all-German parliament for ratification. Taking Kohl at his word, the Two-plus-Four powers agreed, as did the Polish government.

The NATO membership question was not as easily solved. The Soviets had repeatedly resisted the West's insistence that Germany remain in NATO, since communist hard-liners back home would interpret such a concession as "caving-in" to the enemy. An unlikely hero in the search for diplomatic answers was Hans-Dietrich Genscher, the Federal Republic's foreign minister. Until now, Genscher (FDP [Free Democratic Party]) had figured only marginally in the diplomatic negotiations since his boss, Chancellor Kohl, preferred to do most of the work himself.[26] Nevertheless, Genscher set to work to find a compromise on the divisive issue of NATO membership and, on January 31, 1990, presented a possible solution. His plan stipulated that a united Germany should remain in NATO but that no NATO forces would be permitted in the former GDR. This would have created a demilitarized zone that might assuage Soviet fears of further NATO encroachment. In addition, Genscher suggested that NATO eschew its historical military mission in favor of more political goals. Genscher's proposal had obvious advantages for Mikhail Gorbachev. It would allow him to agree to German membership in NATO and to save face, or even perhaps to claim a victory. If nothing else, it could serve as the starting point for discussion.

The United States picked up Genscher's proposals and elaborated on them during a high-level conference in Moscow in early February. In the meeting, Secretary Baker presented his Soviet colleagues with a list of concessions that the United States could give in return for Soviet acceptance of unification. These included border guarantees, a ban on German possession of nuclear weapons, and changes in NATO. During Gorbachev's visit to

Washington in May and June, Baker reiterated these "nine assurances." In one startling White House session, Gorbachev seemed willing to concede that the Germans themselves could choose to be a member of whichever alliance they wished. Bush and Baker realized that, if Gorbachev was serious, this formulation was the key to Soviet acceptance of unification. In more relaxed conversations during games of horseshoes at Camp David, Bush and Gorbachev reached an understanding of each other's position. By the end of the visit, the United States had gained Soviet acceptance that the Germans themselves should decide which alliance they preferred.[27] In return, Gorbachev had a much-needed trade agreement in his pocket. Upon his return to Moscow, Gorbachev announced the arrangement and wondered when his opponents' wrath would descend upon him. Surprisingly, when the Central Committee of the Communist Party of the Soviet Union (CPSU) met three weeks later, it reelected Gorbachev as general secretary, effectively silencing his critics. It appeared that *perestroika* would survive another day.

Why did the CPSU acquiesce so easily? Perhaps the decisions of the NATO London summit, taking place concurrently with the CPSU conference, had an impact. In what may have been the most important international compromise of the entire year, NATO officials agreed to de-emphasize the military aspects of the Atlantic alliance and reshape the treaty into one of political cooperation. The West agreed to reduce traditional troop strengths in Europe and shift its nuclear strategy away from flexible response options popular in the 1960s and 1970s to one of "last resort."[28] As part of the deal, Germany agreed to limit the size of its army and abjure atomic, biological, and chemical weaponry. By any measure, this would enhance Soviet security, and suddenly the loss of East Germany seemed a fair swap.

The final Soviet agreement came two weeks later. Having just survived his CPSU meeting and enlivened by the London NATO declarations, Gorbachev felt secure enough to invite Kohl to Moscow and his home in the Caucasus for face-to-face discussions. On July 14, the most important German-Soviet negotiations since 1939 began. In the next few days, Gorbachev agreed to unification in principle and to the new German borders. He then conceded that the Soviet Union would allow Germany to join whichever alliance it wished, with the understanding that it would choose NATO. Bundeswehr troops, in their role as part of NATO, could be stationed on former GDR territory once Soviet troops left. In return, Kohl offered Gorbachev over three billion dollars in financial support for the beleaguered Soviet economy and money to pay for the maintenance of Soviet troops still in East Germany.

The final Two-plus-Four document paved the way for unification and, remarkably, all sides came out reasonably satisfied. The end result is sufficient to claim that the process was a success. Yet, it is clear that the actual Two-plus-Four sessions were mostly a formality. The real decisions were made the old-fashioned way, in direct one-to-one negotiations. Thus, it is ironic that German unification was made not in Berlin or Bonn but in the Soviet Caucasus and at Camp David in the United States. There is nothing new about this bilateral decision-making approach. What was novel, however, was the degree that each of the four nations had to subordinate or alter its own national interests to accommodate a new political reality. Soviet foreign policy underwent the greatest change, for Soviet troops now had to withdraw from eastern Europe. Similarly, the transformation of NATO signalled a distinct change in U.S. foreign policy that would ultimately lead to a diminution of the American military presence in central Europe. Although Britain and France played negligible roles in affecting the outcome, they were most directly affected. Neither one would occupy the same position within the EC again, once a united Germany entered the market. Perhaps, their marginal participation in the process symbolized this transformation already at work. Germany's rising status as an international power was already making the postwar notions of an Anglo-French–dominated Europe obsolete.

Professor Karl Kaiser once called the diplomacy of German unification "a fortunate case of statecraft." Indeed, the Germans may well marvel at how lucky they were. The twelve months beginning with October 1989 produced a remarkable confluence of events. Had it not been for Mikhail Gorbachev and *perestroika*, East German communism would not have collapsed. Similarly, had it not been for the economic difficulties in the Soviet Union, Gorbachev would not have been as willing to allow Germany to retain NATO membership. Negotiations might have broken down at many critical junctures. However, it would be foolish to attribute the success of Two-plus-Four to good luck alone. Even the most fortuitous events would have been wasted had it not been for the talented diplomats, including Genscher, Shevardnadze, and Baker, who knew how to exploit the events properly. These men made solving the age-old German problem look quite easy. Forging a single community out of the two cultures would prove much more difficult.

NOTES

1. Renata Fritsch-Bournazel, *Europe and German Unification* (New York: Berg, 1992), 172. Mitterand repeated the comment in his interview with the *Wall Street Journal*. See Karen Elliott House and E. S. Browning, "Mitterand Sees Europe at the Crossroads," *Wall Street Journal*, November 22, 1989, p. A6.

2. Manfred Görtemaker, *Unifying Germany, 1989–1990* (New York: St. Martin's Press, 1994), 155.

3. For more on diplomatic French fears vis-à-vis the collapse of East Germany and unification, see D. Yost, "France in the New Europe," *Foreign Affairs* 69 (Winter 1990–91).

4. Martin McCauley, "Gorbachev, the GDR and Germany," in Gert-Joachim Glaessner and Ian Wallace, eds., *German Revolution of 1989* (Oxford: Berg, 1992), 180.

5. Görtemaker, *Unifying Germany, 1989–1990*, 157.

6. Harold James and Marla Stone, eds., *When the Wall Came Down: Reactions to German Unification* (New York: Routledge, Chapman, Hall, 1992), 253–54.

7. Richard Davy, "Grossbritannien und die Deutsche Frage," *Europa-Archiv* 4 (1990): 141.

8. See Connor Cruise O'Brien, "Beware, the Reich Is Reviving," *London Times*, October 31, 1989, and reprinted in James and Stone, eds., *When the Wall Came Down*, 221–23.

9. Peregrine Worsthorne, *Sunday Telegraph*, May 7, 1989. Quoted in Davy, "Grossbritannien," 141.

10. Sheila Rule, "A Sense of Delight, Tempered by Pleas for Caution," *New York Times*, November 11, 1989.

11. "Thatcher Sees East European Progress As More Urgent Than Germans' Unity," *Wall Street Journal*, January 26, 1990, p. A12.

12. Stephen F. Szabo, *The Diplomacy of German Unification* (New York: St. Martin's Press, 1992), 47.

13. The Chequers Memorandum can be found in James and Stone, eds., *When the Wall Came Down*, 233–39, as can the comments of Timothy Garton Ash, who was a participant in the meeting (242–46). The memorandum also has been published in Konrad H. Jarausch and Volker Gransow, *Uniting Germany* (Providence, RI: Berghahn Books, 1994), 129–31.

14. Ridley's extremely unflattering comments eventually cost him his job. See "Saying the Unsayable about the Germans," *The Spectator*, July 14, 1990.

15. Karl Kaiser, "Germany's Unification," *Foreign Affairs* 70 (1990–91): 179.

16. Szabo, *Diplomacy of German Unification*, 13.

17. See the firsthand account in James A. Baker, *The Politics of Diplomacy* (New York: G. P. Putnam's Sons, 1995), 164–65.

18. Kissinger's comments were made at a White House dinner on November 13, 1989. See Michael Beschloss and Strobe Talbott, *At the Highest Levels* (Boston: Little Brown, 1993), 138.

19. Peter H. Merkl, *German Unification in the European Context* (University Park: Pennsylvania State University Press, 1993), 308.

20. See Hannes Adomeit, "Gorbachev and German Unification: Revision of Thinking, Realignment of Power," *Problems of Communism* 39 (July–August 1990): 4.

21. Robert Pear, "War Powers Curb on Kremlin Seen," *New York Times*, October 28, 1989.

22. Szabo, *Diplomacy of German Unification*, 45.

23. See Hans-Peter Riese, "Die Geschichte hat sich ans Werk gemacht: Der Wandel der sowjetischen Position zur Deutsche Frage," *Europa-Archiv* 4 (1990): 125–26 (translated by the author).

24. The plan can be found in Jarausch and Gransow, *Uniting Germany*, 105–6.

25. Douglas Hurd, foreign minister of Great Britain, and his French counterpart Roland Dumas both expressed preference for a four-plus-zero formula that would have excluded the Germans entirely. See Beschloss and Talbott, *At the Highest Levels*, 185; See also Szabo, *Diplomacy of Germany Unification*, 61.

26. Given the two men's antipathy toward each other both politically and personally, it is understandable that Kohl wanted to minimize Genscher's involvement.

27. For a more in-depth account of the Washington meeting and the Camp David session, see Beschloss and Talbott, *At the Highest Levels*, 215–28; see also Philip Zelikow and Condoleezza Rice, *Germany United and Europe Transformed* (Cambridge: Harvard University Press, 1997), 277–83.

28. Britain and France insisted that the nuclear option be kept available, otherwise nuclear disarmament might have been considered as an option.

5

Coming Together—
Remaining Apart

On Unity Day, October 3, 1990, Germans celebrated the political unification of their country. By acceding to the Federal Republic's Basic Law and political system, East Germany assured itself a fairly swift and uneventful assimilation into the legal and political institutions of West Germany. The same cannot be said for social and economic integration. Here, the process of assimilation was much more difficult, even agonizing. Germans who had grown apart by forty years of conflicting ideology were suddenly thrust together and expected to get along. Economic assumptions regarding the nature of the marketplace had to be undone. Social and individual rights needed to be reexamined and the role of citizens in society debated. These were questions that could not be solved overnight.

This chapter and the next present only some of the conflicts attendant to this forced cultural amalgamation. Chapter 5 explores three crises with one common theme: each grew out of the cultural shock of uniting East and West Germany. The topics are meant to be case studies of the economic, social, and intellectual dislocations that East Germans have been forced to endure ever since the collapse of communism. Chapter 6 also examines the shocks of unification. However, the issues it presents cannot be explained away as a by-product of changing ideologies. Instead, Chapter 6 presents case studies of how East and West Germans alike struggled to understand and come to terms with East Germany's past. The thesis of these two chapters is nevertheless similar. Unification turned out to be much more difficult than first imagined. It is, in fact, not a singular event accomplished at the stroke of a pen but a long and arduous process of social and intellectual conflict and compromise that continues to this day.

BACKGROUND—SOCIAL AND ECONOMIC DIVISION

In 1990 those East Germans who refrained from emigrating to the Federal Republic watched helplessly while the Federal Republic came to them. Within the span of a few months, the society they had known all their lives had been replaced by something new and largely alien. This was a fairly complete transformation. Workers found new expectations at their jobs, students discovered a new curriculum at school, and shoppers coped with daily changes in prices for food or clothing. The socialist system that had taken care of much of their social wants was rapidly disappearing, and a new and unfamiliar capitalist system had come to replace it. In the old communist state, everyone had a right to a job. Not so in the capitalist West. East Germans suddenly had to worry about finding and keeping employment, and many had no idea how to go about it. Even the simple things, like checking the newspaper for opportunities, had to be learned. In their former world, where apartment space was controlled by government agencies, there were no rent checks to write, no security deposits to make, and no fire insurance premiums to pay. Living in East Germany meant being told what you could and could not do; now you had to make dozens of choices every day. Although these transformations did not happen overnight, they nevertheless occurred far too rapidly for a smooth transition. For many, it was a dizzying, bewildering transition. For some, it would be their undoing.

THE CHANGING MARKETPLACE

In March 1990, East and West Germany agreed on terms to unite their economic, monetary, and social structures. On July 1, the treaty came into effect. Many East Germans welcomed the change, expecting the introduction of the Deutschmark to be the panacea to all their problems. At once, the East Germans scrapped their worthless Ostmarks and rushed to buy the Western goods they had coveted for so long. In only three months, the formerly socialist nation was submerged in a capitalist marketplace. But the dreams of those who expected an East German economic revival never materialized. The introduction of capitalism to a society that had never known the nuances of a free-market economy had the same effect as throwing a bucket of water on a fire. East German products now faced direct competition from

West German goods which were of much higher quality. One by one, firms that had been the mainstay of the GDR's highly regarded industrial infrastructure began to close, sending their workers to the unemployment offices for government relief. Within months, the East German economy had disintegrated. It would take years to undo the damage.

Why did this collapse occur? Many Western economists were taken aback by the severity of the reversal, since they had believed that East Germany's strong economic base would make the transition to capitalism easier. As it turned out, they had based their prognosis on false evidence. The decline of communism had revealed that the image of East Germany as an economic powerhouse was more a mirage than a reality. Much of the GDR's economic base had been heavily subsidized by the communist government and thus had never been subjected to the tests of competition, even within the communist bloc. Further, the success that East Germany did enjoy in the marketplace was not due to the quality or technological superiority of the goods but to the captive markets available to them behind the Iron Curtain. Consequently, the false demand for goods gave East German industry a patina of stability while underneath the surface its plants and infrastructure were hopelessly out of date. Finally, East Germany's industrial production depended heavily on energy obtained from burning brown coal, a usable but highly sulfuric (and thus environmentally unfriendly) source of energy. Even if East German products had not been inferior to those of the European Union, production would nevertheless have had to be curtailed or modified to suit the environmentally conscious West. These shortcomings hinted that the East German economy would be unable to withstand the pressure of a competitive marketplace. Somehow, this economic mess would have to be integrated with one of the world's most vibrant economies. How should it be done?

In keeping with the rapid unification strategy, the Bonn government opted to ignore the advice of financial experts and proceed with a swift unification of the economic structures. Their thinking was that if hardship should follow it was best to have it come all at once and get it over with rather than to drag out the transition period. Indeed, their decision made a period of hardship inevitable, since it gave East Germany's struggling infrastructure very little time to prepare for the shock of capitalism. To facilitate the transition, the government established the *Treuhandanstalt*, a trustee agency designed to oversee the transfer of East Germany's public property to private ownership. The agency's mission was threefold. The first was the privatization of the East German economy. Those state-run companies that were still economically viable were to be sold to private organizations or persons and the proceeds used to support workers dislocated by the changeover to capitalism. The agency also saw to the aid of those companies that had a reasonable chance for survival by providing financial and logistical aid. Finally, in the most hopeless cases, the *Treuhand* was empowered to shut down and liquidate firms that were no longer economically viable.

At first, the prognosis was fairly optimistic. Experts reckoned that about 82 percent of the East German companies were either salvageable or viable outright. The most optimistic observers believed that once East Germany's companies were in private hands, West German firms would strike up working relationships with them. This in turn would create investment opportunities that would help capitalize the firms and keep them solvent. Therefore, the logic was to keep as many plants operating as possible and find buyers to take over the production. However, as the agency set about its business, the results did not live up to expectations. Western money was slow to come into East Germany for a variety of reasons. Given the hopelessly outdated production facilities in East Germany, the costs of retooling scared away many prosepective investors. Further, Western companies were loathe to enter into partnerships with East German firms since many had accumulated a great deal of real or potential debt. The costs of environmental clean-up were enough to scare away many buyers. Finally, the issue of land ownership and property title rights remained unsettled. Few entrepreneurs wished to risk investing in a company built on expropriated lands for fear that there might be future ownership disputes and litigation.

The *Treuhand* did its best to preserve East German industry. Eventually, however, it became more of a clearinghouse for the selling of East German firms to the highest bidder, which usually turned out to be West Germans. There proved to be many bargains in the process. Some entire corporations that had more debt than working capital were sold to West German firms at pennies to the dollar. Some companies were transferred to owners for no consideration at all beyond vague promises to update facilities and employ a given number of workers. Because of such questionable business decisions, the *Treuhand* drew a great deal of fire from critics. East Germans were especially angered that the *Treuhand* did not seem interested in restructuring firms and thereby saving local jobs. Some radical critics voiced their displeasure in more destructive ways, as the assassination of the *Treuhand*'s chief executive bears witness. Subsequent investigations by government officials and journalists did reveal a great deal of mismanagement, some of it bordering on fraud. Nevertheless, by the end of its first year in operation, the *Treuhand* had sold about 3,000 plants and closed another 600. By early 1992, it still had 10,000 more firms to dispose of.

The efforts of the *Treuhand* notwithstanding, little could be done to avoid a terrible economic catastrophe. By the best estimates, two-thirds of the East German workforce worked in plants that were no longer viable given the new competition with the West. Consider the example of the Halle-Bitterfeld-Merseburg area in the state of Saxony-Anhalt. This area, once known as the "industrial triangle" at the economic heart of East Germany, was home to almost 40 percent of East German chemical production. The large Buna and Leuna chemical plants, which together employed over 40,000 workers, had to lay off close to 10,000 workers just to remain in production. The coal mines of Halle (which produced the cheap but environmentally unfriendly brown coal) went without orders as the industries they supplied curtailed production or tried to become more environmentally responsible. Eventually, one-fourth of all full-time workers in Halle had lost their jobs.[1] As unemployment rates rose, consumer goods production slowed and shops closed. The city drifted into lawlessness as desperate citizens took to thievery to survive. Only the heartiest souls ventured onto the streets at night. A homeless shelter, previously unheard of in the communist years, opened to minister to the destitute.

The conditions in Halle were similar to those throughout East Germany. In the weeks before the introduction of the Deutschmark, Western goods flooded into the GDR. Given a choice for the first time, consumers in East Germany stopped buying products made near their homes for better-quality goods coming from the Federal Republic. East German industrial production sank 7 percent in the first six months of 1990. Fifty-six out of sixty-nine key industries demonstrated decreased productivity over the previous six months. Among the hardest hit were the sugar, chocolate, tea, and coffee industries (–40 percent), the food industry (–23 percent), and the textile plants (–20 percent).[2]

The Federal Government had expected some economic dislocation, but not the catastrophe that actually ensued. The Bundestag hoped that the German Unity Fund, a special fund collected from federal and state sources, would provide sufficient financial aid to support the new areas. A good deal of money was spent for unemployment relief, retirement pensions, and job-training programs. It was, unfortunately, only a fraction of the total amount needed. The remainder was raised either through borrowing or the levying of new or higher taxes. In 1990–1991, the government transferred 85 to 100 million dollars to help the struggling eastern states. Even such large amounts could not begin to halt the free-fall collapse of the economy in the former GDR. Industrial production had dropped to one-third of 1989 levels, and unemployment approached 12 percent.[3]

The eastern states of Germany would not recover from this collapse quickly. In the years to come, this area continued to experience double-digit rates of unemployment. Labor statistics from 1997 reveal that the eastern part of Germany suffers from twice as many unemployed as the western.[4] It is therefore not surprising that the citizenry has voiced a great deal of discontent, some of it manifested in attacks on foreigners and other hate crimes. There is cause for optimism, however. Western companies have moved into the eastern German states. For example, the Eisenach-based plant that used to make Wartburg automobiles is now an Opel factory. Even McDonald's has set up shop in the larger communities. The East Germans themselves are trying to find their own niche in the capitalist system. For some localities, it is tourism. Others hope to lure new industries. Until the new areas can stand on their own, the costs of the transformation will remain the responsibility of the Federal Government. It already has proved to be a major expense. Some estimates place the total amount of aid sent to the eastern states each year since 1990 at 100 to 150 billion dollars. Most of it is going to entitlements, but a fair portion is providing employment to workers engaged in rebuilding and repairing infrastructure, including roads, bridges, and communication systems. And as anyone who has been to Weimar, Leipzig, or Dresden can attest, much more needs to be done to bring these states up to western standards.

SOCIAL DISCORD—THE ABORTION CONTROVERSY

The union of the two Germanys produced not only difficult economic times but also brought to a head the social issues that divided the two societies. Perhaps the most visible elements of this "social divide" are the differences in laws governing a woman's reproductive rights. East Germany, which always had prided itself on its record of sensitivity to the needs of women, had allowed women to obtain an abortion on demand within the first three months of the pregnancy, free of charge. The Federal Republic, on the other hand, had far more restrictive laws. Paragraph 218 of the penal code held that a pregnancy could be terminated only under certain circumstances (including deformity of fetus, rape, and social necessity) and that two doctors had to agree that the reasons were valid before the procedure could be done. Illegal abortions could be punished with fines or imprisonment.

The Federal Government's restrictive approach undoubtedly had its roots in the immediate postwar climate, when the abuses of euthanasia and the eugenics laws of the Nazi era were fresh in people's minds. Conservative supporters of the law pointed to Article 2 of the Basic Law that grants "the right to life and inviolability of the person" as a justification for making abortions difficult. When a liberal revision of Paragraph 218 passed the Bundestag in 1975, the Federal Constitutional Court agreed with the conservative interpretation and struck down the changes as unconstitutional. The impending unification of the two countries meant that unless the Federal Constitutional Court reversed itself, East German territories would lose their liberal abortion rights and find themselves subject to Paragraph 218. Religious and political considerations further complicated the issue. East Germany's predominantly Protestant population did not necessarily have the same religious misgivings toward abortion as did the Catholic population in the south of West Germany. Further, that Catholic population was also the backbone of the ruling CDU/CSU parties. Chancellor Kohl, himself a Catholic, had to balance the desires of the East Germans whom he hoped to woo into his party with the demands of his electoral base at home.

The months of April through September 1990 were difficult ones for German women in general. One by one, East German mothers saw the rights they had come to depend upon disappear with the coming economic catastrophe. First, factory-run kindergartens closed owing to lack of funding. Then, day care became too expensive for many firms now caught in the competitive crunch. Finally, as unemployment skyrocketed, those women who were not yet driven from their jobs were usually the first ones let go. So when the Unification Treaty negotiators took up the issue of Paragraph 218, they found an angry and vocal women's lobby already at work to protect their rights to an abortion on demand. Curiously, these activists found a good deal of support from women in West Germany (including many in the CDU) who agreed that government should have no right to dictate whether a woman had to carry a pregnancy to term or not. Consequently, the abortion law not only threatened to prevent agreement on a unification treaty but reopened an old wound in the Federal Republic.

The battle over a woman's right to choose an abortion was played out in the press and on the Bundestag floor. The acrimonious debate that followed produced many strange political alliances. Both CDU representative Lothar de Maizière and Rudolf Augstein, the liberal editor of *Der Spiegel*, agreed that Paragraph 218 should be repealed.[5] Chancellor Kohl and the CDU/CSU leadership were dead set against any changes. Although consensus seemed far off, many notable compromises emerged. One suggested that a "personal rights of women" article be amended to the Basic Law to clarify the protection-of-life articles. The SPD implored women all across Germany to band together and have Paragraph 218 overturned.[6] The CDU/CSU countered such suggestions by adopting an even more stringent stance, refusing to allow passage of any law that would grant the eastern territories any more than a temporary exemption from the laws. Further, the CDU demanded that women be under the jurisdiction of their home towns. In other words, a West German woman could be held liable if she traveled to the eastern states for an abortion.[7] A possible compromise came from Rita Süssmuth (CDU), the Bundestag president and former family minister, and Irmgard Adam-Schwätzer (FDP). The proposal allowed women to seek an abortion on demand in the first trimester, provided she undergo counseling and think it over for three days before seeing a doctor. Although the "Süssmuth formula" was not well received everywhere, it did pose a "third way" for discussion and debate. Many German women latched on to it as a reasonable solution to a difficult problem, and it became the centerpiece of later compromises with abortion opponents.

As the final weeks of the Unification Treaty negotiations wound down, a resolution was still lacking. Rather than scuttle the entire treaty, the delegates agreed to set the entire issue aside for a two-year transitional period. Thus, the final draft of the Unification Treaty did not solve the controversy but shoved the responsibility onto the future German Bundestag with the mandate to create a unified abortion statute by December 1992. In the meantime, each area would retain its existing abortion laws. In return for accepting a shorter transition period, the SPD and FPD opponents of Paragraph 218 received the concession that women would be under the jurisdiction at the scene of an abortion, not the one in effect in their home town. The end result of the compromise created a situation where an abortion performed in the Treptow district of East Berlin was legal while one in Neukölln (on the other side of the street) in the former western section was not.[8] This dilatory tactic solved nothing and committed Germany to two more years of confusion. As the debate continued into 1991, Irmgard Adam-Schwätzer (FDP) contributed a fresh proposal approach. Adam-Schwätzer's model proposed a term solution along the lines of the Süssmuth proposal, but added mandatory counseling. In all, six separate bills came to the Bundestag floor for consideration, two from the CDU and one from each of the four other parties represented.[9]

The wide disparity of opinions was a clear indication that traditional party politics was an inefficient and illogical approach to solving what was essentially a social, religious, and ethical problem. So when an "institutionalized women's movement"[10] evolved among the female Bundestag members, the chances for a cross-party solution seemed more possible than ever. Headed by the FDP delegate Uta Würfel, female delegates from all parties worked together to advance a draft bill similar to the Süssmuth and Adam-Schwätzer models. Their proposal accepted the Federal Court's ruling protecting the fetus and stipulated that women should seek counseling during the first trimester but then be allowed to decide whether or not to continue the pregnancy. The cornerstones of the group effort were two supplemental proposals. One proposal called for the establishment of government-funded counseling agencies for all matters of family planning; the other to authorize day-care service in kindergartens for all children aged three and older.[11] These addenda were an effort to give women of all socioeconomic ranks the opportunity to raise children and still work. Despite vicious public and private attacks on the group members, they managed to get the entire package passed through the Bundestag and the Bundesrat in July 1992. Their victory was in no small part due to their nonpartisan appeal and to the fact that the ruling CDU/CSU/FDP coalition freed its membership from the traditional party discipline to vote their consciences.

The passage of the laws was a victory for East German and prochoice Western women and simultaneously a decisive defeat for the CDU and a political slap in Chancellor Kohl's face. Unwilling to let the issue rest, abortion opponents within the CDU filed suit in Federal Court to have the justices review the constitutionality of the law. Sure enough, the court granted an injunction and in a landmark—and extremely controversial—decision of May 28, 1993, it struck down the new law as unconstitutional. Further, in an extreme convolution of judicial prerogatives, the court fashioned its own law, which paradoxically asserted the illegality of abortion but provided no punishment if it is carried out in the first three months of a pregnancy and after the woman has seen a counselor who would try to dissuade her from proceeding. While the court's formula seems identical to the legislation, the assertion of illegality is an important distinction. Since state funding could not be used for an "illegal" act, the court's decision effectively created a double standard whereby women of means could get an abortion but poorer women had to seek cheap but unsafe abortions or get none at all. Feminists across Germany were outraged. "This ruling is violence against women,"[12] read one protest banner. Another prominent politician called it a "catastrophe" and "a return to the Middle Ages." One SPD Bundestag member dubbed it "a relapse into a two-class legislation."[13] Oddly, many Catholics and social conservatives also disagreed with the decision. They felt the decision had not gone far enough to limit a woman's ability to get an abortion.

It remained for yet one more law to clarify the issue to the satisfaction of the Constitutional Court. Again, the parties took to traditional political negotiations to produce a compromise, which passed in August 1995.

This version made all abortions illegal except in cases of rape or medical necessity. Women were permitted an abortion within the first trimester and would not be punished, provided they had been to a counselor. As a concession to the poorer classes, national health insurance would pay for such abortions for all women below a certain level of income.[14] Whether this is a final resolution remains to be seen: In August 1996, and in direct conflict with the federal laws, the state of Bavaria passed even tougher abortion restrictions. The courts will most likely again become involved.

The debate over a woman's reproductive rights is certainly not confined to Germany. Other nations have struggled with the same issue. However, in the fragile culture of the new Germany, where citizens must deal with distinctions of east versus west as well as the usual gender, economic, and racial distinctions, the abortion controversy has become doubly divisive. What is intriguing is that East Germans—who had basically capitulated to the economic and political institutions of West Germany—chose this issue to take a stand and fight. Did the East Germans have some pride in the socialist accomplishments of the communist state after all? Perhaps so, but a more likely reason that the East Germans resisted Paragraph 218 is that they finally had grown weary of surrendering so much of their way of life to the West. In the final analysis, no one got exactly what they wanted. The reproductive rights of former West German women have improved while those of East German women have deteriorated, but only slightly. Consequently, neither prolife nor prochoice advocates can claim a clear victory. Perhaps a solution that satisfies no one may prove to be the only possible compromise between two such diametrically opposite social positions.

CONCLUSIONS—THE BARRIERS OF THE MIND

The ongoing battle over abortion rights and the economic dislocation following unification are only two facets of a much larger problem of social integration. The previous case studies clearly illustrate that the unification of the Germanys is still an ongoing process, fraught with difficulties and pitfalls. What may not be as clear is the fact that the East Germans have sacrificed and given up more than their western counterparts. On the surface, this may seem a logical consequence. After all, the collapse of the communist system was prima facie evidence of the "superiority" of West German ways. Yet the wholesale abandonment of socialism, even those aspects that East Germans thought valuable, has had unexpected psychological consequences. Opinion polls from 1990 and 1991 revealed that many East Germans saw themselves as losers, or at least second-class citizens, when compared to West Germans. They described "Wessies" as more confident, disciplined, and tolerant than they, but also as more egotistical, distrustful, and critical.[15] They also tended to stereotype them as overindulgent—materially wealthy but spiritually bankrupt. Many of them would agree with Martin Ahrends's assessment that West Germans were "gray-haired young people . . . with empty faces [filled with] smugness and indifference."[16] West Germans were not without their own unflattering stereotypes. They described "Ossies" or "Zonis" as lazy people who were unwilling to earn life's pleasures through hard work but preferred to have things handed to them. West Germans often took umbrage that they had to pay higher taxes to support people who weren't doing their fair share of production.

These sentiments cast a different light on the economic and social transformations of the past seven years. As East Germans still suffer from economic hardship and unemployment, they tend to see their situation as punishment for the "accident" of their birthplace. And despite their government's appeals to be tolerant and patient, West Germans are tired of the continuing sacrifices they believe they are making for the integration of the eastern states. These ill feelings are the latest obstacles to unification. The barbed wire and guard towers of yesterday may have been dismantled, but East and West Germans still refer to each other as "drüben" (over there). Now, the German people are separated by the barriers they have created in their minds. Such resentments are the product of forty years of lost contact and misunderstandings. They will resolve with time as the two halves get to know each other better. For the time being, at least socially and psychologically, there are still two Germanys.

NOTES

1. "Langsam, aber teuer sterben," *Der Spiegel* 39 (September 24, 1990): 76.

2. Office of Statistics of the DDR, "Mitteilung über die wirtschaftliche und soziale Entwicklung der DDR im 1. Halbjahr 1990," July 19, 1990, German Subject Collection, Box 77 (folder "Politics and Government"), Hoover Institution, Stanford, CA.

3. Thomas A. Baylis, "Transforming the East German Economy: Shock without Therapy," in Michael Huelshoff et al., eds., *From Bundesrepublik to Deutschland* (Ann Arbor: University of Michigan Press, 1993), 83.

4. "Weniger Stellen und noch mehr Arbeitslose," *Süddeutsche Zeitung*, August 7, 1997.

5. "Der par. 218 muss weg!" *Der Spiegel* 31 (July 30, 1990): 24.

6. "Vage Hoffnung," *Der Spiegel* 15 (April 9, 1990): 47–48.

7. See the discussion in Peter H. Merkl, *German Unification in the European Context* (University Park: Pennsylvania State University Press, 1993), 176–80.

8. "Fuss in der Tür," *Der Spiegel* 33 (August 13, 1990): 28.

9. Jeremiah M. Riemer, "Reproduction and Reunification: The Politics of Abortion in United Germany," in Huelshoff et al., eds., *Bundesrepublik to Deutschland*, 176.

10. Sabine Klein-Schonnefeld, "Germany," in Bill Rolston and Anna Eggert, eds., *Abortion in the New Europe* (Westport, CT: Greenwood Press, 1994), 125.

11. Ibid., 126.

12. "German Court Restricts Abortion, Angering Feminists and the East," *New York Times*, May 29, 1993.

13. Monika Prützel-Thomas, "The Abortion Issue Since Unification," *Debatte*, no. 2 (1995): 109.

14. Ibid., 110.

15. "Den Neuen fehlt Selbstvertrauen," *Der Spiegel* 46 (November 12, 1990): 126.

16. From Martin Ahrends, "In the Belly of the Beast," quoted in *World Press Review*, June 1991, p. 21.

6

Expurgation and Atonement

On the night of January 15, 1990, a mob of angry protesters descended upon the headquarters of the East German secret police (Stasi) on the Normannenstrasse in Berlin. Within hours, the heavily fortified building was occupied by thousands of citizens intent on smashing furniture, vandalizing offices, and seizing files. That night's "demonstration" was the first major act of violence in what had been a peaceful revolution, and some commentators drew quick comparisons to the storming of the Bastille by irate French citizens two centuries earlier. However, as Professor Robert Darnton has pointed out, "January 15 was no July 14."[1] No government fell, nor were any prisoners released that night. What was unleashed, however, was forty years of pent-up anger with the police state mentality of the communist regime. Those who had perpetuated that police state were about to become targets themselves.

On that night in January, the Germans started to expunge the worst aspects of the East German communist regime from the "new" united German society. In a frenzied search for "justice" and even revenge, protesters systematically identified and scheduled for trial those individuals who had been responsible for the abuses in the East German society. The most tempting targets were the agents of the state security ministry (Stasi) and the border guards who shot at fleeing citizens. While the bringing of such "criminals" to justice may seem a laudatory goal, the effort created a "purge mentality" that had a tremendous impact on the ongoing process of German unification. Why did this reaction occur? Was this just another historical case of a "revolution eating its children," or was there a rationale unique to the German situation? What do the trials tell us about the way Germans perceive themselves? This chapter presents two case histories of how East and West Germans alike tried to come to grips with the evils of their pasts. These cases illustrate how the unification brought about not just a clash of cultures but also a clash of consciences. They also suggest why such conflicts were not only an inevitable but also a necessary part of the unification process.

COMING TO TERMS WITH THE STASI

The crowds that attacked Stasi headquarters that January night had good reason to vent their anger. Earlier that month, consumer prices jumped dramatically, signaling the onset of inflation and a protracted period of unemployment and hardship. However, this was not a bread riot; it was more an eruption of frustrations that had lain dormant for forty years. Honecker, Krenz, and the old SED regime were finished, but the new one under the reform-minded Hans Modrow did not appear to be an improvement. Modrow's cool treatment of the Round Table delegates did not inspire their trust. Worse, his insistence that East Germany retain some sort of internal security force worried the dissidents, who by now insisted that the Stasi be completely dismantled. The Normannenstrasse demonstrations settled the issue. In deference to the crowd, Modrow backed away from his position. Within weeks, the dreaded Stasi was gone.

With the Stasi officially dead, the citizenry had to figure out what to do with its remains. All across East Germany, concerned individuals spontaneously formed committees to secure Stasi buildings and contents for analysis. Most of the committees were composed of students, dissidents, or ordinary citizens and varied in size from four to one hundred volunteers, depending of the size of the locality. It is impossible to overstate the magnitude of their job. The Stasi had accumulated an estimated 125 miles of shelving loaded with files and reports. Volunteers soon floated in a "sea of paper," making the task of organization almost impossible. In addition, there were tape recordings of telephone conversations, transcripts of wiretaps, and informant identification cards to be arranged and cataloged.

As one worker put it, working in the Stasi files was like being in a "dreamworld."[2] For those who would come to know their contents, it was more like a nightmare. As the committees searched through the captured records, the information gathered over forty years of institutionalized social spying slowly came into public view. All that was needed was for someone to publish the once-secret information. And publish they did. Now, each Stasi file had the potential to became a Pandora's box filled with years of social and personal hardship. Before long, friendships would be destroyed, careers would end, and long-standing relationships would be ripped apart. And in the end, East Germans would be shocked to identify who actually made this grisly police state function. It turned out to be themselves.

The first fruits from this capture were the startling revelations of the size of the Stasi behemoth and the numbers of citizens who willingly fed it information. Official Stasi documents listed as many as 85,000 citizens as "official collaborators" and another 109,000 as "unofficial collaborators."[3] Considering that East Germany's total population may have been about sixteen million, the figures (if accurate) indicate that one out of every eighty citizens was in some way connected to the Stasi. Neighbors informed on each other. Bosses kept track of the political activities of their workers. Confessionals were bugged. Teachers maintained files on the political reliability of their students and spouses informed on the activities of their mates. Since information came from such a wide variety of sources, individuals who were now allowed to apply for permission to view their personal dossiers had to face the shock of reliving the most intimate details of their lives. Following that shock came the horror in discovering which of their closest friends or associates had provided the accounts.

The Stasi's tentacles had reached every level of East German society. Even now, after the agency's demise, those tentacles could still sting. As the names of informants became known, the most notable ones were given to the press for publication. With every passing day, the list grew more impressive. Many intellectuals, including the world-renowned novelist Christa Wolf and the poet Sacha Anderson, had collaborated. Even some clergy, to many the heroes of the dissident movement, had collaborated. Perhaps the interesting case is that of Manfred Stolpe, who had been a Church leader and head of the Evangelical synod. Many had considered him the moral voice of the anti-communist movement and candidate for political office until he admitted that he had had regular contacts with the Stasi ever since his early days in the ministry. Despite criticisms, Stolpe defended himself by claiming that he was merely seeking a rapprochement between the government and the people he represented through his Church office. "I would have met with the devil if it would have helped us," he told one group of reporters.[4]

Politicians made the most juicy targets and were often the subject of specific searches by the committees. The most damaging revelations surfaced in March 1990, around the time of the first free East German elections. By one report, as many as forty (or 10 percent) of the newly elected representatives to East Germany's first democratic Volkskammer had been tied to the Stasi in some way.[5] Some highly visible East German politicians were identified as informants. Wolfgang Schnur, the former lawyer and churchman who headed the Democratic Awakening party (a coalition partner with Kohl's CDU in the "Alliance for Germany") stepped down once a nonpartisan group of citizens in Rostock discovered proof that he had informed for the Stasi and carried out its orders for twenty years. Similar fates befell ex-minister Hans-Wilhelm Ebeling, head of the German Social Union (DSU) Party and Ibrahim Böhme, the leader of the revitalized eastern SPD. The most important victim proved to be none other than Lothar de Maizière, chief of the eastern CDU and prime minister of East Germany. Suspicion descended upon de Maizière after researchers discovered an identification card mentioning an informant named "Czerny" residing at his address. Although he denied the charges as "nonsense," the accusations cast enough of a shadow on his career that he eventually resigned from the seat he had won in the unified Bundestag.

The long arms of the Stasi apparatus even reached across the border into West Germany, as evidence came to light that Stasi spies and informants had been working in the Federal Republic for years. An estimated 4,000 to 6,000 West Germans had benefited materially from Stasi contacts. As the numbers of the implicated grew ever larger, some Bundestag representatives negotiated a general amnesty for all Stasi agents and collaborators. As one SPD representative correctly assumed, the emergent Germany simply "cannot just throw millions out of society." [6] Even Chancellor Kohl himself was in favor of such a plan. Multiparty negotiations moved forward and produced an agreement that granted amnesty to all Stasi agents as part of an overall unification treaty package. However, with the plan seemingly a done deal and just weeks before Unity Day, the CSU Party withdrew its support. Without the votes of its coalition partner, the CDU could not pass the legislation.

Stasi agents were now subject to litigation. Hundreds were indicted and tried for everything from murder to extortion to blackmail. Each new revelation emerging out of Stasi files meant another potential lawsuit. Needless to say, law courts labored for years to get out from under the mass of litigation. Every so often, new suggestions for amnesty reappeared. However, the opponents of amnesty succeeded in tying the issue to a need for "accountability" and "justice," two issues that no politician dared attack. The end result was a messy parade of show trials aimed at bringing high-ranking officials to the bench. Erich Mielke, the Stasi's top-ranking officer, was arrested and charged in rapid succession with election fraud, illegal wiretapping, and a host of other crimes. When one judge refused to try him on these initial charges (citing Mielke's health as reason), prosecutors indicted him for the murder of two policemen, a crime Mielke had supposedly committed in 1931. This time Mielke was tried and convicted. Had he been acquitted, he would most surely have been indicted for some other crime.[7] Markus Wolf, the chief of Stasi secret operations, was convicted in 1993, but his conviction was overturned by the Federal Constitutional Court, which ruled that German courts had no right to try agents of the former East German state for espionage.

Wisely, the Bundestag passed legislation that placed the entire Stasi file collection under the authority of an independent agency. By doing so, everyone could be reasonably assured that the files would not be used by partisan groups for political blackmail. A further law allows any victim of spying or state-sponsored abuse to see his or her file. Therefore, the commission, headed by the former churchman Joachim Gauck, officially opened the records for public inspection on January 1, 1992. Within months, the commission could no longer handle the volume of inspection requests and was forced to give preferential treatment to the applications of those who had been persecuted or were of an advanced age. The rest waited for months to have their applications approved.

As of February 1995, an estimated 400,000 people already had been through the process,[8] but many hundreds of thousands more still had their applications pending. Despite the obvious temptations, many people do not wish to inspect their files. Perhaps their lack of interest stems from the fear of what might show up. After all, why would should they risk disrupting their lives when they could live happily in ignorance? Indeed, one may debate the value of opening such a deep societal wound at all. Still, for those whose lives were irreparably damaged by a vicious regime, the files are the key to compensation and healing. For the historian, the Stasi files reveal a horror that is true about many autocratic governments; namely, that it took the cooperation of ordinary citizens to make the state security agency work. The list of agents—and victims—grows every week.

BORDER GUARDS

Chris Gueffroy was not yet twenty-one years old when he decided to flee across the Wall to West Berlin. He and a friend used the cover of darkness on February 6, 1989, to swim their way through the Tetlow Canal, elude the watchtowers, and climb the steel and concrete obstacles barring their way. They nearly made it, but at the last obstacle the alarms sounded as searchlights turned their way. After shouting "Halt!" border guards fired their automatic weapons and struck Gueffroy, killing him. He proved to be the 78th victim to fall at the hands of East German border guards who opened fire on citizens trying to flee at the Berlin Wall, and the 201st victim of border shootings overall. What makes his death more than just another statistic was the fact that he was the last to be killed. Had he only waited another nine months, he could have walked across the border unscathed.

In the months following the collapse of East Germany and its swift unification with the Federal Republic, Gueffroy's tragic death became the centerpiece of a controversy that would dominate the legal discourse in Germany for another six years. Should the guards be punished? Popular opinion held that they should stand trial, if not for murder (as many had wished), then manslaughter. However, the question raised jurisdictional and legality questions. Could Germany prosecute former East German border guards even though the guards were subjects of a different government at the time of the alleged crime? On the other hand, should individuals blindly follow a government's orders? If such orders are deemed immoral, does one have a duty to disobey? What should be done with those who sanctioned the shootings, perhaps even ordering guards to shoot, but did not actually pull a trigger? Border shootings occurred over a thirty-year period, and perhaps hundreds of guards could be indictable. Should they all be arrested and tried?

Establishing a legal theory to support prosecutions proved a difficult, but not impossible, task. West Germans could always retreat into the construction that the GDR never officially existed, hence the Basic Law applied to all Germans, even ones temporarily living under Soviet domination. Should that argument fail, prosecutors could make the argument that shooting civilians was against an East German law, which read that guards "may shoot" if other means of stopping a fleeing suspect had been exhausted. However, border guards were never schooled in the intricacies of East German law. Most guards recalled that their handlers had insisted that they "must shoot"; indeed, guards who failed to stop an escape in progress were routinely disciplined. Barring all other legal recourse, prosecutors could always invoke the Nuremberg precedent, which holds that some actions are patently illegal, despite the presence or absence of a governing law, because they violate human rights or are immoral.

Such issues of legal precedent were never clearly settled. Instead, German prosecutors rushed blindly into a series of vindictive trials, designed in part to mete out justice and in part to exact revenge for the wrongs of the East German communist past. In September 1991, a Berlin court put four border guards on trial for the killing of Chris Gueffroy. After a four-month trial, former guard Ingo Heinrich was convicted of manslaughter and sentenced to three-and-a-half years' imprisonment. In passing sentence, the judge asserted that "not everything that is legal is right," evoking images of the judgments made at Nuremberg decades before. However, the same judge ruled that Michael Schmidt, Heinrich's field superior who had shouted an order to shoot, was not guilty. In 1993 an appeals court judge overturned the sentences, and when prosecutors again pressed the case, the four defendants dragged themselves to court for another year's trial. This time, a different judge reduced Heinrich's sentence to two years' probation, but concluded that Schmidt, who had issued the order, might have to stand trial after all. In the end, none of the four defendants served any prison time.[9]

Theirs was not the only trial, just the most publicized one. By the end of 1994, at least seventeen trials involving border guards had taken place, resulting in twelve convictions and sentences up to six years' imprisonment. As researchers uncovered the records of border incidents in government files, prosecutors sought indictments against guards who were implicated in the documentary evidence. In one case, charges were brought against a former guard who was accused of shooting and killing a refugee in 1965. Even though the crime had been committed so long ago, he was nevertheless convicted of manslaughter and given an eighteen-month suspended sentence.

Most of these trials focused on bringing those who did the actual shooting to judgment. By late 1992, however, the judicial net also had ensnared those top officials who had either ordered or incited border guards to shoot fleeing citizens. In a trial that lasted almost ten months, some of East Germany's highest leaders and politicians appeared before the bench. The list of defendants began to look like a who's who of East German political and military leaders. Among the first to be given prison sentences were Heinz Kessler, former defense minister, and his deputy Fritz Streletz. Their transgression was that they served on the Defense Council in the 1970s when the shoot-to-kill orders were promulgated. In 1996, six former generals, including one deputy defense minister, were convicted of ordering the shooting of refugees.

It seems logical that this modern witch-hunt eventually extended to the party political brass, since the ultimate decision-making authority rested with them. Erich Honecker's flight into political asylum and ultimate demise allowed him to elude the judgment of the courts. His successors were not as fortunate. Egon Krenz and Günther Schabowski both were indicted in Berlin for manslaughter. Schabowski, the man notorious for the botched press conference that resulted in the opening of the Berlin Wall, accepted the responsibility and expressed shame for the deaths. Not so with Krenz. In his defense, Krenz branded the trials as political shams and questioned the legal authority of the court to try him. Before he was pronounced guilty, Krenz exclaimed: "The cold war is over, but the enemy is still being pursued, even in this courtroom. Our conviction is a foregone conclusion. You want to convict and you will convict, just as certain politicians are demanding. I ask you to give a legal signal for reconciliation among Germans. Do not continue the illegal prosecution of this case. Put an end to it. That would be a step toward true German unity."[10]

It is easy to sympathize with Krenz's assessment that these were politically motivated trials. The entire process might have been understandable had the trials helped bring Germany together, but the trials did little to unite East and West Germany. Instead, the prosecutions helped reinforce the notion, commonly held among easterners, that the Federal Republic saw itself as the "victor" of the German question and would deal with the "vanquished" however it saw fit. It is ironic that many East Germans, who only years before would have delighted in seeing the GDR brass stand trial, could not draw any satisfaction from these proceedings. What is most puzzling is the thirst for revenge that the West Germans demonstrated. Perhaps, by singling out the guilt of the border guards, the "Wessies" were somehow subliminally validating what happened to themselves at the hands of the Allies after World War II. There is one important difference, however. East Germany had acceded, not surrendered, to the Federal Republic, nor was it now subject to a foreign authority or occupation as Germany was in 1945. Yet, many in East Germany felt that was precisely what happened. In their minds, the trials showed that the events of 1990 were not so much a unification but an annexation.

If not to unify Germany, then what purpose did the border guard trials serve? Those who defended the trials reasoned that justice, the rule of law, and general human rights demanded accountability of past wrongs. Others interpreted the trials as little more than a clumsy attempt to satisfy the public's search for vengeance. In the end, that search overtook the concerns for an individual's rights. As Tina Rosenberg wrote, "Trials that seek to do justice on a grand scale risk doing injustice on the small scale."[11] The only certain conclusion is the truism that in history, it is the winners who determine right and wrong.

CONCLUSIONS

The Stasi purges and border guard trials that followed the collapse of the East German communist regime are not unusual to the pages of history. Whenever nations suffer defeat or tragedy, it seems natural to try to identify the internal faults or weaknesses responsible for the debacle. Such was the case after the defeat of Nazi Germany, when first the Allies and then the Germans themselves undertook a denazification program, not just to eliminate Nazis from positions of power but also to cleanse militarism, anti-Semitism, and intolerance from the German society. Similar reactions occurred in France against the Vichy collaborators and in the United States following reports of the My Lai massacre during the Vietnam War. Angry citizens, refusing to accept that people much like themselves could commit such heinous acts, called for the perpetrators to account for their actions. East Germans, unwilling to accept a communal guilt, needed to find someone to pay for the abuses, the killings, and the repression that they had to endure since 1949. Unfortunately, this recent search for justice, like the other examples, all too easily spun out of control and devolved into a search for vengeance.

There is a more positive interpretation. One might interpret the purges as an attempt to bring subconscious anxieties about the German past to the surface for examination in a sort of "group catharsis." Then, once the undesirable parts were identified and eliminated, a true German renewal could begin. Such an interpretation may be psychologically soothing, but the healing that is the end product of the process hardly justifies the means. The legal bickering that went on for six years is proof that there was no firm legal footing for the trials and convictions. Had these individuals become unwilling sacrifices offered up in search of a clear conscience?

Some might draw comfort from the fact that justice was served in the end. That many of these verdicts were eventually overturned, or that sentences were light or reduced, is in the long run immaterial. What was important was not the outcome, but the process itself. Germany's rush for justice was a modern-day ritual designed to assuage the consciences of citizens in both halves of the reunited country. In the long term, it may just accomplish that goal. However, forty years of accumulated antagonisms between the two cultures will take more than this to heal. Considering that Germany is still expunging the ghosts of its Nazi past, this ritualistic cleansing of the communist past seems likely to continue for some time.

NOTES

1. Robert Darnton, *Berlin Journal* (New York: W. W. Norton, 1991), 120.
2. "Jeder Tag ein Alptraum," *Der Spiegel* 17 (April 23, 1990): 50–51.
3. Ibid, 54–55.
4. *Time*, February 3, 1992. Evidently, his candor worked as he retained his post as minister president of Brandenberg.
5. "Es muss alles raus," *Der Spiegel* 13 (March 26, 1990): 26.
6. "Historischer Kompromiss," *Der Spiegel* 26 (June 25, 1990): 31.

7. Tina Rosenberg, *The Haunted Land* (New York: Random House, 1995), 335.

8. "Germans Split on Forgiving Cold War Crimes," *New York Times*, February 15, 1995, sec. A5.

9. Rosenberg, *Haunted Land*, 348.

10. Stephen Kinzer, "Word for Word: On Trial in Germany," *New York Times*, March 24, 1996.

11. Rosenberg, *Haunted Land*, 351.

7

German Unification in Perspective

The political upheaval that gripped Germany in 1989–1990 is now history. Demonstrators who once took to the streets are now Bundestag representatives and state officials, their protest pamphlets and placards filed away in archival boxes or placed on museum display. As time wears on, younger Germans are finding it difficult to recall the specific events from those twelve hectic months. Soon, they too will have to read about their revolution in books. For the time being, however, they need only look around them to gauge the impact of those events. Everywhere, one sees evidence that revolution has given way to evolution. Judging by the numbers of small shops and the ubiquitous product advertising, the former citizens of East Germany have adapted to their new capitalist system fairly quickly. The Federal Republic, on the other hand, still struggles to find ways to weave a "foreign" population into the fabric of Western society. While political and legal incorporation was accomplished easily, social integration, economic parity, and intellectual compatibility are still many years away. There is one irrefutable conclusion to be drawn from these realizations. Germany did not come into being on October 3, 1990. Instead, it is still in a process of "becoming."

What will the final product be like? Will the new Federal Republic of Germany resemble its 1949 counterpart—capitalist by nature, loyal to its allies, and Western in orientation? Could it revert to the habits of the past and pursue a bellicose foreign policy similar to that of the Kaiserreich or the Third Reich? Might unification produce a new and unrecognizable Germany? Unfortunately, the process of "becoming" presently underway in Germany renders any predictions out of date in short order. Indeed, the present path of German development points out the utter futility of making such prognostications. So far, the unification has not reawakened Germany's longing for a new "Reich," nor has it turned Germany into a paragon of democracy, pacifism, and opportunity. Germany's reentry on the world scene has so far proven fairly humdrum and benign. Can we expect that to continue?

This chapter shall try to address these questions. The conclusions herein are based on three premises. The first contends that the revolution holds a significant place in German history, not as an ending or as a beginning, but as another step in the maturation of Germany as a democratic nation. Secondly, this chapter will show that Germany's future development is as much tied to the needs and aspirations of the rest of Europe as it is to the desires of Germans. Finally, this chapter assumes that enough time has elapsed since the unification to allow us to identify those trends that may indicate the course that German evolution will take. Since the future is far from clear, that assumption is problematical.

REVOLUTION, UNIFICATION, AND GERMAN HISTORY

Although unification has certainly been the most pivotal event in the last fifty years of German history, the world still struggles to understand its true significance. There are two very different ways to interpret the events of 1989 and 1990; each purports to make sense of the unification and explain its significance in light of the rest of Germany's past. One interpretation—particularly popular with those who like to compartmentalize history with "eras" or "epochs"—holds that unification was the culmination of a distinct phase in German history that began with the rise of Nazism. Germany's development, this argument claims, was sidetracked by Hitler's accession to power and was forced through an agonizing period of war, defeat, and division. Therefore, the unification is truly a "revolutionary" event (in the purest sense of the word, meaning a return to a previous starting point), marking Germany's return to the path of peaceful, democratic development originally begun during the Weimar Republic.

This interpretation is attractive to some in that it allows its supporters to bring closure to a particularly ugly chapter of German history and declare that all is again set right. However, its weaknesses outweigh its strengths. The interpretation proceeds from the notion that the National Socialist era was somehow an aberration and not a consequence of German history. If one accepts that principle, then the Nazi experience, the defeat, and the postwar division become "accidents" or impositions on Germany's past. This may lead to some worrisome conclusions. The most troubling is that this interpretation undervalues or ignores the importance of the defeat of Nazism, the division of the nation, and the Holocaust as object lessons for the present. Such a deterministic view of German history also invites hasty comparisons of the Germany created in 1990 with both the Weimar Republic and the Kaiserreich. Once that questionable tie is established, it gives license to those who believe that Germany may someday again threaten the peace. Finally, this approach denigrates the East German social and intellectual experience as historically unimportant. Thus, forty years of German communism become irrelevant for the future development of Germany. Given those shortcomings, it seems pointless to pursue this interpretation any further. Those who insist on carving a niche for the unification in the overall scheme of German history would be better served by referring to the unification as the "end of the postwar era." Such a title is less controversial and more to the point, since it connotes the end of direct foreign influence in German affairs.

A more popular interpretation argues that the unification is just one more step in the continuum of Germany's development as a nation. This view denies that German history is somehow "back on track" with some past ideal. Instead, the emergent Germany will be a new entity forged out of the lessons of defeat, occupation, and division and will bear little resemblance to its historical ancestors. The evidence that this interpretation is receiving widespread support can be seen in the preference for the word *unification* (denoting the coming together of two distinct and disparate states) over *reunification* (denoting the return to a previous unity following a temporary division) in the historical literature. Indeed, a great deal of evidence indicates that Germany is becoming a nation quite different from its predecessors.

Take first the geographic evidence. The new Germany is an amalgam of former East German territory comprising 108,000 square kilometers combined with the Federal Republic's area of roughly 272,000 square kilometers. Although this makes Germany one of the largest nations in Europe, this is hardly comparable to the Reichs of old. Alsace and Lorraine have been irrevocably lost to France, and the historically Prussian lands east of the Oder-Neisse River line are today part of Poland. While some Germans may see these territories as a "Germania irredenta," Germany can never again lay claim to these territories. Border assurances were part of the price that Germany had to pay for Europe's acceptance of unification. Consequently, the new Germany must forever be content with an area of 380,000 square kilometers. It will never again be the size it was in 1913 or 1932.

The geographic unification of the two German states points to another interesting change. Following World War II, as bifurcated Germany became the focal point of a great power struggle between the capitalist West and the communist East, there was little doubt about either nation's political orientation. The Federal Republic of Germany, imbued with Western-style institutions, secure in NATO's defensive alliance system, and physically located west of the Iron Curtain, assumed the identity of a Western nation. East Germany, by virtue of its occupation by Soviet forces and the creation of a communist-dominated government, turned in the other direction. All that has changed. Now that the Cold War is over, distinctions between East and West have become meaningless. Germany no longer straddles an ideological line, but is once again a complete entity located in the center of a continent unfettered by spheres of influence. This will undoubtedly bring about a change in the way Germans perceive their international position. For the time being, the Germans still prefer to think of themselves as Western. However, in the next few decades, their Western orientation will become less and less significant. The new Germany will become ever more "European."

Unification has also forever changed the demographic face of Germany. The addition of East Germany's 16 million people to the population of West Germany created a new nation of about 78 million. That figure is presently 83 million, making Germany the most populous state in Europe. Nevertheless, Germany is not without its demographic difficulties. The unification has caused a major population shift, as former East Germans continue to flee to the western states in search of better jobs. Particularly hard hit are the states of Saxony, Thuringia, and Brandenburg; states which cannot attract citizens as they once did. Those who remain are having fewer children than in the past. This depopulation has led to a host of social problems ranging from the concerns over the loss of East German culture to the Federal Republic's overburdened welfare payments system.

Population shifts have also produced a concomitant change in the religious makeup of Germany. Before unification, the vast majority of East German citizens professed either Protestantism or preferred to be considered nondenominational. In contrast, the West German citizenry was almost evenly split between Protestants and Catholics, with the latter holding a slight edge. The combination of the two populations has made Germany more Protestant and less Catholic by proportion.[1] By itself, this may not have tremendously important consequences for German society, but there are a number of important implications for Germany's political system. The CDU always has based its electoral strength in large degree on the votes of the religious (Catholic) right. However, in 1990 it pulled off a major coup by winning over the largely Protestant and unaligned populations of East Germany to its political agenda. Since the CDU's political platform at the time—namely, the fast-track approach to unification—is no longer relevant, the party has had to find other issues to galvanize the East German vote. That has not been easy, as the losses in the 1992–1993 state elections and Chancellor Kohl's own near-defeat in 1994 attest. Either way, the CDU faces a Hobson's choice. It must either adopt a more liberal platform, keeping the interests of Germany's Protestant population in mind, or risk losing the Protestant vote by catering to the more conservative and Catholic wing of the party.

Unification has had other interesting impacts on German electoral politics. As political parties from West Germany rolled into East Germany in preparation for the March 1990 elections, they brought with them the trappings of the political organization that had served the Federal Republic since 1949. Noting the speed with which East Germany acceded to the Basic Law, most political observers expected that the idiosyncrasies of East Germany's communist political superstructure would soon disappear and be supplanted by the West German political party system. This has not quite happened. Remnants of the GDR's political existence live doggedly on in the Federal Republic. Perhaps the most notable change is the persistence of the Party of Democratic Socialism (PDS)—i.e., the remnants of the old Communist Party. Logically, the PDS should have vanished along with the rest of communism. However, despite a lackluster performance in the 1990 all-German elections, the PDS has been able to exploit the postunification recession and has polled remarkably well in recent elections. In the 1994 elections, former East Germans gave almost 20 percent of their votes to the PDS. In Berlin alone, the PDS received roughly 35 percent of all the votes cast. Evidently, East German populations have taken a fresh look at the party that once was the object of their scorn. While the Communist Party may never be a major player in German politics, its presence will doubtless complicate the political machinery by taking votes away from other parties. The declining fortunes of weaker parties (particularly the FDP) and the appearance of the PDS in coalition state governments[2] are evidence that East Germany will not go away lightly.

Perhaps the most important consequences of German unity are not political but financial. The least appreciated fact about the unification of Germany is that the negotiations leading to unity were as much about Deutschmarks as about unity, peace, or security. Thanks to its burgeoning economy, West Germany was able to turn every negotiation to its advantage simply by holding out the carrot of credits, loans, and grants. By far the biggest recipient of this largesse was the Soviet Union. In January 1990, Chancellor Kohl promised to sell the Soviet Union food at low prices subsidized by the Federal Government. In return, Gorbachev agreed to German unification in principle. Months later, at their summit meeting in the Caucasus, Gorbachev and Kohl again traded an agreement for money. In return for Gorbachev's willingness to yield on the NATO question, Kohl promised even more grant money. Their subsequent negotiations touched off an embarrassing bidding war to see how little or how much the Federal Republic would have to spend in return for Soviet acceptance of Germany's continued membership in NATO. After an initial few rounds of haggling, the two men compromised on a sum of fifteen billion Deutschmarks in loans and grants. Kohl got a Soviet agreement on Germany's NATO membership, and Gorbachev got much needed cash to pay for the retraining and relocation of the Soviet troops then stationed in East Germany.[3]

The costs incurred to "purchase" the rights to unify pale in comparison to the money needed following unification. Take, for example, the efforts that were necessary to clean up the East German environment. Years of neglect had left behind a country despoiled by pollutants. The waters of the Elbe River, along whose banks were located many of East Germany's larger chemical, metal, and paper industries, were completely fouled with nitrates, mercury, and pesticides. Groundwater contamination followed, putting at risk millions of inhabitants of the former GDR. Air pollution was equally devastating. Each Trabant and Wartburg vehicle spewed forth as much carbon monoxide as one hundred Western autos.[4] In the towns where industry used brown coal for energy, thousands of tons of sulfur dioxide emissions poisoned the atmosphere. No one dared to guess how much this cleanup would cost. Even the best estimates conceded that it would take billions of Deutschmarks.

Besides budgeting money for the environment, the German government also had to see after the needs of 18 million new citizens. Providing for them would not be an easy task. From the very beginning, East Germany's revolution was motivated as much by the lure of West Germany's living standard as it was by any vague notions of "nation" or "German unity." At least one observer noted that the East Germans were guided "not by 'Deutschland über Alles' but by 'Deutschmark über Alles.' "[5] Unification was supposed to bring the East Germans better jobs and a better life. Instead, most experienced hardship and unemployment. To smooth the transition, the federal government has provided between 100 and 150 billion Deutschmarks in each of the last seven years for social purposes. Much of the money was spent on infrastructure repairs, which did provide some employment for the struggling East German labor force. Unfortunately, the companies best able to provide the services were based in West Germany, and much of the profit flowed away from the localities that needed it most. The remaining sums went to cover unemployment payments. Although Germany has made some progress in bringing prosperity to the eastern part, the former GDR still has disproportionally high unemployment rates. A leveling is no doubt possible, but it will take many years to accomplish.

The eastern states are just now beginning to emerge from their postunification economic cataclysm, and many more reconstruction projects still await completion. Ongoing projects, including the relocation of the government to Berlin (at a projected cost of 50 billion DM), will continue to make demands on the German economy. Since the economic reconstruction of Germany is still a work in progress, future scholars will have to finish a complete accounting of the unification costs. But before all is finished, the price tag attached to German unification will undoubtedly top 2 trillion Deutschmarks. That may prove a conservative estimate.

In the short run, these expenditures have produced quite a strain on the once-mighty German economy. Despite foolhardy predictions that unification could be achieved without higher taxes, the CDU/CSU government has raised taxes and taken out loans to raise capital. Despite the added revenues, expenditures still outstrip income, and the end result is a rapidly increasing government debt with higher interest rates. Chancellor Kohl's government has resorted to making appeals to "sacrifice" and has restricted spending on the entitlement system that West Germans have enjoyed for five decades. Many in the voting public have grown weary of the financial burdens that unification has placed on their shoulders.

These economic strains have had a concomitant negative impact on the fabric of German social and political life. The costs accompanying the economic and social dislocation of East Germany cannot be measured in Deutschmarks alone. As the competition for jobs has intensified, racially motivated hate crimes have reappeared, especially in the depressed eastern states. Most often, the targets are citizens who are not ethnically German. Many are the descendants of the original "guest workers" who contributed so much to the German economic boom of the 1950s. Today, there are those who would deny citizenship to anyone who does not fit a *völkish* definition of *Germanness*. A national debate on German identity continues to this day.

In the long run, however, there is cause for optimism. Germany stands to gain economically from the attention it has paid to the eastern states. When all the streets are repaired, and all the industries retooled, eastern Germany will possess a state-of-the-art infrastructure based on the most modern technology and communication systems. This should attract investment that in turn could bring about a much needed revitalization of eastern German industry. It is conceivable that the chemical and porcelain manufacturing centers of Leipzig, Halle, and Dresden may rival the Ruhr as the industrial heartland of Germany. Should this scenario take place, it might help German society "grow out" of the social turmoil it experienced in the immediate postunification period. For the immediate future, however, Germany must find its way through a long and arduous process of rebuilding.

GERMANY AND EUROPE

The timing of German unification was unfortunate as far as the European Unity movement was concerned. Before 1989, Europe seemed back on track with its goal of "ever-increasing union." Negotiations were underway that would lead to the Maastricht Treaty of 1992, an agreement designed to strengthen the economic interdependency of Europe by creating a single European currency. At first, the collapse of East Germany and the subsequent drive for unification provided an unexpected impetus to the unity movement. Many nations, most notably France, saw the treaty as a way of restraining a rapidly growing Germany. In the subsequent rush to get Maastricht ratified, many European nations overlooked the fact that Germany would have to divert much of its attention to the support of the new eastern states. It should not have come as a surprise that Chancellor Kohl, even though he has always been a staunch supporter of European unity, would put the goals of his nation ahead of those of Europe.

For example, Germany has been very careful about where it spends its money lately. Unification costs have forced West Germany to keep interest rates high in order to forestall inflation. Since other European currencies are tied to the Deutschmark by way of the Exchange Rate Mechanism, many other nations had to follow suit. While Germany might be able to weather the higher interest rates, the weaker economies soon found that their economic position within the European Union had deteriorated. Tensions erupted in 1993. That summer, as the French franc slipped in value, Germany might have rescued the franc by buying francs on the world currency markets. When Germany refused to do so, the noticeably irked French publicly questioned Germany's commitment to currency union. This debacle, coupled with a similar incident with the English pound the year before and the recession of 1991–1994, may have jeopardized the 1999 target date for the introduction of a single European currency. If it does not happen, Europeans will probably heap most of the blame on Germany.

Incidents such as these have led many Europeans to complain that Germany's attentions have been diverted to the integration of the east German states at the expense of European integration. While it is true that the unification has sidetracked Germany's commitment to European unity in the last few years, that commitment has not disappeared. Once Germany's economic problems at home are ironed out, we can reasonably expect the unity movement to go forward with full German cooperation. No one doubts Chancellor Kohl's commitment to European unity, and even the opposition SPD has voted with him on issues of European integration. After all, Germany stands to gain a great deal. As the territories of the former communist bloc apply for associate status, the Common Market is slowly expanding eastward. It is conceivable that the European Union will welcome Poland, the Czech Republic, and Hungary as new members within the next two decades. By virture of its geographic position, Germany can serve as the link between these new markets and the established West. It is well poised to become both the geographic and economic linchpin of an expanding Europe.

How should Europe view this prospect? The reactions have not always been hospitable. Some diplomats have claimed that Chancellor Kohl is accomplishing economically what Hitler failed to do militarily. Evidently, the image of *Mitteleuropa*, or a middle-European empire dominated by Germany, is still on many politicians' minds. Such comments are curious for a number of reasons. First, what is so unusual about a German economic superpower? Even before unification, Germany had the most productive economy on the continent. True, the addition of the former East Germany may make the new nation even more dominant. But is this increased economic might any cause for alarm? Considering how closely tied the German economy is to the rest of Europe, it is quite true that "when Germany prospers Europe prospers." Some Europeans agree with the old adage that "the only thing worse than being dominated by Germany is not being dominated by Germany." A stable and prosperous Germany, firmly grounded within Europe's supranational institutions, should prove profitable for all of Europe's nations.

The course of world events has made Europe's reactions to German unification immaterial. Like it or not, unification is a fait accompli, and little can stop Germany from becoming the world's next economic superpower. The Soviet domination of eastern Europe has ended, and American influence in western Europe is on the wane. In their places, a new *Mitteleuropa* is indeed emerging, one where Germany dominates its neighbors not with Stuka bombers but with Deutschmarks. The first step in accepting this reality is to come to the understanding that Europe cannot exist without Germany.

Ignoring it or isolating it will be a detriment to all. Consequently, Europe's best hope for peace and mutual prosperity is to seek an ever deeper union, one that will absorb Germany's economic and diplomatic energies into a broader European framework.

GERMANY'S PLACE IN WORLD AFFAIRS

What role will the new Germany occupy in the world in the twenty-first century? Is a future conflict between Germany and the world conceivable? Those who believe that it is possible like to equate Germany's recent unification with its first incarnation in 1871. They believe the same German hubris that catapulted Europe into a world war in 1914 will reemerge now that the German state is one again. But the Germany of today is not the Kaiserreich of old. The Federal Republic is a nation ruled by law and the democratic process. It is no longer subject to the whims of a royal family; it responds to the mandates of a voting public. Further, Germany is no longer able to take its own foreign policy path as it did under the Kaisers. As a member of the European Union and NATO, Germany cannot act independently of its allies without suffering severe economic or political consequences. A repeat of past mistakes is not likely.

Germany's recent behavior provides sufficient evidence to back up these contentions. In the 1990–1991 Persian Gulf War, Chancellor Kohl cited constitutional and historical reasons for Germany's not sending troops to the Gulf. Calls for Germany to participate in the recent UN peacekeeping mission to Bosnia met with similar reactions. This time, however, German troops did see limited action as part of the peacekeeping force, once the Constitutional Court ruling of July 1994 allowed for German troops to operate outside Germany. These actions should not be construed as a prelude to expansionism. Kohl's decision to part with Germany's tradition of noninvolvement was merely an effort to respond to criticisms that Germany was not keeping up its part as a member of NATO. Expansionism seems forever relegated to the margins of German politics. At least for now, a Europeanization of Germany seems far more likely than a Germanization of Europe.

German foreign policy notwithstanding, the most impressive deterrent to any future war may be the German population itself. Even though skinhead rioters or demonstrating nationalists will continue to make the headlines, the quiet majority of the population has turned its back on Germany's racist and imperialist past. Most of them cannot even remember the two world wars and the millions of dead, but they seem to understand that those catastrophes must never be repeated. The question, then, is not whether Germany will ever take its place among the civilized nations of the world. The last forty years of German history have settled that issue. As the new Germany enters the twenty-first century, it does so with a sound democracy and institutions that make the prospects for war highly unlikely. The "German Question" is now answered, provided that future generations of Germans remember the lessons of their history.

NOTES

1. Anthony Glees, *Reinventing Germany* (Oxford: Berg, 1996), 260.

2. This has already occurred in the state elections in Saxony-Anhalt. See Gerald R. Kleinfeld, "The Return of the PDS," in David P. Conradt et al., eds., *Germany's New Politics* (Tempe, AZ: German Studies Review, 1995), 193–94.

3. Manfred Görtemaker, *Unifying Germany, 1989–1990* (New York: St. Martin's Press, 1994), 197–98.

4. "Das Land der 1000 Vulkane," *Der Spiegel* 2 (January 8, 1990): 28.

5. Josef Joffe, "One-and-a-half Cheers for German Unification," *Commentary* 89 (June 1990): 27.

The mass exodus from the GDR began in the summer of 1989 when tens of thousands fled to the West through Hungary and Czechoslovakia. Courtesy of German Information Center.

Swept away by joy, this former GDR inhabitant crosses the German-Austrian border to freedom in triumph. Courtesy of German Information Center.

GDR refugees on arrival in the Federal Republic of Germany. They left their families and friends in the GDR with just a few belongings to seek freedom and self-fulfillment in the West. Courtesy of German Information Center.

Hundreds of thousands of citizens protested against the communist regime during the autumn of 1989 (our photo shows the GDR city of Leipzig, calling for freedom and a united Germany. Courtesy of German Information Center.

Millions of Berlin residents venture into the other parts of the previously divided city following the fall of the Wall on November 9, 1989. The encounters at the Brandenburg Gate were particularly moving (above). Previously, border guards and barriers (below) prevented contact. Courtesy of German Information Center.

Under the pressure of mass protests, the communist leadership in East Berlin was forced to open the Berlin Wall and permit unfettered travel between East and West in November 1989. Courtesy of German Information Center.

Inhabitants of both parts of the city have come together to climb the Wall at the Brandenburg Gate (November 9, 1989). Courtesy of German Information Center.

On the Friedrichstrasse, a West Berliner attempts to hack pieces out of the Wall (November 10, 1989). Courtesy of German Information Center.

East German visitors stream across the newly erected border crossing point at the Potsdamer Plats, headed toward West Berlin. Courtesy of German Information Center.

On December 22, and in the presence of Chancellor Helmut Kohl and GDR Minister-President Hans Modrow, two pedestrian crossing points are opened in the Wall at the Brandenburg Gate. Courtesy of German Information Center.

The Wall has fallen, but two German states remained in 1989. A West Berlin policeman (on left) and a GDR People's Policeman stand next to each other at Potsdam Square in Berlin. Courtesy of German Information Center.

"We want a new Germany"—a demand of demonstrators in Dresden. Courtesy of German Information Center.

German federalism: Residents of Leipzig call for the re-establishment of "their" state, Saxony. Courtesy of German Information Center.

Example of reconstruction in eastern Germany: Mühlenstrasse in Stralsund in 1990 before German unity (above) and five years later (below). Courtesy of German Information Center.

Biographies: The Personalities Behind the Unification

Konrad Adenauer (1876–1967)

Konrad Adenauer was the first chancellor of the Federal Republic of Germany, a founder of the Christian Democratic Union (CDU), and the architect of German postwar political revival. Under his leadership, a West German state rose out of the ashes of World War II to become a major European power with an economy envied by nations across the globe. The postwar success of West Germany is a testament to Adenauer's ability to gauge international politics and understand Germany's role in international affairs. He also had the foresight to develop a strategy to guide his nation's affairs with his fellow Germans in Soviet-dominated Europe and stayed the course even when his decisions were unpopular. Despite becoming chancellor at an advanced age (he was seventy-three), Adenuaer served for fourteen years, longer than any other German head of state save Otto von Bismarck and Helmut Kohl. One can justifiably consider Adenauer Germany's most important twentieth-century statesman.

His life story begins in Cologne, the city where he would eventually make his political career. There, on January 5, 1876, he was born to a lower-middle-class professional family. By all accounts, his childhood and upbringing were typical of any young Catholic Rhinelander growing up in imperial Germany. He attended the universities in Munich, Bonn, and Freiburg where he studied law and economics. Following his bar exams, Adenauer got a job working in the Cologne city administration (as his father had done before him) and for a time served as assistant to the mayor. By 1914 Adenauer was a thirty-eight-year-old with medical problems and therefore never served in the military during World War II. This left him free to pursue his political career. During the war, Adenauer became even more active in the Catholic Center Party and was elected mayor of Cologne in 1917.

The lessons he learned in Cologne were extremely valuable in his later political career. As mayor of a large city, Adenauer had to find ways to keep the city functioning in the midst of all the deprivation that followed the defeat of Germany. His success brought him to the attention of the Catholic Center Party's national leadership, and he quickly rose in status within the party. In 1926 Adenauer was asked to stand for nomination as the party's choice for chancellor, but he declined.

Adenauer showed his mettle when Adolf Hitler became chancellor in 1933. As a Catholic and supporter of centrist politics, he made no secret of his intense dislike for Nazism. In early 1933, Adenauer refused to meet with Hitler and would not allow Nazi banners to be flown on a city bridge. In retaliation, the Nazis forced Adenauer out of the mayor's office with trumped-up charges of financial impropriety. He retired from politics and left Cologne for relative seclusion. The Nazis arrested him twice over the next ten years: once in association with the Night of Long Knives (the Röhm purge) in 1934 and again in conjunction with the von Stauffenberg plot to assassinate Hitler in 1944. Despite a brief imprisonment in a concentration camp following the latter arrest, he survived the war.

In the early months of 1945, as the Allies searched desperately to find capable non-Nazis to act as civilian authorities, American troops restored Adenauer to his old position as mayor of Cologne. He served the occupiers well, working diligently to return critical services to the city and to keep the population healthy. Once the war ended and the Allies' zonal administration plan came into effect, the responsibility for Cologne's administration fell to the British, and Adenauer soon fell from favor with the new occupation authority. He was dismissed from office, ostensibly for failing to do his duty on behalf of the citizens of Cologne. Once again, Adenauer was forced to leave his home city and was forbidden to take part in any political activity. Fortunately for the history of West Germany, the British occupiers later rescinded the latter prohibition.

Adenauer's dismissal from civil government may have been fortuitous in the long run, for it enabled him to leave behind the issues of local government so that he could now concentrate on national political affairs. At the time, national political parties were still forbidden, but nascent groups were forming along prewar lines. Adenauer latched on to the fledgling Christian Democratic Union (CDU), which was formed out of conservative and Christian prewar political factions. In early 1946, he became its chairman. Thus, when the Allies relaxed controls on central political activity, Adenauer stood as the most obvious choice to lead the drive for zonal unity. He became the chairman of the Parliamentary Council that oversaw the writing of a new constitution (the Basic Law). At age seventy-three, Adenauer stood as candidate of his party for the office of chancellor. He won by a margin of one vote.

The tasks facing the Federal Republic of Germany in 1949 seemed herculean, yet Adenauer based his government on a series of simple but interconnected premises. First, Adenauer believed that Germany had to regain its sovereignty and retake its position in the family of nations. This could be accomplished only by atoning for the barbarism of the Nazi years through continued denazification and demilitarization. Thus, Adenauer worked throughout the 1950s to prove that his country was peaceful and trustworthy by forging ties with France and championing the common interests of the nations of Europe. His efforts were rewarded in 1955 as West Germany regained it sovereignty and entered the United Nations. Secondly, the West German economy needed to be revived. In the first years of his chancellorship, the Federal Republic made great strides to rebuild its industrial plant, thanks in part to Marshall Plan funds provided by the United States. He and his finance minister Ludwig Erhard also worked to bring the German economy back into world markets. To this end, the Federal Republic entered into the European Coal and Steel Community (a supranational institution to share coal and steel resources across national boundaries) with France and helped pave the way for the Treaty of Rome, which created the Common Market in 1957. Finally, and perhaps most important, Adenauer believed that Germany must be firmly grounded as a Western nation. He saw that Germany's position in central Europe made it the potential battleground of future conflicts, so he committed West Germany to military and political alliances with the United States and the rest of western Europe. The Federal Republic became a member of the North Atlantic Treaty Organization (NATO) in 1955 and rearmed.

The issue of German unity is conspicuously absent from these guidelines. Adenauer was no rabid nationalist; indeed, above all else he was a political realist. He understood that the goal of unification was incompatible with his other goals to integrate Germany with the West, since the Soviet Union would not likely relinquish its war trophy without some compensation. Therefore, despite repeated Soviet attempts to exchange German unity for German neutrality, Adenauer refused to negotiate. Nevertheless, Adenauer did not completely abandon the goal. His basic premise was that if the citizens of the Federal Republic could live in a peaceful and affluent society, their success would act like a "magnet" to attract the Germans living under Soviet domination. Consequently, a free and democratic West Germany would, by virtue of its prosperity, ultimately destabilize the restrictive and bankrupt communist system in East Germany. Thus, unification might someday follow as a consequence. In accordance with this plan, Adenauer's policy was to deny the existence of a separate German state and assert that the Federal Republic was the only legitimate expression of the political will of the German people. While such a stance made him popular with the West, it led to many foreign policy imbroglios and fights with the rival SPD at home that wanted a more immediate rectification of the issue. It would take thirty years, but the flood of East German refugees heading west by the thousands in 1989 eventually drove home the wisdom of his "magnet policy."

It is unfortunate that Konrad Adenauer's brilliant career ended in controversy. In 1962 his government unraveled under the weight of the "Spiegel Affair," a scandal in which police raided the offices of the newsmagazine *Der Spiegel* following the publication of an article critical of government policy. Those involved in this breach of constitutional law eventually implicated Adenauer and his closest aides, reinforcing a growing feeling that the octogenarian had outlived his usefulness. In April 1963, Adenauer resigned his post. He died in the town of Rhöndorf on April 19, 1967.

Bärbel Bohley (1945–   )

The Stasi once called her "the mother of the underground." To her friends, she was the "mother of revolution." Most former revolutionaries would carry such sobriquets proudly. Bärbel Bohley, however, was an uncommon rebel who sought no publicity, fame, or political power for herself. In seven years of political activism, Bohley garnered only imprisonment, deportation, and harassment. All she wanted was to bring about a socialism worthy of its citizens. Hers was a voice of renewal, not destruction. But in a state convinced of its infallibility, she was an enemy.

This intensely private woman was born in Berlin on May 24, 1945, two weeks after the end of the war. Her father was a construction engineer who was also trained as a teacher but who was forced out of the teaching profession when he refused to join the SED.[1] She entered the state art college and graduated in 1974 as a "diploma artist," specializing in painting and sculpture. She eventually became a leading figure in the East German Artist Union.

Bohley made her political debut in 1983, when she protested the creation of a law that allowed the government to draft women into military service. She personally mobilized as many as 150 women to join a "Women for Peace" political group.[2] The organization became a vehicle for Bohley's pacifist and egalitarian agenda of political reform, and its members became immediate targets of Stasi attacks. Many gave up, but not Bohley. On October 16, she and some thirty other women staged a demonstration against the draft law on the Alexanderplatz in East Berlin. She narrowly escaped capture.

Thereafter, Bohley worked to keep her issues alive while dodging Stasi harassment. Out of her efforts emerged the Initiative for Peace and Human Rights, one of East Germany's first peace groups founded outside of the Church's aegis. Unlike many other activists, Bohley believed in cultivating contacts with like-minded individuals in other countries. In this manner, she met Petra Kelly, the West German environmental activist and Green party candidate, who became her good friend. By taking her activism outside the confines of the East German state, Bohley put herself at risk with government charges of treason. Such was the case when, following an interview with foreign journalists, Bohley was arrested in December 1983 and charged with supplying information to the enemy.[3]

The Women's Prison in East Berlin became her home for the next six weeks, until foreign officials pressured the East German government for her release. Unlike many others in her circumstances, Bohley hoped that she would not be deported. She never saw herself as an enemy of East Germany or socialism; rather as someone who wanted to preserve the best of socialism while eliminating the abuses that had accumulated over the past forty years of dictatorship. Such change could be brought about only within the country.

Following her release, Bohley continued her assault on the government. During Honecker's state visit to West Germany in 1987, he was treated to a gift delivered by Petra Kelly. It was a sculpture entitled "No Man's Land," along with a letter from its creator, none other than Bärbel Bohley. In the message Bohley stated that she was convinced that East Germany could create an ideal socialist state, if only the government would open a dialogue with those who wanted to see peaceful change. Honecker didn't answer the letter.

In January 1988, Bohley was again arrested, this time for disrupting the annual observances of the assassination of Rosa Luxemburg and Karl Liebknecht. Once again she was imprisoned "in the same prison, same cell, (with) the same interrogators,"[4] only this time she was exiled to England for six months upon her release. Bohley remembers this as an important time in her development as a political activist. While in exile, she became convinced of the need to go public with her reformist political agenda.[5] Thanks to the efforts of key Evangelical Lutheran Church officials, Bohley was allowed to return to the GDR just in time to put her new political philosophy into action. As the Honecker government started to crumble, Bohley founded the political action group New Forum to bring together all interest groups in a discussion on how to improve society and create a new socialism. Technically, the New Forum was not a political party but an "oppositional alliance."[6] The founders thought the term *alliance* would appear less threatening to state officials, since the primary goal was not to bring down the state but to reform it. Apparently, many of the public agreed with their reformist agenda. Their official application to register the association drew 200,000 signatures.

When the Berlin Wall opened on November 9, Bohley was taken aback. Rather than join in the celebration, she reportedly watched the events on television, had a drink, and turned in for the night.[7] The next day, as the reality of the situation sank in, she stated that she thought everyone, government and citizens alike, had lost their minds.[8] She understood already that the end of the Wall also meant an end to her dreams for socialist renewal. Within a few weeks, Bohley's platform became obsolete. East and West Germany were now clearly on the path of unification.

In an attempt to get on the unification bandwagon, the New Forum leadership dumped Bohley from the very organization she had helped to create. In truth, her continued participation would not have altered the eventual outcome. As the March 1990 election approached, the organizations she helped found (Human Rights Initiative and New Forum) joined with other groups to form Alliance 90, but their attempt to get their political program represented in the East German government fell far short, gaining only 2.9 percent of the vote. East Germany's citizenry had repudiated Bohley's vision for a refurbished East German society based on socialism. They preferred a merger with West Germany.

Bohley has remained critical of unification long after it had become an accomplished fact. Since 1990, she has remained active in the politics of the Federal Republic and has become a protector of the rights of the victims of Stasi persecution. In 1992 she formed an informal group to keep the Stasi files open to public inspection despite appeals to seal them. In 1996 she founded a citizens office to help anyone who had been a victim of the GDR system. In this effort, she was joined by a number of prominent Germans, including Helmut Kohl. Some have criticized her for "selling out to the system," but she pays such attacks little heed. Her idealism is as strong as ever, even if her goals of pacifism and egalitarianism are more than ever out of her grasp.

Willy Brandt (1913–1992)

Willy Brandt was the first socialist (SPD) chancellor of West Germany, serving from 1969 to 1974. A practitioner of the politics of realism, Brandt urged that West Germany's foreign relations should acknowledge the status quo and accept the postwar settlement as it existed in fact. His efforts led to nonaggression treaties with both Poland and the Soviet Union, which in turn led to a better working relationship with East Germany. Chancellor Brandt did more than any other European politician to advance understanding and promote détente between the communist bloc and the capitalist West. He was honored with the Nobel Peace Prize in 1971.

Willy Brandt was born Herbert Ernst Karl Frahm on December 18, 1913. He was raised by his mother and grandfather in the town of Lübeck, a port on the Baltic Sea. It is from his grandfather, a worker and ardent supporter of the SPD, that Herbert got his interest in socialism. As a young boy, he was active in the Falcons, the socialist group for youngsters, and at the age of sixteen became the local leader of the Socialist Youth Organization. He also turned out to be a superb student, and he received scholarship awards permitting him to attend the Johanneum, a prestigious university-preparatory institution in Lübeck.[9] There he developed a flair for writing, and he prepared for a future in journalism.

As the Nazi movement grew in intensity, young Herbert's political energy began to overshadow his academic skills. He found himself involved repeatedly in clashes with the Hitler youth and was tried and acquitted of charges surrounding the death of a Nazi demonstrator. In 1931 he joined the Socialist Workers' Party, a militant offshoot of the SPD and became one of its spokesmen. When the Nazis seized power in 1933, Herbert campaigned actively against them and lived a secretive life underground. Already targeted for arrest, Frahm took the name Willy Brandt as a pseudonym. But even a new identity could not protect him fully. Brandt decided to flee and continue his anti-Nazi work from outside German borders.

Crouched in a small fishing boat, Brandt sailed first to Denmark and then to Norway. In Oslo, he contacted the Norwegian Socialist Party and went to work writing articles for its publications. Brandt also helped to smuggle anti-Nazi propaganda into Germany at considerable risk to himself. He joined the Norwegian branch of the Socialist Workers' Party, learned Norwegian, entered Oslo University to study history and philosophy, and ultimately received Norwegian citizenship (the Nazis had revoked his German citizenship). His work for the party involved a great deal of traveling across Europe. In 1936 he returned to Berlin clandestinely to organize resistance movements and then traveled to Spain to spend the next two years in the civil war. The outbreak of World War II and the invasion of Norway in 1940 again sent Brandt packing, this time for neutral Sweden. In Stockholm, he became secretary of the International Council of Democratic Socialists, an office that afforded him many valuable political contacts.

Brandt returned to Germany at the war's end. Technically still a Norwegian citizen, Brandt went to Berlin as a press attaché for the Norwegian government. In 1946, following a meeting with Kurt Schumacher, one of the founders of the reviving SPD, Brandt was offered a position within the SPD's Berlin office. He gave up his Norwegian citizenship, reclaimed his German heritage, and took the post on January 1, 1948. Brandt again fell on his penchant for writing and immersed himself in the party as editor of the newspaper. His first elected office was as representative to the Berlin House of Representatives in 1950. In 1957 he was elected mayor of Berlin and held the post during the most turbulent period of the city's history. The building of the Berlin Wall and President John F. Kennedy's visit made Berlin the focus of world attention and put Brandt in the national and international spotlight. Twice he ran for chancellor (in 1961 and 1965), but he lost each time. The 1969 elections went otherwise. On October 18, 1969, Willy Brandt became the first Social Democrat of the postwar era to become chancellor of West Germany.

Although he had run on a platform of domestic reform, history remembers Willy Brandt most for *Ostpolitik* ("Eastern policy"), a strategy that completely reoriented West German foreign policy toward the communist bloc nations. In rapid succession, Brandt concluded ground-breaking treaties with former enemies. The August 1970 treaty with the Soviet Union pledged mutual nonaggression and affirmed the present boundaries of the countries of Europe. In December, an agreement with Poland acknowledged the reality of Poland's Oder-Neisse frontier, helping assuage thirty years of ill-feeling between the two nations. A four-power agreement in 1971 guaranteed western access to and from West Berlin and eased travel restrictions to the West. Finally, goaded by the Polish and Soviet agreements, East Germany entered into negotiations to lessen the tensions between the two Germanys. The resultant 1972 accord committed the two states to accept each other's existence and work together to solve matters of mutual importance.

Willy Brandt was reelected as chancellor in 1972, but his second term was short-lived. Just as happened to Konrad Adenauer, a scandal ultimately ended Brandt's career as chancellor. His downfall, known as the "Guillaume affair," began when police arrested one of Brandt's closest advisors, Günther Guillaume, and charged him with spying for the GDR. Brandt took full responsibility for the incident and resigned from office in 1974, even though he was not obliged to do so. Brandt continued to work within the party as its chairman, and in 1976 became the president of the Socialist International. In the 1980s, he worked to forge communication between the SPD and the Peace Movement and often disagreed even with his own party over disarmament issues. He resigned the chairmanship of the party in 1987 and died on October 8, 1992.

If one looks back on Willy Brandt's career through the lens of the 1990 unification, it is tempting to see his term as counterproductive to the cause of German unity. True, *Ostpolitik* did set back the goal of unification, but the contemporary climate of distrust between East and West Germany made the goal unachievable anyway. Brandt's legacy is his realization that the two Germanys would never come together in an atmosphere of confrontation. His policies initiated a more peaceful discourse that made unification at least possible. Theorists called this "Change through Rapprochement." Brandt often put it much more plainly: "What belongs together, will grow together." Seen in this larger context, *Ostpolitik* becomes a logical extension of Adenauer's "magnet" strategy. By opening new avenues of cooperation between the Germanys, East and West Germany did "grow together." More precisely, East Germany grew closer to West Germany.

Lothar de Maizière (1940–   )

Lothar de Maizière was the leader of the East German CDU from November 1989 until the unification of the Germanys in October 1990. He became East Germany's last head of state in March 1990, when elections ousted the PDS and elevated the CDU to power in the East German People's Chamber. In his position as minister president, de Maizière oversaw the negotiations for currency and political unification with the Federal Republic. Although he spent over thirty years in the CDU, Lothar de Maizière does not fit the mold of a typical politician, either physically or mentally. One might guess, judging by his slight build and his bearded and bespectacled face, that he was a professor or a minister but hardly a head of state. Those who have met him describe him as a very complex and learned man who would probably feel more at home in the company of intellectuals than legislators. Indeed, de Maizière became a politician only accidentally. Had it not been for a number of chance happenings that affected his life, he might never have come to politics at all.

De Maizière was born on March 2, 1940, in the town of Nordhausen near the Czech border. He grew up in a well-to-do Huguenot family, whose ancestors fled religious persecution in France during the seventeenth century. In gratitude to their adopted homeland, generations of the de Maizière family served Brandenberg (and later, Prussia) as lawyers and army officers, and they soon developed a reputation as loyal, unselfish civil servants. Consequently, Lothar felt a good deal of pressure to enter one of those professions. He had other intentions, however.

Shortly after he completed his primary studies, Lothar turned his back on family tradition and entered the Music College of East Berlin. He became quite accomplished on the viola and performed with many orchestras, including the East Berlin Symphony. When once asked why he chose music, de Maizière replied, "I was of the opinion that one could play Brahms just as well in Hamburg as in Leipzig."[10] His answer reveals that his decision was influenced by his inability to relate to the East German government. Living in a society that wanted nothing to do with the aristocratic past and even less to do with religion must have been difficult for a devout Christian with a proud family heritage. With its ability to transcend political boundaries, music became de Maizière's means of escape.

Then, in the middle of a promising career, de Maizière was diagnosed with a nerve disorder that would ultimately put an end to his ability to perform. Faced with the need to find a new career at a relatively young age, de Maizière rediscovered his family's tradition. In 1969 he began correspondence courses in law from Humboldt University. By studying in his free time between concerts and performances, de Maizière managed to graduate in six years and in 1976, following a brief law apprenticeship, he entered the East Berlin College of Jurists. Although he was now in a mainstream occupation, this Christian-musician-turned-advocate still did not feel a part of society. He consequently attracted clients who themselves were outsiders, particularly draft dodgers, environmental dissidents, and individuals charged with political crimes. He soon developed a reputation for defending the rights of the common man against the claims of the political system.

His career as a lawyer proved the perfect complement to his activities in politics. As a sixteen-year-old, de Maizière had already joined the CDU in an effort to help bring about change. Unfortunately, the party was little more than a puppet in collaboration with the monopoly SED, so de Maizière remained an inactive member and never held any major offices. Instead of working within the party to achieve change, de Maizière turned to the church. His reputation as a decent and fair Christian got him elected to the synod of the Evangelical Church Union in 1985, and the next year he became a vice president of the synod. In 1987 the CDU leadership chose him to head one of the party's working committees dealing with Church-related issues. Thus, as the revolution of 1989 was about to unfold, de Maizière was well placed within the CDU and the Church but was not part of the decision-making cadre.

The events of October and November 1989 swept away not only the SED but those who had collaborated with the corrupt regime. When Wolfgang Götting, the leader of the bloc CDU, was removed from office, the party rank and file voted de Maizière as their next leader. The choice was logical. He had contacts with the Church, was above reproach, and, most important, had held no previous positions within the party leadership that would have linked him to the corrupt SED past. His goal for the party was simple: the CDU had to become the guardian of the social interests of all East German citizens. This formula would become de Maizière's credo in the turbulent months ahead.

From the outset, de Maizière sought to forge ties with Western political parties. The alliance with the CDU in the Federal Republic was a natural step, but the relationship was not always cordial. De Maizière was soon overshadowed (both in power and stature) by Chancellor Helmut Kohl, his West German counterpart. Many pundits pegged de Maizière as a "junior partner" to Kohl, poking fun not just at his lack of power but also at his short stature. Undaunted, de Maizière worked to bring about electoral co-operation between the two CDU parties, the German Social Union (DSU), and the Democratic Awakening (DA). The resulting entente, called the Alliance for Germany, achieved a stunning victory in the March 1990 elections. Lothar de Maizière had become his country's first (and last) freely elected prime minister.

Two important tasks lay ahead. East and West Germany needed to create a currency union and find a way to integrate the failing communist economy into the capitalist. Likewise, a unification treaty had to be negotiated. In the months ahead, no one worked harder than de Maizière. While many of his cabinet members were on vacation, de Maizière stayed on the job each day, sometimes until the next morning. Hard work was necessary, as he was not negotiating from strength. The rush for Deutschmarks had diminished the influence that his government could wield in the unification process. De Maizière had to struggle to present the views of his East German constituents to the often unsympathetic West German politicians. The press was not always kind either, and allegations that he had been a Stasi informant plagued de Maizière's efforts. Nevertheless, he stuck to his mission, and within months East Germany was united politically and economically. Lothar de Maizière surrendered his position on Unity Day, October 3 ,1990, but he did not leave public life. He entered the Bundestag as CDU representative and was given a position without portfolio in Kohl's cabinet, but the accusations of Stasi involvement ultimately forced his resignation.

History will doubtless remember de Maizière as the politician who presided over the dissolution of East Germany. But if historians forget the sense of duty and obligation with which he represented his people in the unification process, they will do him disservice. His career is analogous to those of many East Germans. The socialist state never commanded his allegiance, so he withdrew into his heritage, his music, and his religion. Millions of other East Germans had similarly abandoned the prevailing ideology for other loyalties. What sets de Maizière apart from the others was his acute sense of altruism. In a remarkably clairvoyant speech delivered on the eve of unity, de Maizière observed:

Our common future will depend on the amount of understanding we show for one another. Those on the one side must not adopt a superior attitude, and those on the other must not merely see themselves as learners with the added burden of their history.

We will only achieve true unity if we are willing to correct the many prejudices stemming from ignorance. This mutual understanding also requires us to respect each other's ideals—even if we do not share them. The end of an ideology which for many was a bitter disappointment should not destroy our belief in all ideals.[11]

In an hour of need, there was once again a de Maizière to do his duty.

Rainer Eppelmann (1943–   )

Rainer Eppelmann's life and career defy adequate categorization. Berliners may remember him for his fifteen years as minister of the Samaritan Church and youth leader in Friedrichshain, a district to the north of the city where he built a reputation as an outspoken and somewhat unorthodox Protestant pastor. Others may remember him as a social activist, an antimilitarist, a political organizer, or a governmental bureaucrat. In fact, he is all of these things. However, as remarkable as his *curriculum vitae* may be, Pastor Eppelmann's biography is above all the story of an ordinary man responding well to the challenges of extraordinary circumstances.

It seems appropriate that a life dedicated to peace should begin in the middle of World War II. Rainer Eppelmann was born on February 12, 1943, in Berlin. As a young boy, he grew up amid the hardships of war, defeat, and occupation by Soviet armies. Although he had become a citizen of the GDR, Eppelmann (like many other youngsters) went to school in West Berlin. He had hoped to become an architect, but the erection of the Berlin Wall in 1961 abruptly cut short his studies. In retaliation for having experienced West

German schools, the East German state ostracized Eppelmann and denied him further education. Eppelmann was reduced to working in construction as an unskilled laborer, knowing that he might never be allowed to finish his schooling.[12]

Perhaps the most important day in Eppelmann's life came in 1966 when he received his letter to report for military service. Looking back, Eppelmann recalled that his draft notice led him to realize just how much impact politicians have on the lives of ordinary individuals. This was his political epiphany.[13] Like many others who by inclination did not wish to bear weapons, he tried to avoid serving. Fortunately for him, the GDR had only two years earlier passed a law to allow conscientious objectors to serve in the *Bausoldaten*, or construction units, thereby avoiding combat training. Given his objections to war and his familiarity with construction, this seemed a logical alternative. Eppelmann entered the *Bausoldaten* but refused to take the oath of allegiance required of all who entered the military. His obstinance landed him in prison for eight months. The experience helped him resolve that the GDR needed to change.

After his discharge and a brief flirtation with college, Eppelmann went back into construction as a mason, but he found it unsatisfying. It was 1968, and as the Soviets intervened in Czechoslovakia's drive for a more open society, Eppelmann's ambitions turned to political activism. At this critical junction of his life, Eppelmann decided to the enter the ministry. He found religion attractive for two reasons. The Church was the only institution where free expression was allowed and, consequently, the best venue for a critic of communism to vent his anger publicly. His decision also had emotional roots. Eppelmann remembered that the only good experiences he ever had in the GDR were those as a youth in Church organizations. Ultimately, he reached the conclusion that the ministry was the only occupation in which he "could have imagined getting old."[14]

Eppelmann entered the seminary in 1969, and five years later became a youth pastor in the Friedrichshain section of Berlin. Soon, he became the pastor of Berlin's Samaritan Church, where he began to fashion a ministry around his personality. Not surprisingly, the church quickly gained notoriety for some rather unorthodox worship services. His most famous efforts were his "Blues Services," which featured a worship liturgy accompanied by jazz musicians. Before long, the church's pews were filled with parishioners, some interested more in syncopation than in salvation. As his reputation grew, he began use the pulpit to question the GDR's military preparedness policies. Seizing upon the Old Testament theme of "swords into ploughshares," Eppelmann became one of the founders of the Peace Movement of the 1970s. In the early 1980s,

Eppelmann stepped up his attack on the increasing militarism of his society. Again he made news by positioning garbage cans at his altar and asking his parishioners to "deposit" their children's military toys.

Eppelmann first came to national prominence during the nuclear missile debate. In January 1982, he and fellow dissident Robert Havemann co-authored a letter criticizing the regime's foreign and domestic policy. Their note urged the Honecker government to enter negotiations with West Germany, demilitarize, and avoid international confrontations. The letter, known as the Berlin Appeal, gained international attention once it was disseminated to the Western press and broadcast media. The letter was openly defiant, calling on the SED to begin public debates on government policy, allow for the free expression of opinions, and to lend support to peace demonstrators. One of its statements, "Make peace without arms"[15] became a popular slogan of the Peace Movement. The East German government considered the letter seditious. Two weeks later, Eppelmann was arrested, but he was released within a day.[16] In the public's view, Eppelman and Havemann both had come to embody the Peace Movement.

The 1989–1990 revolution quickly elevated Eppelmann from dissident to political insider. During the high point of the uprisings in October, Eppelmann teamed with fellow pastors Friedrich Schorlemmer, Heino Falcke, and others to found the Democratic Awakening (DA), a moderate political action group pledged to a democratic renewal of the GDR. As leadership passed from Honecker to Krenz, Eppelmann was chosen to represent the DA in the Round Table discussions. His meteoric rise to power accelerated with Krenz's fall from power. Hans Modrow, the new prime minister, offered Eppelmann a cabinet position in his newly formed Government of National Responsibility. The man who had spent a lifetime attacking politicians had become one himself.

His position in Modrow's government concluded with the March 1990 elections, which brought Lothar de Maizière and a CDU-dominated government to East Germany. In a bold political move, de Maizière approached Eppelmann to serve as minister of defense. Eppelmann now had the chance to be in charge of the very system he had loathed for years. As he later reflected on his decision to accept, "It hit me like a bolt of lightning. Someone just gave you the chance to do what you have talked about for fifteen years. . . . I told him, [that] if it can be called the Ministry of Disarmament and Defense and you accept that it is a program and not just a name, then I'll say yes."[17]

Eppelmann was now in charge of the security of his country, and in that capacity he made decisions that were extremely unpopular. Despite the clear reference to "disarmament" in his title, the avowed pacifist refused to strike down the hated conscription laws, as he felt they were necessary to the country's security. His enemies were quick to point out the irony of a former "draft dodger" protecting the jobs of the East German military. One such detractor claimed that the good pastor was no longer leading sheep but tanks. Eppelmann discounted such criticism and refused to yield to critics, remaining steadfast to his belief that change should be gradual.

Eppelmann had hoped to continue his work toward his disarmament goal even beyond unification. He never got to realize his ultimate goals since the pace of unification politics outran his efforts. The Democratic Awakening merged with the national CDU, and Eppelmann lost his position and his cabinet rank. Once the unification merged the two political systems, Eppelmann had to resign himself to working within the framework of the larger party. He eventually settled into the new Bundestag as a CDU representative from Brandenberg and has taken on a number of party jobs, preferring to work on social issues. For a time, he was the chairman of a government committee on family and senior citizens. Since 1995, he has served as the chairman of a CDU social commission. The next year, he was elected to the CDU leadership. Rainer Eppelmann, the minister who began his career as a political outsider, has become a political insider.

Hans-Dietrich Genscher (1927–)

German unification was won by the efforts of many individuals, most of them by now household names. Men such as Helmut Kohl and Mikhail Gorbachev can feel secure of their place in history. Yet, one of the most pivotal roles in the unification process was played by a man who preferred to remain out of the spotlight and work quietly to achieve his government's ends. Hans-Dietrich Genscher, the West German foreign minister, may be the most underrated figure in the unification drama. He did much of the groundwork to prepare for the meetings between the heads of state and played a crucial role in the negotiations that secured Soviet acceptance of unification.

Genscher was born on March 21, 1927, to a professional family in the small town of Reidenburg. At the age of six, his family moved to the nearby city of Halle, where he remained most of his adolescent years. Like most youngsters, Genscher's dream of continuing his education was interrupted by the war. Before he could complete his basic studies, Genscher was forced to serve as a helper to an anti-aircraft unit for about a year and a half. In mid-September 1944, he received orders to report to boot camp at Helbra in Thuringia; but after only three weeks of training, he was sent to the Ore Mountains (Erzgebirge) to perform two months of compulsory labor service. By December, the authorities deemed him ready for action, and he saw active duty for the next five months.

For Genscher, the end of the war and the immediate postwar period held mixed blessings. On May 7, Allied occupation armies captured and imprisoned him. Released only two months later, he returned to his home in Halle to work as a construction worker while trying to put his law studies back on track. Unfortunately, while he was just about to return to school, Genscher was stricken with tuberculosis, and the illness would continue to plague him the rest of his life. Between his frequent trips to the hospitals and sanatoriums for treatment, Genscher found a way to resume his studies, taking a position at the Martin Luther University in Halle. Two years later, he was able to transfer to the university in Leipzig, where he eventually took his degree. Thereafter, he opened a law practice as a junior barrister.

Perhaps the most important event of Genscher's early life was his decision to leave Halle (then part of the GDR) in 1952 and emigrate through West Berlin to Bremen in the Federal Republic. In Bremen, his political career blossomed. While working for a law firm, he joined the Free Democratic Party (FDP) and quickly scaled its ranks. In 1956 he entered national politics and served as head of the FDP's Bundestag faction from 1959 to 1965. Having gotten a reputation as an outspoken critic of Chancellor Kurt Kiesinger's CDU government, Genscher was selected to hold one of three FDP cabinet positions in the SPD/FPD coalition government of Willy Brandt. Although he had hoped for the finance ministry, he was assigned the post of ministry of interior, where he would concentrate on environmental issues. He remained in this position through Brandt's second cabinet. When his colleague Walter Scheel vacated the foreign ministry upon being elected federal president in 1974, Genscher, though lacking expertise in foreign affairs, moved into the position. Genscher was now the highest ranking FDP member of the SPD/FPD coalition government.

Genscher's career reached another crucial junction in 1982 when the FDP fell at odds with Chancellor Schmidt's SPD over financial policy. In September, Genscher helped to sever his alliance with the SPD and steer his small but important FDP Bundestag faction into a voting coalition with the CDU opposition headed by Helmut Kohl. The resulting constructive vote of no confidence in Schmidt led to Kohl's elevation as chancellor. Genscher managed to keep his party together despite a number of left-wing defections, and he entered the new government as vice-chancellor and foreign minister.

Genscher proved to be an intriguing diplomat. As a former resident of Halle, he was always more interested in intra-German affairs than most other politicians. He soon developed his own distinctive political style that featured an almost rabid longing for détente and improved relations with the Soviet bloc. As result, he was often seen as something of a loose cannon and never given a great deal of important work. He was one of the first West German politicians to grasp the potential of Mikhail Gorbachev's overtures in East Germany as a key to peace. His admiration for *perestroika* and *glasnost* often put him at odds with his own government, which was busy trying to stay in line with the conservatism then popular with its allies, the United States and United Kingdom. Indeed, the word *Genscherism* was soon coined as a pejorative term to describe someone who was too trustful of Gorbachev's promises. This very trust guided Genscher through the magical months of 1989 and helped him chart the diplomatic course that led through the collapse of the GDR to the unification of Germany.

The unmistakable apex of Genscher's popularity was his appearance in Prague during the emigration crisis in autumn 1989. Appearing personally on the balcony of the West German embassy, he announced to the crowd of squatters that they would be allowed to emigrate to West Germany. Thereafter followed months of intense negotiations with West Germany's allies to build an international consensus on the unification movement. In 1990 his suggestion to "neutralize" the territory of the GDR led to the greatest compromise of the unification—namely, that the new Germany could be a member of NATO provided the military threat to the Soviet Union would be no greater (or preferably less) than before.

Genscher's efforts to bring about a peaceful unification brought him much acclaim, especially from those East Germans who considered him one of their own. In the 1990 elections, the FDP took a seat in Halle—a result that was interpreted as a sign of gratitude from his former home town. With the unification behind him, Genscher turned to the foreign policy of his new nation. Among other efforts, he called for a closer union between the peoples of East and West Germany, explored the possibilities for new international diplomatic organizations, and debated the possible German peacekeeping roles in war-torn Yugoslavia. Much to everyone's surprise, Genscher announced in April 1992 that he would step down from his position as foreign minister for health reasons. On May 17, he turned over the office to Klaus Kinkel.

Genscher's own description of himself as "the man in the middle" is a good image to describe this man's remarkable career. During his eighteen years of service as foreign minister (the longest such tenure in German history), his efforts helped guide Germany from division through unification and into a new era in Germany's relations with other nations. For his efforts, he received countless prizes and awards from both German and foreign organizations. Although he was never a head of state, Hans-Dietrich Genscher is justifiably remembered as one of the most important German statesmen of the century.

Erich Honecker (1912–1994)

Erich Honecker was first secretary of the East German Communist Party from 1971 until his dismissal in 1989. During his eighteen years in power, Honecker furthered East Germany's position as the Soviet Union's most advanced industrial ally and a resolute member of the Warsaw Pact while simultaneously seeking rapprochement with the West. Toward the end of his career, Honecker's closed-minded attitude toward the ills of communist society translated into a rigid adherence to the status quo. His refusal to embrace Mikhail Gorbachev's reform initiatives ignited the 1989 revolution that ended the SED's monopoly in governmental affairs. Within a year, the nation he had helped to build ceased to exist.

Honecker was born in the town of Neunkirchen (at that time, Wiebelskirchen) in the Saar on August 25, 1912. He was the son of a poor working-class family. His father worked in the coal mines and following World War I became active in local communist organizations. Young Erich followed in his father's footsteps by joining a communist youth group in 1922 at the age of nine. His party activities at the time consisted mostly of distributing leaflets and collecting money in support of striking mine workers. In less politically charged times, he divided his time working on a farm in Pomerania and learning to be a roofer. At eighteen, he went to Moscow for a year to study at the Lenin School of the Communist International. He returned home to the Saar in 1931 to take a position as secretary of the local Communist Youth Organization. Two years later, he was in charge of youth activities throughout the Ruhr.

His home in the Saar proved an excellent base from which to observe the Nazi seizure of power in 1933. At the time, the Saar was still under French jurisdiction pursuant to the Versailles settlement and therefore (temporarily) out of Hitler's reach. Honecker used this happenstance to help lead the underground resistance to Hitler in the Rhineland and in southern Germany. From time to time, he would cross the border under cover to do clandestine work and on at least one occasion was forced to flee to avoid capture by the Gestapo. In 1935 he worked to convince his fellow Saarlanders to reject reincorporation with Germany, but his leaflet campaign had no effect. Following the plebicite on the question, he fled to Paris and continued his secretive work by organizing communists in Germany. On one such trip in December

1935, Honecker's luck ran out. The Gestapo arrested him in Berlin and, following a trial two years later, he was sentenced to ten years in prison. Honecker spent the next eight years behind bars. Not long before the end of the war, he escaped his captors but was soon reinterred. He regained his freedom only after the Red Army liberated the prison in 1945.

Honecker's travails for the communist movement stood him in good stead with the Russian occupation authorities. Through them, he met Walther Ulbrich and other future SED leaders in early May. As he was still a relatively young man (he was thirty-three), he seemed the natural choice to form and lead the antifascist youth organization that eventually became the Free German Youth (FDJ). In 1958 he again traveled to Moscow for two more years of education, after which he returned to assume a position in the party Central Committee with the title of Minister for State Security. In this capacity, Honecker took charge of the building of the Berlin Wall in 1961 and helped promulgate the "shoot-to-kill" orders that the border guards received at its completion.

Honecker succeeded Walther Ulbricht as first secretary of the SED on May 3, 1971. His early years were productive ones. In 1972 he and Willy Brandt reached agreements to ease travel restrictions between their two countries, and the Federal Republic retreated from its traditional diplomatic policy of treating the GDR as though it did not exist. In 1975 East Germany joined in signing the Helsinki accords on human rights. In the early 1980s, he risked an overt breach of relations with his allies when he publicly disagreed with the Soviet Union over the arms race issue. In 1987 Honecker became the first East German head of state to make an official state visit to the Federal Republic.

Such successes masked discontent latent within East German society. Dissident groups based partly on the peace movement grew and flourished as Honecker's government continued to repress freedom and stifle initiative. As ordinary East Germans suffered without adequate food and Western goods, Honecker retreated into the world of privilege available only to the party brass. As *perestroika* and *glasnost* began to reshape communism all over eastern Europe, Honecker became ever more isolated from the realities of the impending collapse of his government. This isolation was nowhere more evident than at the party meeting in celebration of the GDR's fortieth anniversary, where Honecker spoke of the marvelous advances of his socialist society while protesting citizens paraded their anti-SED placards in the streets. On October 18, 1989, the Central Committee voted to remove Honecker from his position, citing that his recent gall bladder surgery made the move necessary for "reasons of health." On December 3, he was officially excluded from party membership.

As the revelations of the misuse of party resources made headlines, many East Germans demanded that Honecker be brought up on charges. He was thrown in jail in January, but because of his poor health, Honecker was allowed to serve his sentence under house arrest in the home of a Protestant minister. He ultimately fled to the Chilean embassy in Moscow and was extradicted to Germany in 1992. In 1993 a Berlin court again released him and shortly thereafter Honecker moved to Chile. The new German government decided not to put him on trial again. He died of liver cancer on May 29, 1994.

Helmut Kohl (1930–   )

Helmut Kohl has served the Federal Republic of Germany both on the local level as a state minister-president and on the national level as the leader of the CDU. Kohl's leadership of the CDU/CSU/FDP coalition brought electoral victory in 1982 elevating him to the office of chancellor. Kohl's sixteen-year tenure in that office is longer than any other in German history, save that of Otto von Bismarck. Kohl will be remembered primarily as the Chancellor of Unification, but history will also remember his efforts to bring about a closer union of the European states.

Helmut Joseph Michael Kohl was born on April 3, 1930, in Ludwigshafen, an industrial town located in the state of Rhineland-Palatinate. His father Johann had a well-paying job as a civil servant in the government. Consequently, the family managed to live comfortably and even the Depression did not cause any extreme hardship. Although young Helmut was an average student academically, his classmates remember him as one who was not afraid to argue with his teachers—a skill that no doubt helped him in his later political life. Like most other German schoolchildren, Helmut did participate in the Hitler Youth, but he never rose above simple membership. Apparently, he cared more about breeding rabbits and aiding stray animals than practicing military drills.

Nevertheless, the war did eventually catch up with him. Ludwigshafen, home to a number of chemical concerns, was flattened by repeated Allied bombings. In 1944 Helmut's older brother Walther was killed. Then, just before the war ended, Helmut was summoned to Bavaria for training as an anti-aircraft soldier. Fortunately, it was April 1945 and the war was nearly over. As resistance collapsed, Helmut and his friends hid from the advancing Allied armies and from the wrath of Polish laborers who were seeking revenge for their enslavement by the Nazis. When the Nazis surrendered,

Helmut was all of fifteen years old and miles from home. It took him weeks to make it back to his family in the Palatinate.

The immediate postwar years were difficult ones. After a brief stint as a farm hand, Kohl returned to his interrupted schooling. From 1945 to 1950, he worked on his secondary school diploma. Simultaneously, he entered political life. He was one of the youngest members of the Christian Democratic Union (CDU), having joined in 1946 at the age of sixteen. The next year, Kohl became deputy chairperson for Europa-Union, a political group dedicated to forwarding the cause of European unity. Unfortunately, the French occupation armies forbade the association, and Kohl's first foray into political leadership ended rather abruptly.

Kohl spent much of the 1950s working toward a university degree and furthering his political ambitions. By 1955 he had become a member of the board of the CDU in Rhineland-Palatinate. Three years later, he earned his doctorate from the University of Heidelberg and started work for various industrial companies near Ludwigshafen. At age twenty-nine Kohl became chairman of his CDU county organization and then deputy chairman of the state CDU. He worked toward possible election as mayor of Ludwigshafen but was so highly regarded within the party that by 1966 he realized that he could be the next state party chairperson. In 1969 Kohl replaced Peter Altmeier as minister-president of Rhineland-Palatinate and left his position in the chemical industry to devote all his energy to politics.

Once Kohl achieved prominence in the state CDU, word of his ability spread to the higher party levels. As a high-ranking state delegate, Kohl soon became familiar with the nuances of the national party and its leadership. Only two years after his elevation to minister-president, Kohl made a bid for election as national party chairman, but he lost to Rainer Barzel. Undaunted, he was successful only two years later. During these years of SPD ascendancy, Kohl worked to rebuild CDU strength at local levels, thereby amassing a large amount of goodwill among the delegates of his party. That goodwill helped him get reelected repeatedly as party chairman. Following the CDU coalition victory the next year, Helmut Kohl officially became the chancellor of the Federal Republic of Germany.

Kohl ascended to office at a critical time in recent German history. By 1982 the left-wing trends of the previous decade had evaporated. At home, the economy lagged as unemployment rates and taxes soared to ever higher levels. In a manner similar to the tack taken by both Margaret Thatcher and Ronald Reagan, Kohl's CDU platform had called for a social course correction. As he put it in a policy statement, "The question with regard to the future is not how much more the country can do for its citizens. The question of the future is how freedom, dynamic strength and personal responsibility can be newly developed."[18] While evoking images of Adenauer and Erhard, Kohl managed to get elected on promises to free the marketplace from excessive government involvement so as to promote the personal accumulation of wealth.

Although the social platform did attract many voters, it may have been the CDU stance in foreign relations that meant the electoral difference. In the last years of Helmut Schmidt's chancellorship, West German foreign policy was in crisis. Schmidt's Western NATO allies intended to station American Pershing II missiles in central Europe as a deterrent to the threat of the Soviet Union's SS-20s. As the Peace Movement and antinuclear activists took to the streets in opposition to the plans, relations between the Federal Republic and the West hit an all-time low. The ruling SPD was firmly against the deployment, despite the wishes of their chancellor. The internecine row resulted in a Bundestag constructive vote of no confidence in the government of Helmut Schmidt in October 1982, and Kohl got a chance to form a new government based on a coalition with the CSU and FDP. Citing the need to keep West Germany firmly entrenched in the Western alliance, Kohl promised to proceed with the deployment if he were elected. The CDU/FDP victory in the next year's elections signaled the beginning of a new attempt to restore the country's postwar friendships and reaffirm Adenauer's goal of anchoring the Federal Republic in the West.

Helmut Kohl's greatest accomplishment was his successful negotiation of German unification. Nevertheless, his detractors give him little credit for it. Many maintain that he was merely the beneficiary of a confluence of lucky breaks. Others think that Kohl was never serious about unification, claiming that it just "fell into his lap" without much effort on his part. Nothing could be farther from the truth. Although Kohl has never been a starry-eyed idealist, it is nevertheless clear that he believed his entire life that unification was possible. Further, were it not for Kohl's success in reassuring both Presidents Reagan and Bush that West Germany would remain firmly in the Western alliance, the United States would never have agreed to unification.

It is also unfair to say that Kohl has shown no interest in Europe. One need only remember his days with the Europa-Union to see that this criticism is also unwarranted. From his earliest days as chancellor, Kohl worked with François Mitterand to renew the postwar Franco-German partnership, as was so elegantly demonstrated by the image of the two men standing hand-in-hand at Verdun in 1984, paying tribute to the war casualties of both nations. His efforts paid dividends five years later. France had every reason to oppose German unification but in the end did not. Instead, France became a cautious partner in the process, having accepted Kohl's promises to ground unification firmly in the overall context of European unity.

Helmut Kohl is in some ways an enigmatic figure. His ability to act quickly turned out to be a strength in 1990, as he seized the opportunity to bring about unification in a relatively short time span. However, this same decisiveness has often caused him to act first and think about consequences later. Consequently, his career has not been without controversial moments. President Reagan's visit to a military cemetery in Bitberg in 1985 was one such embarrassment. Despite the fact that the graves contained the remains of SS soldiers, the two went ahead with proceedings to honor the war dead of the two nations. Both he and Reagan drew fire from Holocaust survivors and the political opposition on the left for their apparent glorification of the perpetrators of the Nazi horror. Kohl's failure to consult with his allies before issuing the Ten-Point Program and his hesitation to ensure the Polish border were similar misjudgments. After a narrow victory in the 1994 elections, Chancellor Kohl spent his next four years in office trying to weld together the two Germanys in a hostile climate of high unemployment and a rising economic dissatisfaction. His work ended in September 1998, when national elections ousted the CDU/CSU/FDP coalition in favor of a SPD/Greens government. After sixteen years in office, Kohl stepped down as chancellor. Although he has vowed to remain active in CDU politics, Kohl's future within the party is still uncertain. In any event, his place in history is secure.

Egon Krenz (1937–   )

Of all the figures who played a prominent role in the upheaval of 1989, none is more controversial than Egon Krenz. He was simultaneously hero and traitor, reformer and reactionary. Writers have characterized him as everything from a progressive to a feckless sycophant. Regardless of how one interprets his actions, Egon Krenz was afforded an opportunity granted to very few. In those hectic weeks of September and October 1989, he had the ability to change the course of German history, but he proved unequal to the task. Indeed, his biography is the story of many missed opportunities.

Krenz's humble beginnings belie the political respect he eventually commanded. He was born in Kolberg on March 19, 1937, the son of a war widow and her second husband, a department store tailor. Toward the end of World War II, the again-widowed Frau Krenz fled the advancing Russian armies and returned to Damgarten, her home town, with her young son Egon. In the early years of the occupation, Egon had to scrounge in fields for potatoes or along railroad tracks for fuel in order to supplement his mother's meager income. His education was unremarkable. Following grade school, Krenz briefly studied to work as a mechanic. He soon abandoned this training and began studies in Putbus to become a teacher. In 1957 he completed his exams, and entered his two years' military service.

Krenz never seriously pursued teaching, since he realized that he had more opportunities for social mobility in politics. Growing up poor provided him with every prerequisite for political life in a socialist state. Already in his early teens, Krenz entered the Young Pioneers, an arm of the Free German Youth (the communist youth organization) that was then headed by a young Erich Honecker. Krenz's loyalty and ability made an impression on Honecker, and the future party secretary became Krenz's political mentor. Krenz soon advanced to leadership positions in the Free German Youth and was named a candidate for SED membership in 1953. While in the military, Krenz represented the army at the Fifth Party Congress in 1958. He was now committed to a life in politics.

In the early 1960s, Krenz climbed the bureaucratic ladders to become the secretary of the Free German Youth council, the position Honecker had once held. In 1964 Krenz began political studies in Moscow at the Soviet Union's party school and graduated in 1967 with a degree in economics. He then returned to his position in the youth organization where he worked for the next seven years. His big break came in 1971 when he was elected as a representative to the Volkskammer and became a member of its presidium. Five years later, Krenz was named to the SED Politburo, and in 1983 he was given the post of defense secretary. In this capacity, he took charge over both the armed services and the Stasi.

Krenz was still a relatively young man. His elevation to such circles of power seemed odd, considering the generational difference between him and the older Politburo members. These differences were underscored at public appearances where Krenz, wearing the most stylish and casual of modern clothes, looked out of place alongside his fellow party functionaries who were wearing suits and ties. Those who mistrusted him derisively called him "teacher's pet" or the "eternal youth."[19] Admittedly, Krenz did little to conform. His frequenting of discotheques and bars led many to question his lifestyle. He soon gained a reputation as something of a playboy, and rumors of alcoholism followed him through much of his career.

Despite some misgivings about his personal life, Krenz became the clear choice to succeed Erich Honecker. He had done everything in the proper order, followed in his mentor's footsteps, and remained loyal to the movement. However, in many ways, he was trapped between two different visions of East German society. As party functionary, he understood the necessity for propaganda and agitation, but in his position as youth leader he became acquainted with the discontent and despondence of young people. As defense secretary, he received Stasi reports of the discontent latent in society but chose to do nothing. As Krenz himself often admitted, he "should have had the courage earlier"[20] to present problems to the leadership for resolution. Instead, he remained quiet.

His intervention could have made a difference. Having studied in Moscow, Krenz understood the Russian language and culture, including *glasnost* and *perestroika*, perhaps better than most East Germans. Yet as the crisis approached, Krenz seemed more interested in bringing Honecker over to reform than supplanting him as general secretary. Consequently, when he might have used the May elections to introduce an East German *perestroika*, he saw to their usual rigging instead. As the Leipzig demonstrations gained popularity, Krenz claimed that he knew of Kurt Masur's nonviolence initiative and supported it. He also claimed to have urged the troops not to fire that night.[21] When the end came for Erich Honecker on 18 October, Krenz was the choice to take over as party secretary. It must have been a bittersweet victory, gained at the expense of the man who was a father figure.

Egon Krenz did make an attempt to gain public acceptance by promising free elections and the elimination of the SED monopoly on power. His government also opened the Berlin Wall (admittedly by accident) and instituted free travel. These efforts were much too little and too late. The public image of Krenz was that of the party functionary who had supported the suppressing of the Tienanmen Square demonstrations in China a few months earlier. To most, he symbolized the old order and, like the communist system he still supported, had to go. Revelations about the good life lived by party members while the rest of the population had to do without did not help his popularity. Eventually, even his own supporters abandoned him. On December 6, "in order to forestall further endangerment of the party's existence" the Central Committee and Politburo removed Krenz as general secretary after having served only forty-odd days.[22] He resigned all other party positions three days later. A further indignation came on January 21, 1990, when the SED (now renamed the Party of Democratic Socialism and eager to break its ties with the communist past) stripped him of membership. He has spent recent years defending himself in court against charges that he is guilty of murder for his role in directing the shootings of fleeing citizens.

Egon Krenz retired to reflect on his role in the German revolution. His memoirs reveal a man with many misgivings about his past, including his lack of courage, but the book was less than candid about his duplicity. He was the consummate conservative when the milieu called for conservatism.

When the climate changed, however, Krenz tried to position himself as the champion of change. Unlike the chameleon, Krenz could not sense the environment and adapt to it. Instead, he tried moderation when the masses wanted radical change. The wreckage of Egon Krenz's career is sufficient evidence to prove the maxim that the most dangerous time for repressive governments is when they try to reform.

Hans Modrow (1928–   )

Hans Modrow was a dedicated communist his entire life. Over the course of his career, he rose up the SED ladder to occupy high positions in the East German government. Yet, he was not a typical SED functionary. Instead, he was somewhat opinionated and outspoken in a party that valued silent obedience above everything else. Shunned by his comrades and sent to an undesirable party post, Modrow might easily have drifted into obscurity. But, the events that shattered the East German status quo in 1989 catapulted Modrow to the very pinnacle of power, and then just as swiftly removed him from it. Today, most Germans remember Modrow not just as the last SED chairman but as a man who eased East Germany through a very difficult transition period. He is one of few communists who are remembered with some degree of respect.

Hans Modrow was born on January 27, 1928, in the town of Jasenitz, a seaport now in Poland but then part of Germany. His father was a sailor who was injured in World War I. Hans had wanted to take to the sea as his father had, but his education and then World War II both intervened to forestall such a possibility. Modrow was called to duty during the last years of the war and saw action in an anti-aircraft battery. He was subsequently captured by advancing Russian armies and placed in a prisoner-of-war camp, where he worked as a slave laborer felling trees.

While most of his immediate family fled to the West following the war, Modrow remained behind. In 1949 he joined the SED and became a leader in the Free German Youth. Four years later, he became that organization's leader for East Berlin. Modrow held that post until 1961 when he was elevated to the position of SED secretary for the Berlin suburb of Köpenick. In 1967 Modrow reached the ranks of the SED Central Committee and served as secretary of its propaganda and agitation section for East Berlin. All the while, Modrow pursued a degree in social science from the SED school, a certification in economics from the College of Economics in East Berlin, and a doctoral degree in economic sciences from Humboldt College in East Berlin, all by correspondence.[23]

Modrow had the pedigree of a typical party functionary, and his loyalty to communism was legendary. While in Moscow in 1953, Modrow waited in line for twenty-four hours to mourn at Stalin's casket. By contrast, when his mother died in the Federal Republic in 1989, Modrow would not attend the funeral. It would look bad, so he felt, for a party official to travel to the West for personal reasons while so many others were denied such permission.[24] He was not one to wrap himself in the trappings available to the socialist elite. Modrow preferred a simpler life and lived in small apartments similar to those of workers. While one might expect such blind devotion would stand him in good stead with the party brass, it often had the reverse effect. Such loyalty was threatening to those who preferred to pay lip service to Marxism while driving Volvos and living in their party-provided villas. Over time, an enmity developed between Modrow and the party leadership that flared into open distrust and criticism.

In 1971, with Honecker's ascension to power, Modrow became party secretary for agitation and propaganda. Only two years later, he was named district party leader for Dresden, a city so plagued with problems that most in the party saw it as a dead end for one's career. It proved to be just that. Despite repeated efforts to improve the city through rebuilding and infrastructure repair, Modrow was thwarted by those on the Central Committee who preferred to keep him in political limbo. Even though it was common practice to elect party district leaders to the Politburo, Modrow's sixteen years as Dresden's chief never so much earned him even a nomination. He was the only district leader so disgraced. Early in 1989, having already been called on the carpet for "bad socialist work," Modrow was again given a bad evaluation by the Central Committee. He reportedly considered giving it all up to work in a factory.

Being shunned by the party actually worked to his advantage. To the population, Modrow took on the air of an independent thinker who might be able to bring about change within the system. Even those who distrusted socialism saw that this "political black sheep" might be someone with whom the people could reliably deal. As a result, opposition groups and Soviet leaders alike often tossed about his name as someone loyal to socialism but untainted by, and unsympathetic with, the abuses of the present party leadership. His name was mentioned often as someone who might lead an East German *perestroika* and *glasnost*.

In the autumn of 1989, Modrow got his chance. As the trains of refugees headed for Dresden on November 7 bound for the Federal Republic, Modrow became the first party district leader to enter into a dialogue with opposition leaders. Although the demonstrations at the train station got out of hand and required force to contain, Modrow's dialogue with the dissidents helped forestall any widespread violence. Therefore, when the SED relinquished its monopoly status and the power of decision making reverted to the People's Chamber (Volkskammer), its delegates turned to Modrow to replace the departing Willi Stoph as prime minister. Almost by default, Modrow had taken over the government that had so often spurned him. The next elections would either confirm or reject his leadership.

In the meantime, Modrow had to contend with running a government fractured by revolution and hobbled by social and economic discontent. His dealings with the Round Table illustrate the degree of disunity present. Eager to appear conciliatory, Modrow worked with the Round Table when it suited his purposes. But he could not appear to be their puppet either and often refused to cooperate when the civic groups' demands were unreasonable. As he put it, he "had to walk this thin line, not falling into either one of those two traps."[25] For a while, he balanced himself well but tripped when he insisted on retaining an internal security force similar to the dreaded Stasi. The popular outcry and his subsequent backdown damaged his credibility, undermined his status as an independent decision maker, and ruined any chances that his government had for success.

In foreign policy, however, Modrow still had a few cards to play. Following consultations with Moscow, Modrow revealed his plan for a gradual federation between East and West Germany. The plan received little consideration, primarily because Chancellor Kohl (rightly) thought that Modrow's caretaker government would soon be swept away. The elections of March 18 bore out Kohl's evaluation. The CDU victory ended any hope of a renewed socialist state under PDS (SED) governance, and with it ended the Modrow experiment. Modrow handed over his position as head of state to Lothar de Maizière after serving roughly four months.

Hans Modrow continues to work within the PDS to gain electoral votes and Bundestag seats, but his one chance to effect change has passed. In the course of German unification, Modrow was only a transitional figure and, by definition, marginally important to the outcome. But Modrow deserves credit for being one of few party faithful who understood the necessity of change and was willing to confront a corrupt system at the expense of his own livelihood. Like everyone else, Modrow had no way of knowing how much or how little change would satisfy the people. His dream of a renewed socialist state was shattered by the popular cry for union with the Federal Republic. This is not an unfamiliar theme.

NOTES

1. Ernst Elitz, *Sie Waren Dabei* (Stuttgart: Deutsche Verlags-Anstalt, 1991), 29.

2. Dirk Philipsen, *We Were the People* (Durham, NC: Duke University Press, 1993), 134–35.

3. Elitz, *Sie Waren Dabei*, 31.

4. "RDA: Bärbel la rebelle," *Espoir*, October 13, 1989, 35.

5. Philipsen, *We Were the People*, 296.

6. Ibid., 295.

7. Elitz, *Sie Waren Dabei*, 36.

8. Ibid.; see also Philipsen, *We Were the People*, 133.

9. Bernard Cook, "Willy Brandt," in Frank W. Thackeray and John Findling, eds., *Statesmen Who Have Changed the World* (Westport, CT: Greenwood Press, 1993), 57.

10. Elitz, *Sie Waren Dabei*, 185.

11. *The Unification of Germany in 1990* (Bonn: Press and Information Office of the Federal Government, 1991), 144.

12. Philipsen, *We Were the People*, 59.

13. Manfred Richter and Elsbeth Zylla, eds., *Mit Pflugscharen gegen Schwerter: Erfahrungen in der Evangelischen Kirche in der DDR, 1949–1990* (Berlin: Edition Temmen, 1991), 131.

14. Ibid.

15. Philipsen, *We Were the People,* 56. The original in German is "Frieden schaffen ohne Waffen." See also *Der Fischer Weltalmanach—Sonderband DDR* (Frankfurt: Fischer Taschenbuch Verlag, 1990), 266.

16. Gert-Joachim Glaessner and Ian Wallace, eds., *The German Revolution of 1989: Causes and Consequences* (Oxford: Berg, 1992), 135.

17. Richter and Zylla, *Mit Pflugscharen gegen Schwerter*, 133 (translation by author).

18. Günther Müchler and Klaus Hoffmann, *Helmut Kohl* (Bonn: Press and Information Office of the Federal Government, 1992), 69.

19. *New York Times*, October 19, 1989.

20. Elitz, *Sie Waren Dabei*, 47.

21. Egon Krenz, *Wenn Mauern Fallen* (Vienna: Neff, 1990), 204–5 and 134–37.

22. *Der Fischer Weltalmanach—Sonderband DDR*, 277.

23. Philipsen, *We Were the People*, 90; see also *Der Fischer Weltalmanach—Sonderband DDR*, 282.

24. Elitz, *Sie Waren Dabei*, 73.

25. Philipsen, *We Were the People*, 260.

Primary Documents
of the Unification

THE CONSTITUTIONS OF THE GERMAN STATES

For forty years, the German people were governed by two different constitutions, each a product of the postwar animosities between the capitalist West and the communist East. The West German constitution, called the Basic Law, was drafted by a parliamentary council consisting of delegates chosen by the members of the state parliaments. After a long process of deliberation, the document was ratified on May 23, 1949. The East German constitution was written under the supervision of the Soviet occupation authority and ratified by the East German Volkskammer (People's Chamber) on October 7, 1949. It since went through a number of revisions, the most notable in 1974 (reprinted here) in the wake of détente with the West. The following excerpts from the two documents provide a basis for the comparison of two very dissimilar governmental systems.

At first glance, the documents seem strikingly similar. Each stresses the importance of human rights and gender equality, and both accept racial or ethnic diversity. In addition, both aspire to protect the freedom of conscience, assembly, and religion. A closer read will reveal many notable ideological differences. The West German Basic Law is a blueprint for a competitive, capitalist society. It bears many of the same ideas on freedom and social responsibility as other Western, democratic constitutions. The East German constitution, on the other hand, demands the abolition of private property and the creation of a planned socialist economy. It is conspicuously different from its West German counterpart in its codification of the social rights of its citizens, including the right to guaranteed housing (Article 37), health care (Article 35), and work (Article 24). Despite such socialist-inspired laws, the reality of everyday existence in the GDR was that the majority of the guarantees spelled out in the constitution were either circumvented or ignored.

Another issue of interest is that both documents accept the possibility of a future unification of the Germanys. There are some differences in approach, however. The Basic Law claims to have authority over all Germans and contains sections which outline procedures for the accession of other German territories (Article 23), or the complete revision of the document should Germany be reunited (Article 146). Each of these articles was stricken following unification. The original East German constitution mentions that the GDR's goal is to "overcome the division of Germany imposed . . . by imperialism." However, this article and references to Germany proper were dropped in the 1974 revisions as a concession to détente.

Document 1
THE BASIC LAW

[Preamble]
The German People in the Länder of Baden, Bavaria, Bremen, Hamburg, Hesse, Lower Saxony, North Rhine-Westphalia, Rhineland-Palatinate, Schleswig-Holstein, Württemberg-Baden, and Württemberg-Hohenzollern,

- Conscious of its responsibility before God and Men,

- Animated by the resolve to preserve its national and political unity and to serve the peace of the World as an equal partner in a united Europe,

- Desiring to give a new order to political life for a transitional period, has enacted, by virtue of its constituent power, this Basic Law of the Federal Republic of Germany.

It has also acted on behalf of those Germans to whom participation was denied. The entire German people is called on to achieve by free self-determination the unity and freedom of Germany.

I. BASIC RIGHTS

Article 1

1) The dignity of man is inviolable. To respect and protect it is the duty of all state authority.

2) The German people therefore acknowledge inviolable and inalienable human rights as the basis of every community, of peace and of justice in the world.

3) The following basic rights bind the legislature, the executive and the judiciary as directly enforceable law.

Article 2

1) Everyone has the right to the free development of his personality insofar as he does not violate the rights of others or offend against the constitutional order or the moral code.

2) Everyone has the right to life and to inviolability of his person. The freedom of the individual is inviolable. These rights may only be encroached upon pursuant to a law.

Article 3

1) All persons are equal before the law.

2) Men and women have equal rights.

3) No one may be prejudiced or favored because of his sex, his parentage, his race, his language, his homeland and origin, his faith or his religious or political opinions.

Article 4

1) Freedom of faith and of conscience, and freedom of creed, religious or ideological, are inviolable.

2) The undisturbed practice of religion is guaranteed.

3) No one may be compelled against his conscience to render war service as an armed combatant. Details will be regulated by a Federal Law.

Article 5

1) Everyone has the right freely to express and to disseminate his opinion by speech, writing and pictures and freely to inform himself from generally accessible sources. Freedom of the press and freedom of reporting by radio and motion pictures are guaranteed. There shall be no censorship.

2) These rights are limited by the provisions of the general laws, the provisions of law for the protection of youth and by the right to inviolability of personal honor.

3) Art and science, research and teaching are free. Freedom of teaching does not absolve from loyalty to the constitution.

Article 8

1) All Germans have the right to assemble peacefully and unarmed without prior notification or permission.

2) With regard to open-air meetings this right may be restricted by or pursuant to a law.

Article 9

1) All Germans have the right to form associations and societies.

2) Associations, the objects or activities of which conflict with the criminal laws or which are directed against the constitutional order or the concept of international understanding, are prohibited.

3) The right to form associations to safeguard and improve working and economic conditions is guaranteed to everyone and to all trades and professions. Agreements which restrict or seek to hinder this right are null and void; measures directed to this end are illegal.

Article 11

1) All Germans enjoy freedom of movement throughout the Federal territory.

2) This right may be restricted only by a law and only in cases in which an adequate basis of existence is lacking and special burdens would arise to the community as a result thereof or in which the restriction is necessary for the protection of youth against neglect, for combating the danger of epidemics or for the prevention of crime.

Article 16

1) No one may be deprived of his German citizenship. Loss of citizenship may arise only pursuant to a law, and against the will of the person affected it may arise only if such person does not thereby become stateless.

2) No German may be extradited to a foreign country. Persons persecuted for political reasons enjoy the right of asylum.

II. THE FEDERATION AND THE LÄNDER

Article 23

For the time being, this Basic Law applies in the territory of the Länder of Baden, Bavaria, Bremen, Greater Berlin, Hamburg, Hesse, Lower-Saxonia, North Rhine-Westphalia, Rhineland-Palatinate, Schleswig-Holstein, Württemberg-Baden, and Württemberg-Hohenzollern. In other parts of Germany it shall be put into force on their accession.

Article 26

1) Activities tending and undertaken with the intent to disturb peaceful relations between nations, especially to prepare for aggressive war, are unconstitutional. They shall be made a punishable offense.

2) Weapons designed for warfare may be manufactured, transported or marketed only with the permission of the Federal Government. Details will be regulated by a federal law.

XI. TRANSITIONAL AND CONCLUDING PROVISIONS

Article 116

1) Unless otherwise provided by law, a German within the meaning of this Basic Law is a person who possesses German citizenship or who has been admitted to the territory of the German *Reich*, as it existed on December 31, 1937, as a refugee or expellee of German stock or as the spouse or descendant of such person.

2) Former German citizens who, between January 30, 1933 and May 8, 1945, were deprived of their citizenship for political, racial or religious reasons, and their descendants, shall be regranted German citizenship on application. They are considered as not having been deprived of their German citizenship if they have established their domicile in Germany after May 8, 1945 and have not expressed a contrary intention.

Article 146

This Basic Law shall cease to be in force on the day on which a constitution adopted by a free decision of the German people comes into force. Bonn/Rhine, May 23, 1949.

Document 2
THE GDR CONSTITUTION

The Constitution of the German Democratic Republic [as modified 7 October 1974]
[Preamble]

In continuation of the revolutionary traditions of the German working class and in consequence of the liberation from fascism, the people of the German Democratic Republic has, in accord with the processes of historical development in our time, realized its right to socio-economic, political and national self-determination and is building an advanced socialist society.

Imbued with the will freely to decide its own affairs and to continue unswervingly along the road of socialism and communism, peace, democracy and international friendship, the people of the German Democratic Republic has given itself this socialist Constitution.

PART I   FOUNDATIONS OF THE SOCIALIST SOCIAL AND
STATE ORDER

Chapter 1 Political Foundations

Article 1

The German Democratic Republic is a socialist state of workers and farmers. It is the political organization of the working people in town and countryside led by the working class and its Marxist-Leninist party.

Article 2

(1) All political power in the German Democratic Republic is exercised by the working people in town and countryside. Man is the centre of all efforts of socialist society and its state. The Decisive task of the advanced socialist society is the further raising of the living and cultural standards of the people on the basis of a high growth rate of socialist production, increased efficiency, scientific and technological advance and growing labour productivity.

(3) The exploitation of man by man has been abolished for ever. What the hand of man has wrought belongs to the people. The socialist principle: "From each according to his abilities, to each according to his work" is being put into practice.

Article 5

(1) Citizens of the German Democratic Republic exercise their political power through democratically elected popular representative bodies.

(2) The popular representative bodies are the foundation for the system of organs of the state. In their activities they base themselves upon the active participation of citizens in the preparation, implementation and control of their decisions.

Article 6

(1) The German Democratic Republic, faithful to the interests of the people and its international obligations, has eradicated German militarism and nazism on its territory, and pursues a foreign policy serving socialism and peace, international friendship and security.

(2) The German Democratic Republic is for ever and irrevocably allied with the Union of Soviet Socialist Republics. The close and fraternal alliance with it guarantees the people of the German Democratic Republic continued progress along the road of socialism and peace.

The German Democratic Republic is an inseparable part of the community of socialist states. Faithful to the principles of socialist internationalism it contributes to its reinforcement, cultivates and develops friendship, universal cooperation and mutual assistance with all states of the socialist community.

(3) The German Democratic Republic advocates the implementation of the principles of peaceful coexistence between states with differing social systems and, on the basis of equal rights and mutual respect, promotes cooperation with all states.

(4) The German Democratic Republic works for security and cooperation in Europe, for a stable structure of peace in the world and for general disarmament.

(5) Militarist and revanchist propaganda in all forms, warmongering and the manifestation of hatred against creeds, races and nations are punished as crimes.

Article 8

(1) The generally accepted rules of international law serving peace and peaceful international cooperation are binding upon the state and every citizen.

(2) The German Democratic Republic will never undertake a war of conquest or employ its armed forces against the freedom of another people.

Chapter 2

Article 9

(1) The national economy of the German Democratic Republic is based upon the socialist ownership of the means of production. It develops in accordance with the economic laws of socialism on the foundation of socialist relations of production and the systematic implementation of socialist economic integration.

(2) The national economy of the German Democratic Republic serves the strengthening of the socialist order, the constantly improving satisfaction of the material and cultural needs of the citizens, the development of their personality and their socialist relations in society.

(3) The German Democratic Republic bases itself on the principle of the management and planning of the national economy and all other social spheres. The national economy of the German Democratic Republic is socialist planned economy.

Article 15

(1) The land of the German Democratic Republic is one of its most valuable natural resources. It must be protected and utilized rationally. Land used for agriculture and forestry may only be removed from such use with the agreement of the responsible organs of the state.

(2) In the interests of the welfare of citizens, the state and society shall protect nature. The competent bodies shall ensure the purity of the water and the air, and protection for flora and fauna and the natural beauties of the homeland; in addition this is the affair of every citizen.

Article 18

(1) Socialist national culture is one of the foundations of socialist society. The German Democratic Republic fosters and protects socialist culture, which serves peace, humanism and the development of socialist society. It combats imperialist anti-culture, which serves psychological warfare and the degradation of man.

PART II—CITIZENS AND ORGANIZATIONS IN SOCIALIST SOCIETY

Chapter 1

Article 20

(1) Every citizen of the German Democratic Republic has the same rights and duties, irrespective of nationality, race, philosophy or religious confession, social origin or position. Freedom of conscience and freedom of belief are guaranteed. All citizens are equal before the law.

(2) Men and women have equal rights and have the same legal status in all spheres of social, state and personal life. The promotion of women, particularly with regard to vocational qualification, is a task of society and the state.

(3) Young people are especially promoted in their social and vocational development. They have every opportunity for responsible participation in the development of the socialist order of society.

Article 21

(1) Every citizen of the German Democratic Republic is entitled to participate fully in shaping the political, economic, social and cultural life of the socialist community and the socialist state. The principle shall be applied "Participate in working, in planning, and in governing!"

Article 22

(3) The management of the elections by democratically formed electoral commissions, popular discussion on basic questions of policy, and the nomination and examination of candidates by the voters, are inalienable socialist electoral principles.

Article 24

(1) Every citizen of the German Democratic Republic has the right to work. He has the right to employment and its free selection in accordance

with social requirements and personal qualifications. He has the right to pay according to the quality and quantity of the work. Men and women, adults and young people have the right to equal pay for equal work output.

Article 27

(1) Every citizen of the German Democratic Republic has the right, in accordance with the spirit and aims of this Constitution, to express his opinion freely and publicly. This right is not limited by any service or employment relationship. Nobody may be placed at a disadvantage for using this right.

(2) Freedom of the press, radio and television are guaranteed.

Article 28

(1) All citizens have the right to assemble peacefully within the framework of the principles and aims of the Constitution.

(2) The use of material prerequisites for the unhindered exercise of this right, of assembly buildings, streets and places of demonstration, printing works and means of communication, is guaranteed.

Article 35

(1) Every citizen of the German Democratic Republic has the right to the protection of his health and working capacity.

(3) Material security, medical aid, medicaments and other medical benefits are granted free of charge in case of illness and accidents on the basis of a social insurance system.

Article 36

(1) Every citizen of the German Democratic Republic has the right to social care in case of old age and invalidity.

Article 37

(1) Every citizen of the German Democratic Republic has the right to dwelling space for himself and his family in accordance with economic possibilities and local conditions. The state is obligated to implement this right by promoting the construction of housing, the maintenance of existing housing, and public control of the just distribution of dwelling space.

Article 38

(1) Marriage, family and motherhood are under the special protection of the state. Every citizen of the German Democratic Republic has the right to respect for, protection, and promotion of his marriage and family.

(2) This right is guaranteed by the equality of man and wife in married life and family, by social and state assistance to citizens in promoting and encouraging their marriage and family. Large families, mothers and fathers liv-

ing alone receive the care and support of the socialist state through special measures.

(3) Mother and child enjoy the special protection of the socialist state. Maternity leave, special medical care, material and financial support during childbirth and children's allowances are granted.

Article 39

(1) Every citizen of the German Democratic Republic has the right to profess a religious creed, and to carry out religious activities.

(2) The churches and other religious communities conduct their affairs and carry out their activities in conformity with the Constitution and the legal regulations of the German Democratic Republic. Details can be settled by agreement.

> [Part III, which is omitted here, deals with the functioning organs of state government. Part IV outlines the justice system and contains the following article on the right to petition.]

Article 103

(1) Every citizen may submit petitions (proposals, suggestions, applications or grievances) to the popular elected bodies and their deputies, or to state and economic organs. This right also applies to social organization and collectives of citizens. They may be exposed to no disadvantage as a result of exercising this right.

(2) The organs responsible for a decision must deal with such proposals, suggestions or grievances of citizens or collectives with the legally-prescribed time and notify the applicants of the results.

> [The constitution concludes with Part V, which contains two brief articles stressing the primacy of the laws and the amendment procedure.]

Source: The Constitution of the German Democratic Republic (as modified October 7, 1974) (Berlin: Staatsvertrag der Deutschen Demokratische Republik, 1974).

Document 3
EAST GERMAN TRAVEL DECISION

> Following Erich Honecker's dismissal in October 1989, the newly formed government of Egon Krenz tried to form an East German *perestroika* by drafting a law giving the East German citizenry the right to travel abroad. Early drafts of the law were poorly received as not going far enough to halt the exodus of citizens. On November 9, 1989, Krenz gave party information secretary Günther Schabowski a new and less

restrictive draft of the law and instructed him to hold a press conference to present the draft to the news media. Although the legislation was still pending, Schabowski's answers to questions implied that the new ordinances would go into effect immediately. His misstatement resulted in a flood of citizens streaming to border checkpoints to see if the impossible had come true. The Berlin Wall was now irrevocably, albeit accidentally, opened.

The following document is a transcript of the news bulletin released by ADN, the official East German news agency, which echoes the interpretation that the policy had already been approved and put into motion.

EAST GERMAN TRAVEL DECISION

The Government spokesman told ADN [the official East German news agency] the Council of Ministers of East Germany has decided immediately to set in force the following stipulations for private journeys and permanent emigration until a corresponding parliamentary law comes into effect:

1. Private journeys into foreign countries can be applied for without fulfilling preconditions (reasons for travel, relatives). Permission will be given at short notice.

2. The relevant passport and registration offices of the regional offices of the People's Police in East Germany have been ordered to issue visas for permanent emigration immediately without the present preconditions for permanent emigration having been fulfilled. Application for permanent emigration is also possible as before at departments of internal affairs.

3. Permanent emigration is allowed across all border crossing points between East Germany and West Germany and West Berlin.

4. Because of this the temporary issuing of permits in East German missions abroad and permanent emigration using East German identity cards through third countries will no longer apply.

Source: Historic Documents of 1989. Washington, DC: Congressional Quarterly, 1990.

Document 4
THE LIFTING OF GDR TRAVEL RESTRICTIONS:
NOVEMBER 9, 1989

Instead of curbing the emigration of citizens, the announcement of unrestricted travel abroad accelerated the flight to the West. More numerous, however, were those individuals and families who jumped into their Trabants to take a scenic drive or shopping tour. The West German newspaper *Frankfurter Allgemeine Zeitung*, picked up the ADN release and printed the following version. It reiterates the immediacy of the new ordinance.

The GDR opens its Borders to West Germany:

"Temporary Regulation Pending Passage of a Corresponding Ordinance"

West Berlin, 9 November—GDR residents wishing to leave the country can do so at all border crossings of the GDR into the FRG, effective immediately. This resolution by the Council of Ministers was announced Thursday evening in East Berlin by SED Politburo member Günther Schabowski. According to a report by the GDR news agency ADN, the actual text of the resolution was as follows:

"Applications for private travel outside the country can be made without satisfying any prerequisites (reason for travel, family relationships). Permits will be issued on short notice. Permission will be rejected only in exceptional cases. The Passport and Registration Departments of the Volkspolizei district offices have been told to issue visas for permanent emigration without delay, even if the prerequisites for permanent emigration, which are still in effect, are not fulfilled. Applications for permissions for permanent emigration remain possible through the Department for Domestic Affairs. Permanent emigration can occur at any border crossing between the GDR and the FRG or West Berlin. This eliminates the need either for temporary issuance of permits in the foreign offices of the GDR, or for permanent emigration [to the FRG] via third countries, using a GDR identity card."

Regarding the Berlin Wall, Schabowski said that a clarification of the travel issue did not answer the question "of the reason for a fortified national border." That would require consideration of additional factors concerning, for example, the FRG and NATO. A positive factor would be firm resolve on the parts of the FRG and NATO to take steps toward disarmament.

Source: Konrad H. Jarausch and Volker Gransow, *Uniting Germany: Documents and Debates, 1944–1993* (Providence, RI: Berghahn Books, 1994).

Document 5
NEW YORK TIMES COVERAGE OF THE EAST GERMAN EXODUS

News organizations around the world had been following the plight of East German citizens leaving through Hungary and Czechoslovakia as their country continued its rapid descent toward collapse. Among the best reporting of the events are the articles written by columnists Ferdinand Protzman and Serge Schemann for the *New York Times.* Their pieces chronicle both the official and the human side of the upheaval. This article, submitted to the *Times* for publication just before the opening of the Berlin Wall, is set in Hof, a small town located near West Germany's border with Czechoslovakia. It graphically depicts the reasons why many East Germans fled to the West, and illustrates the frustration and desperation that led many to decide to flee.

Tales Émigrés Tell: Why Life in East Germany Proved Finally Intolerable
by Ferdinand Protzman
Hof, West Germany, Oct. 5

The thousands of people who have left East Germany in recent weeks have seized opportunities for escape as they arose, first through Hungary and then through Czechoslovakia. Seen from afar, their flight seemed to be a mass exodus. But in this West German border city, as the tired travelers disembarked, individual voices testified to often difficult choices; personal dramas emerged from the chorus of cheers.

In interviews during their first hours in the West, East Germans who had besieged the West German Embassy in Prague in a last-ditch effort to emigrate, described why they left, what they left behind and what they hope the future holds.

PLAYING THE WRONG TUNE

Henry Albrecht, 30 years old, from Wittenberge, a city near the West German border that is about 75 miles northwest of Berlin, said: "Until I was 18, I believed in the validity of the East German state. I was raised as an East German citizen and my mother is a Communist Party member. One gets so much indoctrination from an early age that believing is just natural. And everything was going well for me. I did well in school, and was one of two people chosen in 1977 from 80 applicants to study law at the university."

His fortunes changed when as a disc jockey in a student club he played a song suggesting that the Berlin Wall should come down, "They immediately expelled me. And since there is no possible rehabilitation, that meant I could never study at a university again. Finally, I found a job as a brewery worker. After working there for a while, I got a break and was allowed to study chemistry at a technical school. Then I was given a position as a clerk in a small chemical company."

In an office argument with a drunken cleaning woman, he scornfully called her a red sow. "I got 15 months in maximum-security prison for that," he said. "She went straight to the police."

This summer, Mr. Albrecht, who is married and has a child, saw a chance to get out of East Germany. After his visa application for Hungary was rejected, he and two friends pooled their money, bought an old car and drove to Prague.

"I had to—that's all—I had to go. My wife and child are still there, and she will suffer for this, I'm sure. We figure she will be arrested. I hope I can get them out, but I don't know. I acted only for myself."

DETERMINED BROTHERS

Thomas Vorwerg, 29, and his brother Michael, 26, are also from Wittenberge, both of them mechanics. They are single and have many relatives in West Germany.

"Did we discuss leaving?" Thomas Vorwerg said. "All summer long. It is the number one topic of conversation in East Germany. We left now because after the 40th anniversary on Oct. 7, the Government will shut the country up tight. Only the party elite will be able to go on vacation outside East Germany.

"So we got in the car and drove straight to Prague. There was no time to waste. If you can't get out now, you had better be prepared to spend the rest of your life locked in there, because they are not going to change. Reforms are not about to happen."

Michael Vorwerg added: "They held us at the Czech border for two hours. We were strip-searched and they went over every millimeter of the car. Once we got to Prague, we were driving around, trying to figure out where the West German Embassy was. A taxi stopped in front of us. The guy asked us if we wanted to be taken to the embassy.

"He took us right there, got us past the police; they went away after we gave them a case of canned pineapples. The cabbie charged us nearly all our East German money, and he took the car. But that's fine with me, he did right by us."

"I don't know what a mechanic makes here, or what qualifications I will need to get a job," Michael Vorwerg said. "I really didn't think of any of that. My concern was with what I wanted for the rest of my life. And I knew it wasn't living in East Germany. I had known that for a long time."

LOVED ONES LEFT BEHIND

Rüdiger is a 23-year-old from Leipzig, who does not want his family name used. He arrived on the first train to reach Hof at 5:48 A.M. on Thursday. Standing on the platform, he seemed stunned by the swirl of people around him.

"My parents are still there," he said. "So is my girlfriend. We talked about it for weeks, we watched the people leaving every night on West German TV. I kept saying this is it, we have to try.

"But my parents didn't want to go now, and my girlfriend finally decided she wanted to stay where her friends and family are. I had applied to leave legally and was turned down because it wasn't in the interest of the state. My visa application for Hungary was also rejected, so I saw this as my last chance. I went to Prague with a colleague from work but we were separated. I don't know if he got out."

Rüdiger said he was well paid by East German standards, "more than 1,000 marks" a month. This is equivalent to $530 at the official rate of exchange, but because prices for many basic items are subsidized, it is indeed a good salary.

"Life is not that bad there," he said. "I had money and we lived O.K. Although I was a bit tired of living with my parents, I never tried to get an apartment. It just wouldn't be possible. I didn't leave for better shopping possibilities.

"Things aren't going to change, no matter what West German TV commentators say. You know whom the East German press talks about all the time now? China. They laud them as our best friends, as exemplary socialists. That's a message, man. We saw what happened when the army cleaned Tiananmen Square on Western TV. Don't think the Government won't do the same in East Germany."

NOT LIKE GRANDMA

Bettina is a 20-year-old retail saleswoman from Plauen, a city less than 20 miles northeast of Hof. She arrived on the fifth train, passing through her hometown.

"That was weird, very weird," she said. "The station was completely empty. It had been cleared by the police. You could see them all around; they had made a corridor no one could get through—lines of police, barricades and vehicles."

Bettina, who is married, noted that she had wanted to emigrate since 1986.

"I applied three times to leave," she said, "and each time they turned me down, saying there was no humanitarian reason, even though my parents had already left. I got a visa for Hungary, but I was afraid to go. Then they started taking visas for Hungary away from people who already had them. It happened to two women I work with. State security came to their homes and took back the visas. So I went to Prague the day before they closed the border. My husband couldn't go because his passport expired."

Along with her husband, she leaves behind her grandmother, who is 83.

"Grandma has such strong feelings for her homeland that she can't leave," she said. "That's the awful part of all this. I hate it. She's worried about who will take care of her and about being alone. I know this sounds awful, but she is old, she has lived her life. I'm young and I want to live mine. I love her, but that is the way it is."

THE COOK'S LIFE SOURED

Frank Brandenburg, 27, his wife Simone, 28, and their children, Sarah, 8, and Benjamin, 3, left East Berlin at 6 A.M. Tuesday, heading for Prague.

They arrived in Hof on Thursday morning and immediately bought tickets for Neunkirchen in Saarland state in West Germany near the French border, where his sister-in-law has lived since August.

The Brandenburgs applied for an exit permit five years ago. They were turned down "because we were considered too young, and young people were not dispensable in East Germany," Mrs. Brandenburg said. "We wanted to leave because of the general political and economic situation. It is a depressing feeling when you see that nothing changes in your country, in contradiction to all the promises. Everything is falsehood and deceit."

She trained to be a cook and worked for the last six years in the kitchen of a big canteen.

"We only had simple can openers that one uses in family households," she complained. "They were broken after the third use on the big cans. So we opened cans with a hatchet. And as soon as one suggested any improvement, one was considered an agitator."

Mr. Brandenburg also trained to be a cook but ended up working as a window and building cleaner because there was no possibility of sharpening his professional skills.

"I would really like to work as a cook again," he said. "My wife would also like to get a part-time job in a restaurant as well."

They left behind a car, a three-room apartment with a bathroom and a kitchen, all their furniture and nearly all their personal belongings.

"We locked the apartment, and gave the keys to my sister so she has a chance to get some personal things out before the state security police confiscate it all," he recalled.

The Brandenburgs said all they expect in West Germany is the chance to lead a normal life. "We will work like in East Germany, but we will work for a better existence, and work on our personal identity," Mr. Brandenburg said. "Over there, we only worked for the apartment and for our clothes."

"There is a political side to the exodus," he continued. "I support the idea of reunification because German is German and there is a certain feeling of homeland that Germans share. But the exodus will have a contrary effect. Now they will close the border much tighter, and I fear that after the celebrations of Oct. 7, the situation will become as bad as in China or Rumania."

THE COURAGE TO LEAVE

Horst Hartmann, 28, his wife Heike, 26, and their children Dominique, 6, and Morice, 2, come from Erfurt. They applied for an exit permit in December 1988, but it was rejected. Then they applied for a visit to West Germany to see Heike's parents, who live in Wuppertal, near Düsseldorf. The authorities fined them for that.

"We left because we just did not want to deal any more with the daily difficulties over there. You cannot do anything because you don't get anything. Whatever you plan, it won't work because of shortages here and there. You can only get things if you pay a lot of money or if you pay in hard currency," Mr. Hartmann said. "In East Germany, I worked about 16 hours a day to make our living. My wife used to work in a kindergarten, but after she gave birth to our second child she could not return to her job because somebody else took it."

He is trained as a lathe operator and hopes to find work in West Germany.

The Hartmanns are optimistic about their future, "although our friends in the West warned us that one is left of one's own and has to make one's way." Mrs. Hartmann said, adding:

"We are not afraid to start again. We are ready to work hard."

Their first plans are to get an apartment and maybe take a vacation.

"A lot of our friends in East Germany are very unhappy, but they lack the courage to leave," Mr. Hartmann added. "You must be ready to leave everything behind."

Source: New York Times, October 9, 1989, p. A-6.

Document 6
CHANCELLOR KOHL'S TEN-POINT PROGRAM
FOR GERMANY UNITY

The rapid pace of events in November disoriented and confused even the most seasoned politicians. Amid popular calls for German unification, Chancellor Helmut Kohl decided that it would be politically expedient to go on record with a suggestion for a unification procedure and timetable. Although his Ten-Point Program (reproduced here in excerpt) contained provisions designed to assuage the worries of other nations, the plan drew intense fire in many foreign capitals following its presentation to the Bundestag on November 28. The governments of both France and England made highly critical comments about it, primarily because Kohl had neglected to consult them before making the plan public. Consequently, Kohl shelved the proposal, and once the public's desire for unity became clear, he discarded it.

Nevertheless, the document yields an interesting glimpse into the Chancellor's thinking regarding East Germany's deteriorating situation. First, the document is evidence that West Germany's primary concern was not to topple East German communism but to stabilize the

GDR, at least temporarily. It is important to remember that this unification plan was drafted in November 1989 during the height of the exodus from the East. The weight of the numbers of East German refugees had severely strained West German relief services. Thus, despite the ostensible purpose to promote continued good-neighborly relations with the GDR, the ulterior motive of points one through five was to ease the burden on the West German government. Second, points six through ten make it clear that Kohl understood the realities of unification in an international context. Germany's European allies would not accept a unification that would allow Germany to return to its old ways and chart its own course in European and world affairs. Therefore, the final points are a concession to demands that unification take place within a European-wide framework. The latter assumptions continued to guide West German policy long after the Ten Points became a dead issue.

A TEN-POINT PROGRAM FOR OVERCOMING THE DIVISION OF GERMANY AND EUROPE

[Excerpts]

1. Immediate measures are called for as a result of events of recent weeks, particularly the flow of resettlers and the huge increase in the number of travelers. The federal government will provide immediate aid where it is needed. We will assist in the humanitarian sector and provide medical aid if it is wanted and considered helpful.

2. The federal government will continue its cooperation with the GDR in all areas where it is of direct benefit to the people on both sides, especially in the economic, scientific, technological, and cultural fields. It is particularly important to intensify cooperation in the field of environmental protection. Here we will be able to make decisions on new projects shortly, irrespective of other developments.

3. I have offered comprehensive aid and cooperation, should the GDR bindingly undertake to carry out a fundamental change in the political and economic system and put the necessary measures irreversibly into effect. By "irreversible" we mean that the GDR leadership must reach agreement with opposition groups on constitutional amendments and a new electoral law.

4. Prime Minister Modrow spoke, in his government policy statement, of a "treaty community." We are prepared to adopt this idea. The proximity of our two states in Germany and the special nature of their relationship demand an increasingly close network of agreements in all sectors and at all levels.

5. We are also prepared to take a further decisive step, namely, to develop confederative structures between the two states in Germany with a view to

creating a federation. But this presupposes the election of a democratic government in the GDR.

6. The development of intra-German relations remains embedded in the pan-European process, that is to say, in the framework of East-West relations. The future architecture of Germany must fit into the future architecture of Europe as a whole. Here the West has shown itself to be pacemaker, with its concept of a lasting and equitable peaceful order in Europe.

7. The attraction and aura of the European Community are, and remain, a constant feature of pan-European development. We want to and must strengthen them further still.

8. The CSCE [Conference on Security and Cooperation in Europe] process is a central element of the pan-European architecture and must be vigorously promoted in the following forums:

- the human rights conferences in Copenhagen, in 1990, and in Moscow, in 1991;
- the Conference on Economic Cooperation in Bonn, in 1990;
- the Symposium on Cultural Heritage in Cracow, in 1991; and,
- last but not least, the next follow-up meeting in Helsinki.

9. Overcoming the division of Europe and Germany presupposes far-reaching and rapid steps in the field of disarmament and arms control. Disarmament and arms control must keep pace with political developments and thus be accelerated where necessary.

10. With this comprehensive policy we are working for a state of peace in Europe in which the German nation can recover its unity in free self-determination. Reunification—that is, regaining national unity—remains the political goal of the federal government. We are grateful that once again we have received support in this matter from our allies in the declaration issued after the NATO summit meeting in Brussels in May.

Source: German Information Office, New York.

Document 7
HELMUT KOHL'S SPEECH AT THE RUINS OF THE CHURCH OF OUR LADY IN DRESDEN, DECEMBER 19, 1989

Even though the rapid collapse of communism made the prospects for German unity seem better than ever, no one believed it would happen quickly. Even Chancellor Helmut Kohl's Ten-Point Program envi-

sioned a gradual coming-together of the two nations. However, as the
March 1990 elections approached, Kohl had committed his party to a
rapid unification. When did his change of mind take place? The defining moment may well have been Kohl's appearance at a political rally in
Dresden in mid-December to drum up support for his CDU party. The
crowd's chants and placards calling for "one people and one nation"
may have convinced him that the East Germans wanted union with the
Federal Republic without delay. Kohl obliged them, and his gamble
eventually paid off in the electoral victory in March 1990. Reprinted
here is the text of his speech that evening.

Ladies and gentlemen, my dear young friends, dear fellow countrymen and
countrywomen!

First of all I would like to thank all of you for such a friendly welcome. My
dear friends, hundreds of journalists from all over Europe have come to us
and I think that together we should show them how we are able to hold a
peaceful rally in the heart of Germany. Hence my most sincere request
that—despite all our enthusiasm—we now concentrate together in these few
minutes on the business of our meeting.

The first thing I want to pass on to you is a warm greeting from all your
fellow citizens in the Federal Republic of Germany.

The second thing I would like to communicate to you is my recognition
and admiration for this peaceful revolution in the GDR. We are experiencing
for the first time in German history a nonviolent revolution that is taking
place with such great seriousness and in a spirit of solidarity. I thank you all
very much for that. It is a demonstration for democracy, for peace, for freedom, and for the self-determination of our nation. And self-determination
means for us—us in the Federal Republic, as well—that we respect your
opinion. We will not and do not want to patronize anymore. We will respect
what you decide for the future of this country.

Dear friends, I came here today to the talks with your Prime Minister,
Hans Modrow, in order to help the GDR in this difficult situation. We will
not abandon our fellow countrymen and countrywomen in the GDR. And we
know—allow me to say that here, even in view of this enthusiasm, which de-
lights me greatly—how difficult this road to the future is. But together we
will travel this road into the German future! Today was my first meeting with
Prime Minister Modrow. Both of us are aware that in this historical
hour—regardless of our different political heritages—we must try to do our
duty for our people.

It was a first discussion, it was also a serious discussion, and it accomplished positive results. We agreed to work intensely in the next few weeks

so that as early as spring we will be able to ratify a treaty about cooperation between the Federal Republic of Germany and the GDR. We seek close cooperation in all areas: in the spheres of economics, transportation, environmental protection, in the domains of social policy and of culture. Above all, we seek in the sphere of economics the closest possible cooperation, with the clear aim of improving living conditions here in the GDR as quickly as possible. We want people to feel comfortable here. We want them to remain in their homeland and be able to find happiness here. It is decisive for the future that people in Germany be able to come together, that free movement in both directions be permanently guaranteed.

We want people in Germany to be able to meet wherever they want to. Dear friends, in the coming year you will have free elections. You will decide freely who will sit in your parliament, provided with your trust. You will have a freely elected government. And then the time will have come for what I have called "confederative structures"—that means: joint governmental committees, joint parliamentary committees—so that in Germany we can live with as many common interests as possible. And let me also say, on this square that is rich in tradition, that my goal is—whenever the historical hour allows it—the unity of our nation.

Dear friends, I know that we can reach this goal and that this hour will come if we work for it together—and if we do it with reason and with good judgment, with a sense for what is possible. It is a difficult road, but it is a good road; our common future is at stake. I also know that this cannot be reached from one day to the next. We Germans do not live alone in Europe and in the world. A glance at the map demonstrates that everything that changes here must have consequences for our neighbors, for our neighbors to the east and for our neighbors to the west. It makes no sense not to acknowledge that many will watch with apprehension, and some even with fear, as we take this road. But no good can come of fears. As Germans we have to tell our neighbors: Considering the history of this century, we understand some of these fears. We will take them seriously.

Naturally, we want to represent the interests we have as Germans. We affirm the right of self-determination to which all people of this world are entitled—even the Germans. But if we want to realize this right of self-determination for the Germans, we cannot disregard the security needs of others. We want a world with more peace and more freedom, a world that knows more togetherness and no more confrontation. The "German house"—our common house—must be built under a European roof. That must be the aim of our politics. In a few days the nineties will begin, the last decade of this century. It has been a century in which, above all in Europe and also here in Germany, there has been much poverty, much misery, many deaths, much sorrow—a century that laid upon us Germans a special responsibility—in view of the terrible things that happened.

Here at the ruins of the Church of Our Lady in Dresden, a memorial to those killed in Dresden, I laid down a wreath—to commemorate the suffering and remember those who died in this spectacularly beautiful old German city. In 1945—and I say this to the young people here on the square—I was 15 years old, a schoolboy, a child. I then had the chance to grow up "on the other side," in my homeland in the Palatinate, and I belong to that young generation who took an oath after the war—just as you did here—"Never again war, never again violence!" I would like to add to this oath, while standing here in front of you: in the future, only peace should ever have its source on German soil—that is the aim of our commonality!

But, dear friends, true peace is not possible without freedom. That is why you are fighting, that is why you are demonstrating for freedom in the GDR, that is why we support you, and that is why you deserve our solidarity. Dear friends, we are only a couple of days away from Christmas—the celebration of peace. Christmas, that is the holiday for family and friends. Especially in these days, we in Germany feel ourselves to be a German family again. All of us have felt this during these weeks and days. Let me remind us all of the moving images we saw in the middle of Germany in September, in October, in November—of those images that showed how friends and relatives met each other again; we waited for that for over forty years. We are thankful that we can experience this now. All this did not happen by itself. Many people helped bring it about, not least of whom were the citizens on the streets and squares of the GDR. But in the outside world many also helped. And I have good reasons for mentioning Michail Gorbachev's politics of *perestroika*, which also created these possibilities, the Solidarity freedom movement in Poland, the reformers in Hungary.

Dear friends, we are thankful for this. Now it is a matter of continuing peacefully down this road in the time that lies ahead of us, with patience, with good judgment, and together with our neighbors. Let us work together for this goal, let us help each other in a spirit of solidarity. I greet from here in Dresden all our fellow countrymen and countrywomen in the GDR and in the Federal Republic of Germany. I wish all of you and us a peaceful Christmas, a happy 1990.

God bless our German fatherland!

Source: Richard R. Gray and Sabine Wilke, eds. and trans., *German Unification and Its Discontents* (Seattle: University of Washington Press, 1996).

Document 8

GÜNTHER GRASS ATTACKING THE POPULAR
IMPULSES FOR REUNIFICATION

The idea of unification had widespread appeal within the East German populace. Nevertheless, there was a minority composed mainly of intellectuals and professionals that had no desire to see East Germany lose its independence.

Günther Grass is perhaps the most well known and most vocal of these critics of unification. Born in Danzig (now Gdansk) in 1929, Grass grew up during the Nazi years and came to loathe militarism and war. In the 1950s Grass put his antimilitarism to paper in his novel *The Tin Drum*, a work that launched his career and thrust him into the world literary spotlight. His works since then have elevated him to Germany's best-known living author.

Grass never hid the fact that he was against unification. In his own writings and in interviews with the news media, he repeatedly expressed his misgivings about West German capitalism and the loss of those East German socialist freedoms he thought might have been preserved. Grass's position on unification has not softened with time. His 1995 book *A Wide Field* (*Ein Breites Feld*) attests to his continuing distrust of the new Germany. The following essay is taken from *Two States—One Nation?*, a collection of compositions published in 1990, in which Grass gives his personal reflections on the unification drive.

SHORT SPEECH BY A ROOTLESS COSMOPOLITAN (1990)

Shortly before Christmas, on my way to Lübeck from Göttingen, I was changing trains in Hamburg when a young man approached me, practically cornered me, and called me a traitor to the fatherland. He left me standing there with the phrase echoing in my ears. Then, after I had more or less calmly bought myself a newspaper, he approached me again, now with no mild threat but the statement that it was time to do away with my kind.

My initial anger I managed to shake off while still on the platform, but my thoughts kept returning to the incident as I continued on to Lübeck. "Traitor to the fatherland." The expression, paired with the term "rootless cosmopolitan," belongs to the special vocabulary of German history. Perhaps the young man was right when he spoke that way in cold rage. Isn't it true that I don't give a damn for a fatherland for whose sake my kind should be done away with?

The fact is, I fear a Germany simplified from two states into one. I reject this simplification, and would be much relieved if it did not come about—

either because we Germans finally saw the light, or because our neighbors put their foot down.

I realize, of course, that my position will arouse protest—or, worse, hostility—and I'm thinking not only of the young man in the Hamburg railroad station. These days the *Frankfurter Allgemeine Zeitung* is making short work of those it labels leftist intellectuals. The paper's publishers aren't satisfied to see that communism is bankrupt; they want democratic socialism too to be defunct, including Dubček's dream of socialism with a human face. Our capitalists and communists have always had one thing in common: out of hand they condemn the Third Way. That is why any suggestion that the German Democratic Republic and its citizens have finally achieved autonomy immediately gets shouted down with statistics on the number of people who have fled to the West. That a new identity, painfully acquired over the course of forty years of suppression, has at last asserted itself in a revolution—this is permitted to appear only in small print. The headlines meanwhile create the impression that what triumphed in Leipzig and Dresden, in Rostock and East Berlin, was not the people of the GDR but Western capitalism. And already they are cashing in.

No sooner does one ideology loosen its grip than another swoops down and seizes the prey. The new instrument of torture will be the market economy. If you don't toe the line, you won't get anything. Not even bananas.

No, I don't want an obscenely boastful fatherland fattened by swooping down and seizing—though I have nothing at my disposal to prevent the creation of this monster, nothing except a few ideas. Already I fear that reunification, under whatever subterfuge, is inevitable. The strong Deutschmark will see to that; the Springer press conglomerate, with its mass circulation, now in concert with Rudolf Augstein's flippant epistles in each Monday's *Spiegel*, will see to that; and German amnesia will do its part.

In the end we'll number eighty million. Once more we'll be united, strong, and our voice—even if we speak softly—will be loud and clear. Eventually, because enough is never enough, we'll succeed, with our strong currency and after formal recognition of Poland's western border, in subjugating economically a large chunk of Silesia and a small chunk of Pomerania, and so once more—following the German fairy-tale pattern—we will be feared and isolated.

I am already a traitor to this fatherland. Any fatherland of mine must be more diverse, more colorful, more neighborly—a fatherland that has grown, though suffering, wiser and more open to Europe.

It comes down to a choice between a nightmare and a dream. Why can't we help the German Democratic Republic, through the institution of a just and long overdue *equalizing of the burden*, to achieve enough economic and democratic stability that its citizens will find it easier to stay home? Why do we insist on saddling the idea of a German confederation—an idea that could be acceptable to our neighbors—with vague notions borrowed from the 1848 constitutional assembly at St. Paul's in Frankfurt, or, as if we had no other choice, with the model of a super-Federal Republic? Isn't a German confederation already more than we ever dared hope for? An all-embracing unity, expanded territory, concentrated economic power—is this the goal we should pursue, or isn't all that far too much?

Since the mid-sixties, in speeches and articles I have spoken out against reunification and in favor of a confederation. Here, once more, I will answer the German Question. Briefly—not in ten points, but in five:

1. A German confederation puts an end to the postwar relationship of the two German states, that of one foreign country to another. It eliminates a vile border that also has divided Europe; at the same time it respects the concerns, even fears, of Germany's neighbors by constitutionally renouncing the goal of unifying into a single state.

2. A confederation of two German states does not do violence to the postwar evolution of either state. Rather, it permits something new: an independent togetherness. At the same time, a confederation is sufficiently sovereign to fulfill both states' obligations to their respective alliances, thereby reinforcing the European security concept.

3. A confederation of two German states dovetails better with the current process of European integration than does a single powerful state, since an integrated Europe will itself be confederate in structure and must therefore transcend the traditional divisions into nation-states.

4. A confederation of two German states points the way to a new, different, and desirable self-definition that would include joint responsibility for German history. This understanding of cultural nationhood takes up where the efforts of the St. Paul's assembly failed. It implies a modern, broader concept of culture, and embraces the multiplicity of German culture without needing to assert unity in the sense of a nation-state.

5. A confederation of the two states that make up the German cultural nation would provide an example for the solution of different yet comparable conflicts throughout the world, whether in Korea, Ireland, Cyprus, or the Middle East—wherever one political entity has aggressively established borders or seeks to extend them at the expense of another. A German confederation could become a model to emulate.

A few additional comments. A unified German state existed, in varying sizes, for no more than seventy-five years: as the German Reich under Prussian rule; as the Weimar Republic, precarious from the outset; and finally, until unconditional surrender, as the Greater German Reich. We should be aware—as our neighbors are—of how much grief this unified state caused, of what misfortune it brought to others and to ourselves as well. The crime of genocide, summed up in the image of Auschwitz, inexcusable from whatever angle you view it, weighs on the conscience of this unified state.

Never before in their history had the Germans brought down upon themselves such terrifying shame. Until then, they were no better and no worse than other peoples. But the megalomania born of their complexes led them to reject the possibility of being a cultural nation within a federation to insist instead on the creation of a unified state in the form of a Reich—by any and all means. This state laid the foundation for Auschwitz. It formed the power base for the latent anti-Semitism that existed in other places as well. It helped provide an appallingly firm foundation for the racial ideology of National Socialism.

There is no way to avoid this conclusion. Anyone thinking about Germany these days and looking for an answer to the German Question must include Auschwitz in his thoughts. That place of terror, that permanent wound, makes a future unified German state impossible. And if such a state is nevertheless insisted upon, it will be doomed to failure.

More than two decades ago in Tutzing the notion of "change through rapprochement" was formulated; argued over for a long time, the concept eventually proved correct. By now, rapprochement has become accepted policy. In the GDR, change has occurred as a result of the revolutionary will of the people. What hasn't changed yet is the Federal Republic of Germany, whose people have been watching the events over there with a mixture of admiration and condescension: "We don't want to tell you what to do, but . . . "

Already they are poking their noses in. Help—real help—is given only on West German terms. Property, yes, they say, but no "people's property," please. The western ideology of capitalism, which aims to wipe out every other kind of ideological ism, announces, as if holding a gun to the East Germans' head: A market economy or else.

And who wouldn't put up his hands and surrender to the blessing of one whose lack of human decency is so plainly outweighed by his strength and success? I am afraid that we Germans will also let this second chance for self-definition slip by. To be a cultural nation in confederative pluralism apparently does not satisfy us; and "rapprochement through change" is asking too much—because it's too expensive. But the German Question can't be solved by working it out in marks and pfennigs.

What was it that young man in the Hamburg railroad station said? He was right. If sides must be drawn, let me be numbered among the rootless cosmopolitans.

Source: Günther Grass, *Two States—One Nation?* (Frankfurt am Main: Luchterhand Literaturverlag GmbH, 1990; English translation, San Diego: Harcourt, Brace, Jovanovich, 1990).

Document 9
NATO'S LONDON DECLARATION

What may be the single most important document of the German unification period is often overlooked. Unification would not have been possible without the consent of the four victorious allies from World War II. The main stumbling block to such consensus was the Soviet Union, where Mikhail Gorbachev was under pressure from conservative hardliners critical of *glasnost* and *perestroika*. The loss of the GDR to a new Germany, and the entry of that new state into the North Atlantic Treaty Organization (NATO), might just be the provocation that the right wing of the Communist Party of the Soviet Union could use to oust Gorbachev and end his experiment. Gorbachev, therefore, could not consent to unification unless the West made some concomitant assurances that German unification and entry into NATO posed no threat to the Soviet Union.

The London Declaration of July 6, 1990, actually concedes more than Gorbachev needed. Although it does recapitulate the defensive nature of the alliance, it calls for reductions in the amount of NATO troops and weaponry as a response to decreased Soviet involvement in central Europe. Further, the declaration envisions that the former Warsaw Pact nations would eventually receive an invitation to join the alliance. In short, the document provides a blueprint for the transformation of NATO. It would now deemphasize its historical character as a military alliance in order to reconstitute itself as a social and political cooperative of nations.

1. Europe has entered a new, promising era. Central and Eastern Europe is liberating itself. The Soviet Union has embarked on the long journey toward a free society. The walls that once confined people and ideas are collapsing. Europeans are determining their own destiny. They are choosing freedom. They are choosing a Europe whole and free. As a consequence, this Alliance must and will adapt.

2. The North Atlantic Alliance has been the most successful defensive alliance in history. As our Alliance enters its fifth decade and looks ahead to a new century, it must continue to provide for the common defense. This Alliance has done much to bring about the new Europe. No one, however, can

be certain of the future. We need to keep standing together, to extend the long peace we have enjoyed these past four decades. Yet our Alliance must be even more an agent of change. It can help build the structures of a more united continent, supporting security and stability with the strength of our shared faith in democracy, the rights of the individual, and the peaceful resolution of the disputes. We reaffirm that security and stability do not lie solely in the military dimension, and we intend to enhance the political component of our Alliance as provided for by Article 2 of our Treaty.

3. The unification of Germany means that the division of Europe is also being overcome. A united Germany in the Atlantic Alliance of free democracies and part of the growing political and economic integration of the European Community will be an indispensable factor of stability, which is needed in the heart of Europe. The move within the European Community towards political union, including the development of a European identity in the domain of security, will also contribute to Atlantic solidarity and to the establishment of a just and lasting order of peace throughout the whole of Europe.

4. We recognize that, in the new Europe, the security of every state is inseparably linked to the security of its neighbours. NATO must become not only an institution where Europeans, Canadians and Americans work together not only for the common defense, but to build new partnerships with all the nations of Europe. The Atlantic Community must reach out to the countries of the East which were our adversaries in the Cold War, and extend to them the hand of friendship.

5. We will remain a defensive alliance and will continue to defend all the territory of all our members. We have no aggressive intentions and we commit ourselves to the peaceful resolution of all disputes. We will never in any circumstance be the first to use force.

6. The member states of the North Atlantic Alliance propose to the member states of the Warsaw Treaty Organization a joint declaration in which we solemnly state that we are no longer adversaries and reaffirm our intention to refrain from the threat or use of force against the territorial integrity or political independence of any state, or from acting in any other manner inconsistent with the purposes and principles of the United Nations Charter and with the CSCE [Conference on Security and Cooperation in Europe] Final Act. We invite all other CSCE member states to join us in this commitment to non-aggression.

7. In that spirit, and to reflect the changing political role of the Alliance, we today invite President Gorbachev on behalf of the Soviet Union, and representatives of the other Central and Eastern European countries to come to

Brussels and address the North Atlantic Council. We today also invite the governments of the Union of Soviet Socialist Republics, the Czech and Slovak Federal Republic, the Hungarian Republic, the Republic of Poland, the People's Republic of Bulgaria and Romania to come to NATO, not just to visit, but to establish regular diplomatic liaison with NATO. This will make it possible for us to share with them our thinking and deliberations in this historic period of change.

8. Our Alliance will do its share to overcome the legacy of decades of suspicion. We are ready to intensify military contacts, including those of NATO Military Commanders, with Moscow and other Central and Eastern European capitals.

9. We welcome the invitation to NATO Secretary General Manfred Wörner to visit Moscow and meet with Soviet leaders.

10. Military leaders from throughout Europe gathered earlier this year in Vienna to talk about their forces and doctrine. NATO proposes another such meeting this Autumn to promote common understanding. We intend to establish an entirely different quality of openness in Europe, including an agreement on "Open Skies."

11. The significant presence of North American conventional and US nuclear forces in Europe demonstrates the underlying political compact that binds North America's fate to Europe's democracies. But, as Europe changes, we must profoundly alter the way we think about defense.

12. To reduce our military requirements, sound arms control agreements are essential. That is why we put the highest priority on completing this year the first treaty to reduce and limit conventional armed forces in Europe (CFE) along with the completion of a meaningful CSBM [Confidence- and Security-Building Measures] package. These talks should remain in continuous session until the work is done. Yet we hope to go further. We propose that, once a CFE [Conventional Forces in Europe] Treaty is signed, follow-on talks should begin with the same membership and mandate, with the goal of building on the current agreement with additional measures, including measures to limit manpower in Europe. With this goal in mind, a commitment will be given at the time of signature of the CFE Treaty concerning the manpower levels of a unified Germany.

13. Our objective will be to conclude the negotiations on the follow-on to CFE and CSBMs as soon as possible and looking to the follow-up meeting of the CSCE to be held in Helsinki in 1992. We will seek through new conventional arms control negotiations, within the CSCE framework, further far-reaching measures in the 1990s to limit the offensive capability of conventional armed forces in Europe, so as to prevent any nation from maintain-

ing disproportionate military power on the continent. NATO's High Level Task Force will formulate a detailed position for these follow-on conventional arms control talks. We will make provisions as needed for different regions to redress disparities and to ensure that no one's security is harmed at any stage. Furthermore, we will continue to explore broader arms control and confidence-building opportunities. This is an ambitious agenda, but it matches our goal: enduring peace in Europe.

14. As Soviet troops leave Eastern Europe and a treaty limiting conventional armed forces is implemented, the Alliance's integrated force structure and its strategy will change fundamentally to include the following elements:

> NATO will field smaller and restructured active forces. These forces will be highly mobile and versatile so that Allied leaders will have maximum flexibility in deciding how to respond to a crisis. It will rely increasingly on multinational corps made up of national units.

> NATO will scale back the readiness of its active units, reducing training requirements and the number of exercises.

> NATO will rely more heavily on the ability to build up larger forces if and when they might be needed.

15. To keep the peace, the Alliance must maintain for the foreseeable future an appropriate mix of nuclear and conventional forces, based in Europe, and kept up to date where necessary. But, as a defensive Alliance, NATO has always stressed that none of its weapons will ever be used except in self-defense and that we seek the lowest and most stable level of nuclear forces needed to secure the prevention of war.

16. The political and military changes in Europe, and the prospects of further changes, now allow the Allies concerned to go further. They will thus modify the size and adapt the tasks of their nuclear deterrent forces. They have concluded that, as a result of the new political and military conditions in Europe, there will be a significantly reduced role for substrategic nuclear systems of the shortest range. They have decided specifically that, once negotiations begin on short-range nuclear forces, the Alliance will propose, in return for reciprocal action by the Soviet Union, the elimination of all its nuclear artillery shells from Europe.

17. New negotiations between the United States and the Soviet Union on the reduction of short-range nuclear forces should begin shortly after a CFE agreement is signed. The Allies concerned will develop an arms control framework for these negotiations which take into account our requirements

for far fewer nuclear weapons, and the diminished need for sub-strategic nuclear systems of the shortest range.

18. Finally, with the total withdrawal of Soviet stationed forces and the implementation of a CFE agreement, the Allies concerned can reduce their reliance on nuclear weapons. These will continue to fulfill an essential role in the overall strategy of the Alliance to prevent war by ensuring that there are no circumstances in which nuclear retaliation in response to military action might be discounted. However, in the transformed Europe, they will be able to adopt a new NATO strategy making nuclear forces truly weapons of last resort.

19. We approve the mandate given in Turnberry to the North Atlantic Council in Permanent Session to oversee the ongoing work on the adaptation of the Alliance to the new circumstances. It should report its conclusions as soon as possible.

20. In the context of these revised plans for defense and arms control, and with the advice of NATO Military Authorities and all member states concerned, NATO will prepare a new Allied military strategy moving away from "forward defense," where appropriate, towards a reduced forward presence and modifying "flexible response" to reflect a reduced reliance on nuclear weapons. In that connection, NATO will elaborate new force plans consistent with the revolutionary changes in Europe. NATO will also provide a forum for Allied consultation on the upcoming negotiations on short-range nuclear forces.

21. The Conference on Security and Cooperation in Europe (CSCE) should become more prominent in Europe's future, bringing together the countries of Europe and North America. We support a CSCE Summit later this year in Paris which would include the signature of a CFE agreement and would set new standards for the establishment, and preservation, of free societies. It should endorse, inter alia:

> CSCE principles on the right to free and fair elections;

> CSCE commitments to respect and uphold the rule of law;

> CSCE guidelines for enhancing economic cooperation, based on the development of free and competitive market economies; and

> CSCE cooperation on environmental protection.

22. We further propose that the CSCE Summit in Paris decide how the CSCE can be institutionalized to provide a forum for wider political dialogue in a more united Europe. We recommend that the CSCE governments establish:

> a programme for regular consultations among member governments at the Heads of State and Government or Ministerial level, at least

once each year, with other periodic meetings of officials to prepare for and follow up on these consultations;

a schedule of CSCE review conferences once every two years to assess progress toward a Europe whole and free;

a small CSCE secretariat to coordinate these meetings and conferences;

a CSCE mechanism to monitor elections in all the CSCE countries, on the basis of the Copenhagen Document;

a CSCE Centre for the Prevention of Conflict that might serve as a forum for exchanges of military information, discussion of unusual military activities, and the conciliation of disputes involving CSCE member states; and

a CSCE parliamentary body, the Assembly of Europe, to be based on the existing parliamentary assembly of the Council of Europe, in Strasbourg, and include representatives of all CSCE member states.

The sites of these new institutions should reflect the fact that the newly democratic countries of Central and Eastern Europe form part of the political structures of the new Europe.

23. Today, our Alliance begins a major transformation. Working with all the countries of Europe, we are determined to create enduring peace on this continent.

Source: Historic Documents of 1990 (Washington DC: Congressional Quarterly, 1991).

Document 10
RESOLUTION ON THE GERMAN-POLISH FRONTIER

The transformation of NATO did much to persuade the Soviet Union to accept German unification, but it did little to relieve Polish anxieties over the issue of their border with East Germany. Theoretically, a newly united Germany might lay claim to the Oder-Neisse territories that were ceded to Poland at the end of World War II. Some sort of agreement seemed necessary.

Although he was more than willing to grant such assurances, Chancellor Kohl could do little better than promise a joint resolution of the West German and East German legislators, with the understanding that the first order of business of the Bundestag of a reunited Germany would be a treaty with Poland recognizing existing borders. The following resolution was debated and passed by the West German Bundestag on June 21, 1990, just before the Two-plus-Four talks began. That same day, the East German People's Chamber passed an identical resolution.

RESOLUTION OF THE GERMAN-POLISH FRONTIER

The German Bundestag,

- conscious of its responsibility in the light of German and European history,

- firmly resolved to help achieve in free self-determination the unity and freedom of Germany so that Germany will serve the peace and freedom of the world as an equal partner in a united Europe based on the rule of law and respect for human rights,

- anxious to make a contribution through German unity to the development of a peaceful order in Europe in which frontiers no longer divide, which enables all European nations to live together in mutual trust and engage in comprehensive co-operation for the common benefit, and which ensured lasting peace, freedom and stability,

- conscious of the terrible suffering inflicted on the Polish people through crimes perpetrated by Germans and in the name of Germany,

- conscious of the great injustice done to millions of Germans who have been ex-pelled from their native regions,

- desiring that a united Germany and the Republic of Poland, mindful of the tragic and painful chapters of history, systematically continue the policy of understand-ing and reconciliation between Germans and Poles, shape their relations with a view to the future and thus set an example of good-neighborliness,

- convinced that special importance attaches to the young generation's commit-ment to reconciliation of the two nations,

- expecting the freely elected People's Chamber of the GDR to issue simultane-ously an identical declaration,

expresses its will that the course of the frontier between the united Germany and the Republic of Poland be definitively confirmed, by a treaty under in-ternational law, as follows:

The course of the frontier between the united Germany and the Republic of Poland shall be as specified in the "Agreement between the German Democratic Republic and the Polish Republic concerning the Demarcation of the Established and Existing German-Polish State Frontier" of 6 July 1950 as well as the accords implementing and supplementing the aforemen-tioned agreement (Treaty of 22 May 1989 between the German Democratic Republic and the Polish People's Republic on the Delimitation of the Sea Areas in the Oder Bay. Instrument of 27 January 1951 confirming the De-marcation of the State Frontier between Germany and Poland) and by the "Treaty between the Federal Republic of Germany and the Polish People's

Republic concerning the basis for Normalizing their Mutual Relations" of 7 December 1970.

The two sides reaffirm the inviolability of the frontier existing between them now and in the future and undertake to respect each other's sovereignty and territorial integrity without restriction.

The two sides declare that they have no territorial claims whatsoever against each other and that they will not assert such claims in the future.

The Government of the Federal Republic of Germany is formally called upon to communicate this resolution to the Republic of Poland as the expression of its will.

Source: The Unification of Germany in 1990: A Documentation (Bonn: Press and Information Office of the Federal Government, 1991).

Document 11
TREATY OF AUGUST 31, 1990, BETWEEN THE FEDERAL REPUBLIC OF GERMANY AND THE GERMAN DEMOCRATIC REPUBLIC ON THE ESTABLISHMENT OF GERMAN UNITY (UNIFICATION TREATY)

The Unification Treaty laid out the agreement necessary for the amalgamation of East German and West German institutions into common German institutions. Negotiations began in July 1990 and culminated with the signing less than two months later. Representing West Germany in the negotiations was Wolfgang Schäuble, federal minister of the interior. GDR State Secretary Günther Krause headed the negotiation team from East Germany. The process was not without major disagreements. Financial and property matters proved to be difficult issues. What role should the new states play in the overall taxation and revenue distribution scheme of a new German nation? Should the new state address the claims of property owners who had their land appropriated by the communist state? Some social issues, including women's reproductive rights, proved too vexing to solve within the time framework and were left for future resolution.

Considering that two German states had existed apart for forty years with differing institutions and laws, it is telling of East Germany's desire for immediate unification that a consensus could be reached at all. On August 31, 1990, the principles signed the treaty in East Berlin. The treaty came into force the day East Germany acceded to the Basic Law (October 3, 1990). What follows are excerpts from the treaty.

TEXT OF THE TREATY (WITHOUT ANNEXES)

The Federal Republic of Germany and the German Democratic Republic,

Resolved to achieve in free self-determination the unity of Germany in peace and freedom as an equal partner in the community of nations,

Mindful of the desire of the people in both parts of Germany to live together in peace and freedom in a democratic and social federal state governed by the rule of law,

In grateful respect to those who peacefully helped freedom prevail and who have unswervingly adhered to the task of establishing German unity and are achieving it,

Aware of the continuity of German history and bearing in mind the special responsibility arising from our past for a democratic development in Germany committed to respect for human rights and to peace,

Seeking through German unity to contribute to the unification of Europe and to the building of a peaceful European order in which borders no longer divide and which ensures that all European nations can live together in a spirit of mutual trust,

Aware that the inviolability of frontiers and of the territorial integrity and sovereignty of all states in Europe within their frontiers constitutes a fundamental condition for peace,

Have agreed to conclude a Treaty on the Establishment of German Unity, containing the following provisions:

Chapter I
Effect of Accession

Article 1
Länder

(1) Upon the accession of the German Democratic Republic to the Federal Republic of Germany in accordance with Article 23 of the Basic Law taking effect on 3 October 1990 the Länder of Brandenburg, Mecklenburg-Western Pomerania, Saxony, Saxony-Anhalt and Thuringia shall become Länder of the Federal Republic of Germany. The establishment of these Länder and their boundaries shall be governed by the provisions of the Constitutional Act of 22 July 1990 on the Establishment of Länder in the German Democratic Republic (Länder Establishment Act) (Law Gazette I, No. 51, p. 955) in accordance with Annex II.

(2) The 23 boroughs of Berlin shall form Land Berlin.

Article 2
Capital City, Day of German Unity

(1) The capital of Germany shall be Berlin. The seat of the parliament and government shall be decided after the establishment of German unity.

(2) 3 October shall be a public holiday known as the Day of German Unity.

Chapter II
Basic Law

Article 3
Entry into Force of the Basic Law

Upon the accession taking effect, the Basic Law of the Federal Republic of Germany, as published in the Federal Law Gazette Part III, No. 100–1, and last amended by the Act of 21 December 1983 (Federal Law Gazette I, p. 1481), shall enter into force in the Länder of Brandenburg, Mecklenburg--Western Pomerania, Saxony, Saxony-Anhalt and Thuringia and in that part of Land Berlin where it has not been valid to date, subject to the amendments arising from Article 4, unless otherwise provided in this Treaty.

Article 4
Amendments to the Basic Law Resulting from Accession

The Basic Law of the Federal Republic of Germany shall be amended as follows:

1. The preamble shall read as follows:
"Conscious of their responsibility before God and men,
Animated by the resolve to serve world peace as an equal partner in a united Europe, the German people have adopted, by virtue of their constituent power, this Basic Law.

The German in the Länder of Baden-Württemberg, Bavaria, Berlin, Brandenburg, Bremen, Hamburg, Hesse, Lower Saxony, Mecklenburg-Western Pomerania, North-Rhine/Westphalia, Rhineland-Palatinate, Saarland, Saxony, Saxony-Anhalt, Schleswig-Holstein and Thuringia have achieved the unity and freedom of Germany in free self-determination. This Basic Law is thus valid for the entire German people."

2. Article 23 shall be repealed.

3. Article 51 (2) shall read as follows:
"(2) Each Land shall have at least three votes; Länder with more than two million inhabitants shall have four, Länder with more than six million inhabitants five, and Länder with more than seven million inhabitants six votes."

4. The existing text of Article 135a shall become paragraph 1. The following paragraph shall be inserted after paragraph 1:
"(2) Paragraph 1 above shall be applied mutatis mutandis to liabilities of the German Democratic Republic or its legal entities as well as to liabilities

of the Federation or other corporate bodies and institutions under public law which are connected with the transfer of properties for the German Democratic Republic to the Federation, Länder and communes (Gemeinden), and to liabilities arising from measures taken by the German Democratic Republic or its legal entities."

5. The following new Article 143 shall be inserted in the Basic Law:
"Article 143

(1) Law in the territory specified in Article 3 of the Unification Treaty may deviate from provisions of this Basic Law for a period not extending beyond 31 December 1992 in so far as and as long as no complete adjustment to the order of the Basic Law can be achieved as a consequence of the different conditions. Deviations must not violate Article 19 (2) and must be compatible with the principles set out in Article 79 (3).

(2) Deviations from sections II, VIII, VIIIa, IX, X, and XI are permissible for a period not extending beyond 31 December 1995.

(3) Notwithstanding paragraphs 1 and 2 above, Article 41 of the Unification Treaty and the rules for its implementation shall remain valid in so far as they provide for the irreversibility of interferences with property in the territory specified in Article 3 of the said Treaty."

6. Article 146 shall read as follows:
"Article 146

This Basic Law, which is valid for the entire German people following the achievement of the unity and freedom of Germany, shall cease to be in force on the day on which a constitution adopted by a free decision of the German people comes into force."

Article 5
Future Amendments to the Constitution

The Governments of the two Contracting Parties recommend to the legislative bodies of the united Germany that within two years they should deal with the questions regarding amendments or additions to the Basic Law as raised in connection with German unification, in particular

- with regard to the relationship between the Federation and the Länder in accordance with the Joint Resolution of the Minister Presidents of 5 July 1990,

- with regard to the possibility of restructuring the Berlin/Brandenburg area in derogation of the provisions of Article 29 of the Basic Law by way of an agreement between the Länder concerned,

- with considerations on introducing state objectives into the Basic Law, and

- with the question of applying Article 146 of the Basic Law and of holding the referendum in this context.

Chapter III
Harmonization of Law

Article 8
Extension of Federal Law

Upon the accession taking effect, federal law shall enter into force in the territory specified in Article 3 of this Treaty unless its area of application is restricted to certain Länder or parts of Länder of the Federal Republic of Germany and unless otherwise provided in this Treaty, notably Annex I.

Article 9
Continued Validity of Law of the German Democratic Republic

(1) Law of the German Democratic Republic valid at the time of the signing of this Treaty which is Land law according to the distribution of competence under the Basic Law shall remain in force in so far as it is compatible with the Basic Law, notwithstanding Article 143, with the federal law put into force in the territory specified in Article 3 of this Treaty and with the directly applicable law of the European Communities, and unless otherwise provided in this Treaty. Law of the German Democratic Republic which is federal law according to the distribution of competence under the Basic Law and which refers to matters not regulated uniformly at the federal level shall continue to be valid as Land law under the conditions set out in the first sentence pending a settlement by the federal legislator.

(2) The law of the German Democratic Republic referred to in Annex II shall remain in force with the provisos set out there in so far as it is compatible with the Basic Law, taking this Treaty into consideration, and with the directly applicable law of the European Communities.

(3) Law of the German Democratic Republic enacted after the signing of this Treaty shall remain in force to the extent agreed between the Contracting Parties. Paragraph 2 above shall remain unaffected.

Article 10
Law of the European Communities

(1) Upon the accession taking effect, the Treaties on the European Communities together with their amendments and supplements as well as the international agreements, treaties and resolutions which have come into force in connection with those Treaties shall apply in the territory specified in Article 3 of this Treaty.

(2) Upon the accession taking effect, the legislative acts enacted on the basis of the Treaties on the European Communities shall apply in the territory specified in Article 3 of this Treaty unless the competent institutions of

the European Communities enact exemptions. These exemptions are intended to take account of administrative requirements and help avoid economic difficulties.

(3) Legislative acts of the European Communities whose implementation or execution comes under the responsibility of the Länder shall be implemented or executed by the latter through provisions under Land law.

Chapter IV
International Treaties and Agreements

Article 11
Treaties of the Federal Republic of Germany

The Contracting Parties proceed on the understanding that international treaties and agreements to which the Federal Republic of Germany is a contracting party, including treaties establishing membership of international organizations or institutions, shall retain their validity and that the rights and obligations arising therefrom, with the exception of the treaties named in Annex I, shall also relate to the territory specified in Article 3 of this Treaty. Where adjustments become necessary in individual cases, the all-German Government shall consult with the respective contracting parties.

Article 12
Treaties of the German Democratic Republic

(1) The Contracting Parties are agreed that, in connection with the establishment of German unity, international treaties of the German Democratic Republic shall be discussed with the contracting parties concerned with a view to regulating or confirming their continued application, adjustment or expiry, taking into account protection of confidence, the interests of the states concerned, the treaty obligations of the Federal Republic of Germany as well as the principles of a free, democratic basic order governed by the rule of law, and respecting the competence of the European Communities.

(2) The united Germany shall determine its position with regard to the adoption of international treaties of the German Democratic Republic following consultations with the respective contracting parties and with the European Communities where the latter's competence is affected.

(3) Should the united Germany intend to accede to international organizations or other multilateral treaties of which the German Democratic Republic but not the Federal Republic of Germany is a member, agreement shall be reached with the respective contracting parties and with the European Communities where the latter's competence is affected.

Chapter VII
Labour, Social Welfare, Family, Women, Public Health and Environmental Protection

Article 30
Labour and Social Welfare

(1) It shall be the task of the all-German legislator

1. to recodify in a uniform manner and as soon as possible the law on employment contracts and the provisions on working hours under public law, including the admissibility of work on Sundays and public holidays, and the specific industrial safety regulations for women;

2. to bring public law on industrial safety into line with present-day requirements in accordance with the law of the European Communities and the concurrent part of the industrial safety law of the German Democratic Republic.

(2) Employed persons in the territory specified in Article 3 of this Treaty shall be entitled, upon reaching the age of 57, to receive early retirement payments for a period of three years, but not beyond the earliest possible date on which they become entitled to receive a retirement pension under the statutory pension scheme. The early retirement payment shall amount to 65 percent of the last average net earnings; for employed persons whose entitlement arises on or before 1 April 1991 early retirement payments shall be raised by an increment of five percentage points for the first 312 days. The early retirement payments shall be made by the Federal Institute for Employment along similar lines to unemployment pay, notably the provisions of Section 105c of the Employment Promotion Act. The Federal Institute for Employment may reject an application if it is established that there is a clear lack of manpower in the region to carry out the occupational duties so far discharged by the applicant. The early retirement payments shall be refunded by the Federation in so far as they reach beyond the period of entitlement to unemployment pay. The provisions on early retirement payments shall be applied to new claims up to 31 December 1991. The period of validity may be prolonged by one year.

In the period from this Treaty taking effect up to 31 December 1990, women shall be entitled, on reaching the age of 55, to receive early retirement payments for a period not exceeding five years.

(3) The social welfare supplement to pension, accident and unemployment payments introduced in the territory specified in Article 3 of this Treaty in conjunction with the Treaty of 18 May 1990 shall be limited to new

cases up to 31 December 1991. The payments shall be made for a period not extending beyond 30 June 1995.

(4) The transfer of tasks incumbent upon the social insurance scheme to separate agencies shall take place in such a way as to ensure that payments are made and financed and sufficient staff is available to perform the said tasks. The distribution of assets and liabilities among the separate agencies shall be definitively settled by law.

Article 31
Family and Women

(1) It shall be the task of the all-German legislator to develop further the legislation on equal rights for men and women.

(2) In view of different legal and institutional starting positions with regard to the employment of mothers and fathers, it shall be the task of the all-German legislator to shape the legal situation in such a way as to allow a reconciliation of family and occupational life.

(3) In order to ensure that day care centres for children continue to operate in the territory specified in Article 3 of this Treaty, the Federation shall contribute to the costs of these centres for a transitional period up to 30 June 1991.

(4) It shall be the task of the all-German legislator to introduce regulations no later than 31 December 1992 which ensure better protection of unborn life and provide a better solution in conformity with the Constitution of conflict situations faced by pregnant women—notably through legally guaranteed entitlements for women, first and foremost to advice and public support—than is the case in either part of Germany at present. In order to achieve these objectives, a network of advice centres run by various agencies and offering blanket coverage shall be set up without delay with financial assistance from the Federation in the territory specified in Article 3 of this Treaty. The advice centres shall be provided with sufficient staff and funds to allow them to cope with the task of advising pregnant women and offering them necessary assistance, including beyond the time of confinement. In the event that no regulations are introduced within the period stated in the first sentence, the substantive law shall continue to apply in the territory specified in Article 3 of this Treaty.

Article 34
Protection of the Environment

(1) On the basis of the German environmental union established under Article 16 of the Treaty of 18 May 1990 in conjunction with the Skeleton Environment Act of the German Democratic Republic of 29 June 1990 (Law

Gazette 1, No. 42, p. 649), it shall be the task of the legislators to protect the natural basis of man's existence, with due regard for prevention, the polluter-pays principle, and cooperation, and to promote uniform ecological conditions of a high standard at least equivalent to that reached in the Federal Republic of Germany.

(2) With a view to attaining the objective defined in paragraph 1 above, ecological rehabilitation and development programmes shall be drawn up for the territory specified in Article 3 of this Treaty, in line with the distribution of competence under the Basic Law. Measures to ward off dangers to public health shall be accorded priority.

Article 37
Education

(1) School, vocational or higher education certificates or degrees obtained or officially recognized in the German Democratic Republic shall continue to be valid in the territory specified in Article 3 of this Treaty. Examinations passed and certificates obtained in the territory specified in Article 3 or in the other Länder of the Federal Republic of Germany, including Berlin (West), shall be considered equal and shall convey the same rights if they are of equal value. Their equivalence shall be established by the respective competent agency on application. Legal provisions of the Federation and the European Communities regarding the equivalence of examinations and certificates, and special provisions set out in this Treaty shall have priority. In all cases this shall not affect the right to use academic professional titles and degrees obtained or officially recognized or conferred.

(2) The usual recognition procedure operated by the Conference of Ministers of Education and Cultural Affairs shall apply to teaching diploma examinations. The said Conference shall make appropriate transitional arrangements.

(3) Examination certificates issued under the trained occupation scheme and the skilled workers' training scheme as well as final examinations and apprentices' final examinations in recognized trained occupations shall be considered equal.

(4) The regulations necessary for the reorganization of the school system in the territory specified in Article 3 of this Treaty shall be adopted by the Länder named in Article 1. The necessary regulations for the recognition of examinations under educational law shall be agreed by the Conference of Ministers of Education and Cultural Affairs. In both cases they shall be based on the Hamburg Agreement and the other relevant agreements reached by the said Conference.

(5) Undergraduates who move to another institution of higher education before completing their studies shall have their study and examination record up to that point recognized according to the principles laid down in Section 7 of the General Regulations of Degree Examination Procedures (ABD) or within the terms of the rules governing admission to state examinations.

(6) The entitlements to study at an institution of higher education confirmed on leaving certificates issued by engineering and technical schools of the German Democratic Republic shall be valid in accordance with the resolution of 10 May 1990 of the Conference of Ministers of Education and Cultural Affairs and its Annex B. Further principles and procedures for the recognition of technical school and higher education certificates for the purpose of school and college studies based on them shall be developed within the framework of the Conference of Ministers of Education and Cultural Affairs.

Article 45
Entry into Force of the Treaty

(1) This Treaty, including the attached Protocol and Annexes I to III, shall enter into force on the day on which the Governments of the Federal Republic of Germany and the German Democratic Republic have informed each other that the internal requirements for such entry into force have been fulfilled.

(2) The Treaty shall remain valid as federal law after the accession has taken effect.

Done at Berlin on 31 August 1990 in duplicate in the German language.
For the Federal Republic of Germany
Wolfgang Schäuble

For the German Democratic Republic
Günther Krause

Source: The Unification of Germany in 1990: A Documentation (Bonn: Press and Information Office of the Federal Government, 1991).

Document 12
TREATY ON THE FINAL SETTLEMENT WITH RESPECT TO GERMAN (12 SEPTEMBER 1990)

The Treaty on the Final Settlement with Respect to Germany (or simply Final Settlement) was the culmination of months of international negotiation. The document was basically a formality, since most of the critical issues already had been solved by face-to-face negotiations and codified by separate agreements. Nevertheless, the treaty finally did settle external questions (such as borders) that remained unresolved since the breakdown of quadripartite control of Germany in 1947. In that respect, the document is truly the "final settlement" of issues from World War II.

The Federal Republic of Germany, the German Democratic Republic, the French Republic, the Union of Soviet Socialist Republics, the United Kingdom of Great Britain and Northern Ireland and the United States of America,

- Conscious of the fact that their peoples have been living together in peace since 1945;
- Mindful of the recent historic changes in Europe which make it possible to overcome the division of the continent;
- Having regard to the rights and responsibilities of the Four Powers relating to Berlin and to Germany as a whole, and the corresponding wartime and post-war agreements and decisions of the Four Powers;
- Resolved in accordance with their obligations under the Charter of the United Nations to develop friendly relations among nations based on respect for the principle of equal rights and self-determination of peoples, and to take other appropriate measures to strengthen universal peace;
- Recalling the principles of the Final Act of the Conference on Security and Cooperation in Europe, signed in Helsinki;
- Recognizing that those principles have laid firm foundations for the establishment of a just and lasting peaceful order in Europe;
- Determined to take account of everyone's security interests;
- Convinced of the need finally to overcome antagonism and to develop cooperation in Europe;
- Confirming their readiness to reinforce security, in particular by adopting effective arms control, disarmament and confidence-building measures; their willingness not to regard each other as adversaries but to work for a relationship of trust and cooperation; and accordingly their readiness to consider positively setting up appropriate institutional arrangements within the framework of the Conference on Security and Cooperation in Europe;
- Welcoming the fact that the German people, freely exercising their right of self-determination, have expressed their will to bring about the unity of Germany as a state so that they will be able to serve the peace of the world as an equal and sovereign partner in a united Europe;
- Convinced that the unification of Germany as a state with definitive borders is a significant contribution to peace and stability in Europe;
- Intending to conclude the final settlement with respect to Germany;

- Recognizing that thereby, and with the unification of Germany as a democratic and peaceful state, the rights and responsibilities of the Four Powers relating to Berlin and to Germany as a whole lose their functions;

- Represented by their Ministers for Foreign Affairs who, in accordance with the Ottawa Declaration of February 13, 1990, met in Bonn on May 5, 1990, in Berlin on June 22, 1990, in Paris on July 17, 1990 with the participation of the Minister of Foreign Affairs of the Republic of Poland, and in Moscow on September 12, 1990;

Have agreed as follows:

Article 1

(1) The united Germany shall comprise the territory of the Federal Republic of Germany, the German Democratic Republic and the whole of Berlin. Its external borders shall be the borders of the Federal Republic of Germany and the German Democratic Republic and shall be definitive from the date on which the present Treaty comes into force. The confirmation of the definitive nature of the borders of the united Germany is an essential element of the peaceful order in Europe.

(2) The united Germany and Republic of Poland shall confirm the existing border between them in a treaty that is binding under international law.

(3) The united Germany has no territorial claims whatsoever against other states and shall not assert any in the future.

(4) The Governments of the Federal Republic of Germany and the German Democratic Republic shall ensure that the constitution of the united Germany does not contain any provision incompatible with these principles.

Article 2

The governments of the Federal Republic of Germany and the German Democratic Republic reaffirm their declarations that only peace will emanate from German soil. According to the constitution of the united Germany, acts tending to and undertaken with the intent to disturb the peaceful relations between nations, especially to prepare for aggressive war, are unconstitutional and a punishable offense. The governments of the Federal Republic of Germany and the German Democratic Republic declare that the united Germany will never employ any of its weapons except in accordance with its constitution and the Charter of the United Nations.

Article 3

(1) The Governments of the Federal Republic of Germany and the German Democratic Republic reaffirm their renunciation of the manufacture and possession of and control over nuclear, biological and chemical weap-

ons. They declare that the united Germany, too, will abide by these commitments. In particular, rights and obligations arising from the Treaty on the Non-Proliferation of Nuclear Weapons of July 1, 1968 will continue to apply to the united Germany.

(2) The Government of the Federal Republic of Germany, acting in full agreement with the Government of the German Democratic Republic, made the following statement on August 30, 1990 in Vienna at the Negotiations on Conventional Armed Forces in Europe:

"The Government of the Federal Republic of Germany undertakes to reduce the personnel strength of the armed forces of the united Germany to 370,000 (ground, air and naval forces) within three to four years. This reduction will commence on the entry into force of the first CFE agreement. Within the scope of this overall ceiling no more than 345,000 will belong to the ground and air forces which, pursuant to the agreed mandate, alone are the subject of the Negotiations of Conventional Armed Forces in Europe. The Federal Government regards its commitment to reduce ground and air forces as a significant German contribution to the reduction of conventional armed forces in Europe. It assumes that in follow-on negotiations the other participants in the negotiations, too, will render their contribution to enhancing security and stability in Europe, including measures to limit personnel strengths."

The government of the German Democratic Republic has expressly associated itself with this statement. . . .

Article 5

(1) Until the completion of the withdrawal of the Soviet armed forces from the territory of the present German Democratic Republic and of Berlin in accordance with Article 4 of the present Treaty, only German territorial defense units which are not integrated into the alliance structures to which German armed forces in the rest of German territory are assigned will be stationed in that territory as armed forces of the united Germany. During that period and subject to the provisions of paragraph 2 of this Article, armed forces of other states will not be stationed in that territory or carry out any other military activity there.

(2) For the duration of the presence of Soviet armed forces in the territory of the present German Democratic Republic and of Berlin, armed forces of the French Republic, the United Kingdom of Great Britain and Northern Ireland and the United States of America will, upon German request, remain stationed in Berlin by agreement to this effect between the Government of the united Germany and the governments of the states concerned. The

number of troops and the amount of equipment of all non-German armed forces stationed in Berlin will not be greater than at the time of signature of the present Treaty. New categories of weapons will not be introduced there by non-German armed forces. The government of the united Germany will conclude with the governments of those states which have armed forces stationed in Berlin treaties with conditions which are fair taking account of the relations existing with the states concerned.

(3) Following the completion of the withdrawal of the Soviet armed forces from the territory of the present German Democratic Republic and of Berlin, units of German armed forces assigned to military alliance structures in the same way as those in the rest of German territory may also be stationed in that part of Germany, but without nuclear weapon carriers. This does not apply to conventional weapon systems which may have other capabilities in addition to conventional ones but which in that part of Germany are equipped for a conventional role and designated only for such. Foreign armed forces and nuclear weapons or their carriers will not be stationed in that part of Germany or deployed there.

Article 6

The right of the united Germany to belong to alliances, with all the rights and responsibilities arising therefrom, shall not be affected by the present Treaty.

Article 7

(1) The French Republic, the Union of the Soviet Socialist Republics, the United Kingdom of Great Britain and Northern Ireland and the United States of America hereby terminate their rights and responsibilities related to Berlin and to Germany as a whole. As a result, the corresponding, related quadripartite agreements, decisions and practices are terminated and all related Four Powers institutions are dissolved.

(2) The united Germany shall have accordingly full sovereignty over its internal and external affairs.

Article 8

(1) The present Treaty is subject to ratification or acceptance as soon as possible. On the German side it will be ratified by the united Germany. The Treaty will therefore apply to the united Germany.

(2) The instruments of ratification or acceptance shall be deposited with the government of the united Germany. That government shall inform the governments of the other Contracting Parties of the deposit of each instrument of ratification or acceptance.

Article 9

The present Treaty shall enter into force for the united Germany, the French Republic, the Union of the Soviet Socialist Republics, the United Kingdom of Great Britain and Northern Ireland and the United States of America on the date of deposit of the last instrument of ratification or acceptance by those states.

Article 10

The original of the present Treaty, of which the English, French, German and Russian texts are equally authentic, shall be deposited with the government of the Federal Republic of Germany, which shall transmit certified true copies to the governments of the other Contracting Parties.

Done at Moscow on 12 September 1990.

> For the Federal Republic of Germany
> Hans-Dietrich Genscher
> For the German Democratic Republic
> Lothar de Maizière
> For the French Republic
> Roland Dumas
> For the Union of Soviet Socialist Republics
> Eduard Shevardnadze
> For the United Kingdom of Great Britain and Northern Ireland
> Douglas Hurd
> For the United States of America
> James A. Baker III

Source: The Unification of Germany in 1990: A Documentation (Bonn: Press and Information Office of the Federal Government, 1991).

Document 13
ADDRESS BY CHANCELLOR KOHL ON THE EVE
OF GERMAN UNITY, OCTOBER 2, 1990

With all the diplomacy, negotiation, bickering, and confrontation behind them, East and West Germans alike could indulge in a brief period of national celebration. Across both countries, parades and parties marked the end of an era of separation and the beginning of a new future as one nation. On the eve of unification, Chancellor Kohl took to the radio and television to deliver an address outlining his dreams and goals for the future. His speech (reprinted here in its entirety) calls for a future where prosperity and justice is available for all Germans. It also envisions a nation at peace, firmly allied with the world's democracies.

However, amid his optimism for the future were words of caution. Economic problems remained and the social and psychological wounds of forty years would not be healed quickly. Kohl did not dwell on those issues, but preferred to summarize the collective fears and joys of 80 million Germans. This was a time for celebration—the hard work began the day after unification.

My fellow countrymen,

In a few hours a dream will become reality. After over forty bitter years of division Germany, our fatherland, will be reunited. This is one of the happiest moments of my life. From the many letters and conversations I have had, I know the great joy also felt by the vast majority of you.

On such a day we naturally look ahead. Yet despite our great joy, we must first think of those who particularly suffered from the division of Germany. Families were cruelly torn apart. Political prisoners were incarcerated. People died at the Wall.

Fortunately, this is now a thing of the past. It must never be allowed to happen again, and thus must never be forgotten. We owe it to the victims to recall this. We owe it to our children and grandchildren. They must be spared such experiences for ever. For the same reason we have not forgotten those to whom we owe the unity of our country. We would never have achieved it on our own. Many played a part in this process.

When has a nation ever had the opportunity of overcoming decades of painful separation in such a peaceful manner? We are reestablishing German unity in freedom in full agreement with our neighbours.

We should like to thank our partners and friends. In particular, we thank the United States of America and above all President George Bush. We also thank our friends in France and Great Britain. They all stood by us in troubled times, and for decades safeguarded the freedom of the Western part of Berlin. They supported our goal of achieving unity in freedom. The close links and friendship between us will endure.

Our thanks are also due to the reformist movements in Central, Eastern and South Eastern Europe. Just over a year ago, Hungary permitted the refugees to leave. This was the first crack in the Wall. The movements for freedom in Poland and Czechoslovakia gave the people of the GDR the courage to stand up for their right of self-determination. Now we are addressing the task of realizing a lasting reconciliation between the German and the polish nations.

We thank President Gorbachev. He recognized the nations' right to pursue their own path. Without this decision, we would not have experienced the way of German Unity so soon.

The fact that this day is already here is thanks particularly to those Germans who overcame the SED's dictatorship through the power of their love of freedom. Their peacefulness and level-headedness remain exemplary.

We Germans have learned from history. We are a peace-loving, freedom-loving people. We will never leave our democracy to the mercy of the enemies of peace and freedom. For us, patriotism, love of freedom and the spirit of good-neighbourliness belong together. We want to be reliable partners and good friends. Thus there is only one place for us in the world: at the side of the free nations.

We also want to be good neighbours at home. This includes being open-minded towards those around us, respecting those with other views and showing friendship towards our fellow citizens from abroad. Our free democracy must be marked by diversity, tolerance and solidarity.

Particularly at this moment, we Germans must show solidarity towards one another. A difficult path lies before us. We want to proceed along it together. If we stick together and are prepared to make sacrifices, we will have every chance of joint success.

Economic conditions in the Federal Republic are excellent. At no time have we been better prepared to master the economic tasks of reunification than now. We will be assisted in this by the diligence and application of the people in the former GDR. Through our joint efforts and a social market economy policy, Brandenburg, Mecklenburg-Western Pomerania, Saxony, Saxony-Anhalt and Thuringia will have become flourishing regions within only a few years.

We will be able to solve the economic problems: not overnight, it is true, but within the foreseeable future. What is more important, however, is that we show understanding towards one another and are prepared to approach each other. We must do away with the notion that Germany is still divided into "over here" and "over there."

Over forty years of communist dictatorship have cut deep wounds, particularly in people's hearts. The state based on the rule of law has the task of establishing justice and domestic peace. We all face a difficult test in this respect. Grave injustice must be made good, but we also need strength for inner reconciliation.

We call upon all Germans to show that we are worthy of our shared freedom. The third of October is a day of joy, gratitude and hope. The young generation of Germans, more than any other previous generation, have every Chance of spending their whole lives in peace and freedom. We know that our joy is shared by many people throughout the world. With them we share our feelings at this moment: Germany is our fatherland, the united Europe is our future!

Source: The Unification of Germany in 1990: A Documentation (Bonn: Press and Information Office of the Federal Government, 1991).

Glossary of Selected Terms

Basic Law: The constitution of Germany. It was framed by representatives from the three western zones of occupied Germany in 1948–1949. In the absence of the Germans under Soviet occupation, the Basic Law was designated as such in order to avoid the impression that it created a permanent division of Germany. It outlines the rights of German citizens and the structures of the institutions of government.

Bizonia: The name given to the German territory resulting from the fusion of the British and United States zones on January 1, 1947. The French zone would later merge with Bizonia to form the territory that became the Federal Republic of Germany (West Germany) in 1949.

Bundestag: The lower house of the West German (and now German) legislature. It is composed of representatives elected directly by the German people.

Christian Democratic Union (CDU): A political party whose membership is predominantly Christian and politically conservative. Founded after the end of World War II, it was the dominant political party in West Germany from 1949 to 1969. A list of the more prominent CDU members includes Konrad Adenauer, Ludwig Erhard, and Helmut Kohl.

Christian Social Union (CSU): A small, independent party of voters concerned primarily with protecting the interests of Roman Catholics. Its political platform is so similar to the CDU's that it has voted with the CDU on almost every major issue. It is generally considered a loyal ally of the larger national CDU party.

Civic Actions Group(s): Any of a number of unofficial political parties or interest groups created by East German citizens in response to their distrust of the government. Groups represented a variety of agendas and interests, ranging from women's issues to environmental protection. Some civic action groups allied with the CDU to form Alliance 90, the coalition that achieved a stunning victory in the March 1990 elections. Others groups faded into insignificance as their causes were absorbed or ignored by other parties once Germany headed toward unification.

COMECON: An acronym for Council for Mutual Economic Assistance. It was an economic agreement forged between the members of the Soviet bloc of nations in 1949. It eventually evolved into an organization similar to the western Common Market and attempted, unsuccessfully, to remove trade barriers between the member nations.

Common Market: A commonly used term to refer to the European Economic Community. Established by the Treaty of Rome in 1957 to break down tariff barriers to trade between member nations, the Common Market has progressively widened the scope of its supranational decision-making ability to include a common European court and parliament. It was later transformed into the European Community and the European Union.

Deutschmark: Standard unit of currency in Germany. It has long been considered one of the world's most stable currencies.

German Democratic Republic (GDR): Official term for East Germany. Founded in 1949 in response to the creation of the Federal Republic of Germany, the German Democratic Republic was the institutionalization of communist rule in the former Soviet zone of occupation.

Glasnost: Russian term meaning "openness." Touted by Mikhail Gorbachev as a solution to the ills of the Soviet Union, *glasnost* promised to reform the Soviet system by making the decision-making more responsive to the wishes of the people. It implied that the communist party would henceforth conduct competitive elections within the party and encourage an open debate of critical issues.

Marshall Plan: The popular name for the American effort to send money and provide technical assistance to the democratic nations of Europe following World War II. Officially credited to General George Marshall, the plan eventually sent billions of dollars in grants to Europe for the reconstruction of those economies devastated by war. The only stipulations attached to the grants were that the countries applying had to have democratic governments and that the European nations themselves should decide how best the money should be spent.

NATO: Acronym for the North Atlantic Treaty Organization. Created primarily to ensure the common defense of Europe against Soviet aggression, NATO evolved into both a political and military organization. It maintains a multinational troop force under international leadership stationed in the member nations. Since the collapse of the Soviet Union, NATO has deemphasized its historical military mission and has forged new political relationships with its former enemies, including Russia.

Party of Democratic Socialism (PDS): A small political party pledged to Marxist principles. Begun following the breakdown of the East German government and the removal of the constitutional monopoly it had over politics, the former members of the SED purged itself of its most stalwart bureaucrats and refashioned itself into a traditional political party. Under the leadership of Gregor Gysi and Hans Modrow, the party has managed to survive unification and continues to advance a Marxist agenda in German politics.

Perestroika: Russian word meaning "restructuring." Part of Mikhail Gorbachev's program of reform, *perestroika* promised a removal of the monolithic bureaucracy that had been responsible for the decline and decay of Soviet society.

Socialist Democratic Party (SPD): A political party pledged to bring more social responsibility to the economic marketplace. The SPD is the heir to the tradition of German socialism dating back to the 1870s. At one time a party that stood for government intervention in the marketplace, the modern SPD has abandoned its Marxist past to assume a more contemporary role as the guardian of the economic well-being of the average citizen. Among its most notable members are Helmut Schmidt and Willy Brandt.

Socialist Unity Party (SED): The official name of the East German communist party. Forged in 1948 by the forced amalgamation of the socialist (SPD) and communist parties, the SED enjoyed a constitutionally guaranteed monopoly over the exercise of decision making in the East German state. Headed by Walther Ulbricht and then Erich Honecker, the SED enforced political and social uniformity through its Ministry for State Security (Stasi).

Stasi: The common term for the dreaded East German Ministry for State Security (Ministerium für *Sta*at*si*cherheit). Essentially a secret police force, the Stasi encouraged citizens to spy on each other in order to root out subversive elements in East German society. It ceased to function following the storming of the Stasi barracks in Berlin in January 1990 and soon thereafter was officially legislated out of existence.

Trabant: German word for "satellite," and the brand name of the mass-produced automobile most readily available in East Germany. The Trabant's small engine and lack of pollution-control equipment made it clearly inferior to just about any other automobile manufactured in Europe. Once the borders opened to travel and shopping, East Germans abandoned their Trabants by the thousands in favor of cars made in the West. It has since become a symbol of the technological and social backwardness of the East German state.

Volkskammer: Translation is "People's Chamber," the German term for the East German pseudolegislative body. Comprised of representatives elected by the people from slates of government-approved candidates, the Volkskammer made into law the decisions of the SED leadership. The Volkskammer ruled

East Germany as a democratically elected body from January 1990 to October 1990. Under the leadership first of Hans Modrow and then Lothar de Maizière, Volkskammer committees worked to hammer out the unification agreement with the Federal Republic. It legislated itself out of existence on October 2, 1990.

Warsaw Pact: The military arm of COMECOM and the eastern European counterpart to NATO. The Warsaw Pact maintained multinational troops ostensible for the protection of the member nations. On at least one occasion, the suppression of the Czech Spring in 1968, the troops also were used to quell democratic or dissenting movements within the Soviet bloc. The treaty establishing the alliance ceased to be in force once the Soviet Union disintegrated.

Annotated Bibliography

Author's note: The following bibliography is a highly selective listing of the best works on the history of Germany and the unification available in English. Unfortunately, there is a wealth of information that has not been translated and is therefore inaccessible to those readers who are not proficient in German. Those works are not included here. Readers who wish to consult German-language publications may find the notes following each chapter useful.

BOOKS

General Histories of the Two Germanies

Childs, David. *The GDR: Moscow's German Ally*. London: George Allen and Unwin, 1983. A good general history of East Germany and its relations with the Soviet bloc.

Dennis, Mike. *The German Democratic Republic: Politics, Economics and Society*. London: Pinter Publishers, 1988. The most recent general account of the history and status of the GDR. An interesting read given the date of publication. Part of the Marxist Regimes Series, this work remains the most definitive contemporary account of how well (or poorly) the GDR functioned, especially in economic and social matters.

Prittie, Terence. *The Velvet Chancellors: A History of Postwar Germany*. London: Frederick Muller, 1979. A readable, if somewhat dated, account of German history since 1945.

Turner, Henry Ashby, Jr. *Germany from Partition to Reunification*. New Haven: Yale University Press, 1992. A revision of his earlier work, *The Two Germanies Since 1945*, the best single-volume introduction to the history of postwar Germany available in English. Although it has only one chapter on unification, the book is still a good starting point for readers seeking an understanding of the background of German history since Hitler.

Biographical

Brandt, Willy. *My Life in Politics*. London: Hamisch Hamilton, 1992. Brandt's memoirs are an intriguing look into his life and career. The book was originally published in German in 1989, and the English language version of 1992 has but one short chapter about the unification.

Honecker, Erich. *From My Life*. Oxford: Pergamon Press, 1981. Erich Honecker's life and work in his own words. Written at the height of his power, the work is basically an antifascist, pro-Marxist polemic. Still, it is an interesting firsthand account of life in German communist circles, if the reader doesn't mind wading through the mass of rhetoric and propaganda.

Klein, Hans, ed. *The German Chancellors*. Carol Stream, IL: Edition Q, 1996. Translation of works by German journalists on the lives and careers of the six chancellors. Less biographical and more an excursion in how personality shapes policy.

Müchler, Günther, and Klaus Hoffmann. *Helmut Kohl: Chancellor of Unity*. Bonn: Press and Information Office of the Federal Government, 1992. A more official, and consequently less probing, biography of Helmut Kohl. Relies heavily on information from speeches and press releases.

Pruys, Karl Hugo. *Kohl: Genius of the Present*. Chicago: Edition Q, 1996. An overly laudatory account of the federal chancellor's life and career. At times difficult to read but filled with insights into Kohl's character.

Documents and Interviews

Gray, Richard T., and Sabine Wilke, eds. and trans. *German Unification and Its Discontents: Documents from the Peaceful Revolution*. Seattle: University of Washington Press, 1996. Valuable compilation of documents, many presented in English for the first time.

Heins, Cornelia. *The Wall Falls: An Oral History of the Reunification of the Two Germanies*. London: Grey Seal, 1994. An interesting look at the personal recollections of Germans and their experiences during the unification.

James, Harold, and Marla Stone, eds. *When the Wall Came Down: Reactions to German Unification*. New York: Routledge, Chapman, Hall, 1992. A compendium of documents gleaned from contemporary journals and speeches illustrating viewpoints on the revolution and unification.

Jarausch, Konrad H., and Volker Gransow. *Uniting Germany: Documents and Debates, 1944–1993*. Providence, RI: Berghahn Books, 1994. Excellent

volume of primary source material; speeches, articles, debates. Fine com-
panion piece to Jarausch's *The Rush to German Unity* (see below).

Philipsen, Dirk. *We Were the People: Voices From East Germany's Revolutionary
Autumn of 1989*. Durham, NC: Duke University Press, 1993. An excellent volume transcribing interviews with key government officials and
dissidents.

The Unification of Germany in 1990: A Documentation. Bonn: Press and Information Office of the Federal Government, 1991. Government publication
that provides full-text transcriptions of the key documents.

Revolution and Unification—General Accounts

Ash, Timothy Garton. *In Europe's Name: Germany and the Divided Continent*.
New York: Vintage Press, 1994. A superb account of the German question written by one of Europe's most prominent journalists. Must reading
for anyone who wants to gain a deeper understanding of the German
revolution and unification and their effect on the continent.

Darnton, Robert. *Berlin Journal*. New York: W. W. Norton, 1991. A well-written
chronicle of the events of 1989–1990 by a prolific French historian, who
was in Berlin at the time. Darnton is strongest in his depictions of the local scene and his personal reflections on the events.

Fritsch-Bournazel, Renata. *Europe and German Unification*. New York: Berg,
1992. A translation of an earlier German volume. It is most useful when
describing historical perspectives of the unification issue. Also a good
source book for documentary information.

Görtemaker, Manfred. *Unifying Germany, 1989–1990*. New York: St. Martin's
Press, 1994. A detailed study of the unification process and its ramifica-
tions, with special emphasis on the role of German unification in the context of the changes occuring concurrently in Europe.

Hämäläinen, Pekka. *Uniting Germany: Actions and Reactions*. Boulder, CO:
Westview Press, 1994. A basic survey of the events culminating in Germany's unification.

Jarausch, Konrad H. *The Rush to German Unity*. New York: Oxford University
Press, 1994. The best single volume on German unification available in
English. Extensive use of German language sources makes this book the
definitive account.

Long, Robert Emmet, ed. *The Reunification of Germany*. New York: H. W. Wil-
son, 1992. Eighteen articles from popular news and opinion periodicals.

Specialized Analyses

Allen, Bruce. *Germany East: Dissent and Opposition*. Montreal: Black Rose
Books, 1989. A useful look at the origins and actions of GDR dissent
groups before the revolution.

Baker, James A. *The Politics of Diplomacy*. New York: G. P. Putnam's Sons, 1995. Reminiscences of the former secretary of state.

Beschloss, Michael, and Strobe Talbot. *At the Highest Levels*. Boston: Little, Brown, 1993. Analysis of Bush administration foreign policy by two men who were actually involved.

Gallis, Paul E. *The Unification of Germany: Background and Analysis of the Two-plus-Four Talks*. Washington, DC: Congressional Research Service, 1990. A probing analysis of the international diplomacy of 1990.

Glaessner, Gert-Joachim, and Ian Wallace, eds. *The German Revolution of 1989: Causes and Consequences*. Oxford: Berg, 1992. Eleven analytical articles, written by European experts, on the political, social, and international aspects of the collapse of the GDR.

Goeckel, Robert F. *The Lutheran Church and the East German State: Political Conflict and Change under Ulbricht and Honecker*. Ithaca, NY: Cornell University Press, 1990. The definitive study of the role of the clergy and the "church in socialism."

Grass, Günther. *Two States—One Nation?* San Diego: Harcourt, Brace, Jovanovich, 1990. A commentary critical of reunification from contemporary Germany's most respected literary figure.

Grosser, Dieter, ed. *German Unification: The Unexpected Challenge*. Providence, RI: Berg Publishers, 1992. An excellent compendium of articles by German political scientists. It is strongest in its analysis of the collapse of the GDR and in placing the unification issue in many different contexts, including social, historical, economic, and diplomatic.

Jones, Alun. *The New Germany: A Human Geography*. Chichester: J. Wiley and Sons, 1994. Basically a demographic analysis of Germany following unification that also looks into problems of modernization and Germany's changed role in European affairs.

Joppke, Christian. *East German Dissidents and the Revolution of 1989: Social Movement in a Leninist Regime*. New York: New York University Press, 1995. An excellent look into the peace and human rights movements in East Germany.

Keithly, David M. *The Collapse of East German Communism*. Westport, CT: Praeger Publishers, 1992. A tight, well-thought-out account of the events leading up to the decline and disintegration of the East German state.

Merkl, Peter H. *German Unification in the European Context*. University Park: Pennsylvania State University Press, 1993. A scholarly, in-depth account of the impact of the revolution.

Opp, Karl-Dieter, Peter Voss, and Christiane Gern. *Origins of a Spontaneous Revolution: East Germany, 1989*. Ann Arbor: University of Michigan Press, 1995. An indispensible volume that asks the question "why" the revolution happened in order to determine the conditions conducive to spontaneous peaceful revolution. The authors' examinations of the motivations of the demonstrators and the degree of spontaneity that the demonstrators exhibited in the rallies are extremely revealing.

Osmond, Jonathan. *German Reunification: A Reference Guide and Commentary*. Harlow, Essex (UK): Longman Group, 1992. Articles that present different aspects of unification and their effects. Intended to be a guide to further study.

Pond, Elizabeth. *Beyond the Wall: Germany's Road to Unification*. Washington, DC: The Brookings Institution, 1994. An account of the unification from public policy and foreign affairs viewpoints. Based predominantly on a wealth of personal interviews with the participants. Exceptionally strong on US State Department efforts.

The Revolution of the Candles: Christians in the Revolution of the German Democratic Republic. Macon, GA: Mercer University Press, 1996. English translation of *Die Revolution der Kerzen*. A collection of personal reminiscences, poems, and sermons from the months of October and November 1989. Contains interesting recollections of arrests, street demonstrations, and the attempts to achieve change peacefully.

Szabo, Stephen F. *The Diplomacy of German Unification*. New York: St. Martin's Press, 1992. Well-researched, tightly written book on diplomacy leading up to and through the Two-plus-Four talks. Emphasizes US and USSR diplomatic efforts.

Verheyen, Kirk. *The German Question: A Cultural, Historical, and Geopolitical Explanation*. Boulder, CO: Westview Press, 1991. A well-researched look at the historical development of the question of two Germanys and the possibilities of unification. Final chapter treats unification itself.

Zelikow, Philip, and Condoleezza Rice. *Germany United and Europe Transformed*. Cambridge: Harvard University Press, 1997. This book, written by two state department insiders, is a controversial account of German foreign policy leading up to unification. It argues that Kohl abandoned *Ostpolitik* to negotiate with the collapsing Soviet Union from a position of strength.

VIDEO AND OTHER MEDIA SOURCES

The German Revolution of 1989 and the unification the following year are among the most well-documented political events in history. One source of audiovisual accounts is the Hoover Institution on War, Revolution and Peace at Stanford University, which holds a collection of videos and audiotapes of speeches and interviews with politicians and dissidents. Other useful video materials include:

- *The German Democratic Republic in Change*. Chicago, IL: Brittanica, 1990.

- *Germany Reunites*. PBS Adult Learning Satellite Service, 1992.

- *The Nation Returns*. Princeton, NJ: Films for the Humanities and Sciences, 1994.

- *The Reunification of Germany.* Los Angeles, CA: Churchill Films, 1992.

- *Reunification—One Year Later.* Cologne and Corvallis, OR: Deutsche Welle, 1991.

- *Test the West! Metamorphosis in East Germany.* San Diego, CA: Bronco Video, 1991.

- *The "Turnaround."* Ellensburg: Central Washington University Media Development and Production, 1992.

- *Wie Die Mauer Fiel (How the Wall Fell).* Agoura Hills, CA: ATN Deutscher Fernseh-Club, 1992.

Computer enthusiasts may be fortunate to find the now out-of-print CD-ROM entitled Seven Days in August (Burbank, CA: Time Warner Interactive Group; Edenquest, 1993). The disk contains information on the fall of the Berlin Wall, the Round Table negotiations, and social implications of the revolution.

Index

About the Author

RICHARD A. LEIBY is Assistant Professor of History at Rosemont College in Rosemont, Pennsylvania, where he teaches both German and European history. He has written on Jean Monnet, the European Unity Movement, and the Nazi resettlement policy in occupied France. He is working on an anthology dealing with the effects of World War II on European cultural and political institutions.